NUCLEAR SUBURBS

NUCLEAR SUBURBS

COLD WAR TECHNOSCIENCE AND THE PITTSBURGH RENAISSANCE

PATRICK VITALE

UNIVERSITY OF MINNESOTA PRESS
MINNEAPOLIS • LONDON

A different version of a portion of chapter 1 was published in "Anti-Communism, the Growth Machine, and the Remaking of Cold-War-Era Pittsburgh," *International Journal of Urban and Regional Research* 39 (2015): 772–87. Copyright 2015 by Urban Research Publications Limited; published by permission of John Wiley & Sons, Inc.
A different version of chapter 2 was published as "Cradle of the Creative Class: Reinventing the Figure of the Scientist in Cold War Pittsburgh," *Annals of the American Association of Geographers* 106, no. 6 (2016): 1378–96; reprinted by permission of the publisher, Taylor & Francis Ltd., http://www.tandfonline.com.
A different version of chapter 3 was published as "Making Science Suburban: The Suburbanization of Industrial Research and the Invention of 'Research Man,'" *Environment and Planning A* 49, no. 12 (2017): 2813–34.

Published by the University of Minnesota Press
111 Third Avenue South, Suite 290
Minneapolis, MN 55401-2520
http://www.upress.umn.edu

ISBN 978-1-5179-0028-1 (hc)
ISBN 978-1-5179-0029-8 (pb)
A Cataloging-in-Publication record for this book is available from the Library of Congress.

Printed in the United States of America on acid-free paper

UMP BmB 2021

Contents

Abbreviations

ACCD	Allegheny Conference on Community Development
AEC	Atomic Energy Commission
AIChE	American Institute of Chemical Engineers
AIEE	American Institute of Electrical Engineers
AIME	American Institute of Mining and Metallurgical Engineers
Alcoa	Aluminum Company of America
ANS	American Nuclear Society
ASCE	American Society of Civil Engineers
ASME	American Society of Mechanical Engineers
BR3	Belgian Reactor-3
BTR	*Bettis Technical Review*
DPA	Defense Production Administration
EPIC	East Pittsburgh Improvement Company
ESWP	Engineering Society of Western Pennsylvania
FBI	Federal Bureau of Investigation
G20	Group of 20
JCAE	Joint Committee on Atomic Energy
NSC	National Security Council
PAD	Plant Apparatus Division
PAIDC	Pittsburgh Area Industrial Dispersion Committee

PBPE	Pittsburgh Board of Public Education
PET	Pittsburgh Engineering Trust
Pitt	University of Pittsburgh
PPG	Pittsburgh Plate Glass
PRPA	Pittsburgh Regional Planning Association
PURA	Pittsburgh Urban Redevelopment Authority
PWR	pressurized water reactor
R&D	research and development
RIDC	Regional Industrial Development Corporation
ROTC	Reserve Officer Training Course
SHARE	South Hills Association for Racial Equality
STS	science and technology studies
UE	United Electrical, Radio, and Machine Workers
UET	United Engineering Trust
USIA	United States Information Agency
WABCO	Westinghouse Air Brake Company

Introduction

Engineering the Bubble

We are always writing the history of the same war, even when we are writing the history of peace.

—Michel Foucault, *"Society Must Be Defended"*

Somewhere out there beyond the firmament, past the asteroid belt, there were other worlds where children did not regularly fear for their bodies.

—Ta-Nehisi Coates, *Between the World and Me*

As a child growing up in the 1980s in Pittsburgh's well-to-do eastern suburbs, I thought that most adult men were engineers and scientists. Three of our five immediate neighbors were nuclear engineers who worked for the Westinghouse Electric Corporation. A house up the street was continuously rented to visiting engineers from Sweden. A nearby subdivision was home to several engineers from Britain who emigrated during a "brain drain." My first school was a small preschool run by the wife of a Westinghouse physicist in the basement of their home. Many of my classmates were the children of engineers and scientists.

As a child, I had little understanding of what these scientists and engineers actually did. I only recognized that there were many of them in my neighborhood and that my father, a manager at a construction company, was not one of them. I also became aware on various trips into the city that we, my neighbors and I, were different from many of the Pittsburghers I saw from the window of our Buick Park Avenue. My neighborhood was overwhelmingly white and affluent—Pittsburgh was not.

Pittsburgh itself also looked different from the suburb where I grew up. My neighborhood was full of big yards and enormous, new houses. Pittsburgh looked worn. Faded aluminum-sided row houses perched precariously on hillsides. Steel mills sat empty, littering the landscape with collapsing warehouses and rusting blast furnaces. There were no steelworkers in our neighborhood. In fact, I had never met a steelworker. During the early 1980s, my parents read about mill closings in the *Pittsburgh Post-Gazette,* yet oddly one of the most devastating industrial collapses of the twentieth century had no impact on our lives. While workers protested in the streets of Pittsburgh, occupied the U.S. Steel Building, attempted to reopen their mill, and returned home exhausted, my family and many others sat on our lush patios talking about school, swim practice, and dad's day at work.

Residents often referred to our town of big houses, sprawling green lawns, and engineers and scientists as the bubble, a term used to refer to many affluent American suburbs. The bubble alluded to our self-imposed isolation—our ability to keep things out; our sense that nothing ever went wrong in our town. Poverty, homelessness, violence, racism, deindustrialization, and war—these were the problems of the rest of the world, not of our community. My suburban neighborhood was not unique in Pittsburgh or in the United States. During the Cold War, tens of millions of white middle- and working-class Americans saw the suburbs as a place that offered security, wealth, and happiness. Yet while suburbanites felt isolated on their back patios and in their Buick Park Avenues, they were not. The neocolonial facades and green lawns of the suburbs were intended to project a state of normalcy, security, and comfort, but the relationships that created these bubbles, both within and outside homes, were intrinsically violent and unequal, and spanned far beyond the tidy boundaries of suburban communities.

Suburbs and suburbanites, as numerous scholars have repeatedly demonstrated, are diverse. For much of the late nineteenth and early twentieth centuries, industries' pursuit of ideal sites for manufacturing and the working class's for home ownership drove suburbanization.[1] Prior to World War II, African Americans sought out freedom from racial oppression in the suburbs, and in recent decades, suburbs have been key entry points for many immigrants moving to the United States.[2] There is not one singular type of suburb.[3] However, despite the diversity of suburbs and suburbanites, many Americans, especially in the years following World War II, lived in suburban bubbles like the one where I grew up. These communities were predominantly home to white middle-class professionals who had college degrees. Residents lived in large, unattached homes that they owned. Homes in these communities accrued value and school systems were well funded and sent the vast majority of graduates to postsecondary institutions. A stark gender division of labor defined these communities, with men predominantly responsible for earning income and women for caring for children and maintaining homes. This extremely common type of suburb hosted social structures that helped reproduce the race, class, and gender advantages of white middle-class men.

There was also a narrower subtype of suburban bubble that is the subject of this book: suburbs that housed large numbers of scientists and engineers. These technoscientific suburbs, located near suburban research and office facilities, became a ubiquitous feature of many metropolitan areas, from Boston to Los Angeles, during the early Cold War.[4] Beginning in the 1940s, a constellation of facilities devoted to nuclear reactor research and development began to develop in Pittsburgh's southern and eastern suburbs. For the duration of the Cold War, the majority of reactors for naval vessels and power plants, vital elements of the U.S. economic and military infrastructure, were developed in these suburbs. The communities around these facilities, including my hometown, housed one of the largest concentrations of nuclear engineers and scientists on Earth. Meanwhile, beginning immediately after World War II, a coalition of Pittsburgh's business and political elite began an aggressive and celebrated effort—called the Pittsburgh Renaissance—to remake the economy and built environment of the region. Along with new skyscrapers, pollution and flood control, and urban renewal, they celebrated and encouraged the growth of nuclear and other technology industries as a way to move the region beyond its reliance on heavy manufacturing. For Pittsburgh's elite, the presence of nuclear scientists and engineers became important symbols of the new Pittsburgh and its postindustrial economy.

Nuclear Suburbs: Cold War Technoscience and the Pittsburgh Renaissance follows nuclear engineers and scientists throughout and beyond the Pittsburgh region, from suburbs to submarines to urban renewal sites, in order to understand how the politics of technoscience and the Cold War were embedded in daily life.[5] It explores the convergence between the growth of technoscience in the suburbs, urban renewal, and the Cold War. The book asks how suburbs—key sites for the social reproduction of scientists and engineers as classed, gendered, and racial subjects—were involved in the remaking of cities, technoscience, and the Cold War. It investigates why and how scientists and engineers were able to insulate themselves socially, physically, and emotionally from the problems they helped create. The book examines why and how local leaders enrolled scientists and engineers as symbols of a modern and remade industrial region. Ultimately, *Nuclear Suburbs* exposes the imbricated historical geographies of class, gender, race, violence, and injustice that created places like the one that produced me.

Suburban Bubbles and the Cold War

One of the primary purposes of middle-class residential suburbs, like those described in this book, was to provide residents with the promise of access to power, privilege, status, and security as well as steadily increasing property values. The designers, developers, and residents of these suburban bubbles intended them as places that prioritized order, stability, and control. More often than not, they adopted methods of exclusion in order to realize this shared vision.[6] By design and practice, suburban bubbles obscured or displaced the harmful effects of the processes that reproduced the power and privilege of their residents.[7]

Cold War suburban bubbles were a spatial expression of the dichotomy between prosperity and poverty that capitalism necessarily creates, but they were also what Richard Walker terms "solutions" to economic, social, and political crises. As Walker shows, suburbanization and the spending that results have long served as means of delaying or preventing capitalist economic crises.[8] Suburban bubbles were also part of the bourgeoisie's ceaseless search for security and the need to obscure the state power that is vitally necessary for this security to be realized.[9] The history of residential middle-class suburban bubbles in North America—from the earliest suburbs in places such as Llewellyn Park, New Jersey, to the present-day gated community—is in part intended to displace or obscure capitalism's crises: to ensure that the exploitation, toxicity, poverty, misery, conflict, and violence intrinsic to capitalism are invisible and take place elsewhere. Thus suburban bubbles are spatial fixes in two senses: they provide a needed outlet to invest surplus capital, but they are also a place of sanctuary and retreat from always imminent crisis.[10]

During the Cold War, suburban bubbles offered suburbanites the opportunity to escape or obscure capitalism's crises, while a heightened trust in technoscience produced a myth that the expert work of scientists and engineers could resolve the world's problems. At the close of World War II, as

Vannevar Bush and many others boldly forecast, science and technology promised limitless power, food, leisure, productivity, health, and wealth to all people.[11] Through their work, scientists and engineers would free humankind from the chains of industrial capitalism, totalitarianism, and communism, ushering in new technologies for the benefit of all. By connecting capitalism, suburbs, and technoscience, business and political leaders created one of the defining myths of the Cold War: that American technological ingenuity and entrepreneurship would allow the entire world to live freely and prosperously like American suburbanites.[12]

The linking of American suburbs and technoscience was more than just a myth. In Pittsburgh and elsewhere, suburbs became highly productive sites for technoscience during the Cold War. Corporations, universities, and the state created research and office parks as places that would buffer scientists and engineers from the crises that they were supposed to resolve.[13] These suburban, technoscientific bubbles were meant to serve two contradictory purposes: to shelter scientists and engineers from the war, violence, inequality, and imminent crisis that they were often integrally involved in creating, while offering these shelters as vitally important sites for formulating solutions to these crises. As I show in part II of this book, these suburban, technoscientific bubbles were always simultaneously both a retreat from and an engagement with capitalism.

Scientists and engineers sought out suburban bubbles not only as sites of work but also as places of leisure, residence, and community. During the Cold War, as Elaine Tyler May argues, white middle-class Americans saw their suburban homes as peaceful, domestic retreats from their Cold War anxieties. Suburbanites hoped to alleviate their fears of communist infiltration and nuclear annihilation through their embrace of the nuclear family, heteronormative relationships, and the residential suburb.[14] Yet despite the sanctuary that suburban homes were supposed to represent, all was not peaceful at home or abroad during the Cold War.[15] Suburban bubbles were an essential element of postwar racial capitalism. In law and practice, concrete and brick, they ensured that the white middle class benefited from the economic prosperity of the Keynesian warfare state, while people of color predominantly bore its ill effects. As Ruth Wilson Gilmore and others argue, the security of white suburban homeowners was based in continual structural and nonstructural violence against African Americans. Systemic white privilege was created through systemic exclusion of African Americans from employment, education, housing, income, savings, and relative safety from state violence. The promise of the heavily subsidized American suburb and the military-industrial complex was secured in part through the solidification of the borders of the racial ghetto and the criminal justice system.[16]

Thus, as Catherine Lutz observed at the inception of the "war on terror," "physical and structural violence" should be understood as "indistinguishable and interdependent."[17] Postwar American prosperity was the direct result of growing American political, economic, and military influence around the world as well as prolific spending on the military. American imperialism and military Keynesianism were vital ingredients of the postwar economic growth that allowed many Americans to obtain home ownership, postsecondary educations, and upward socioeconomic mobility.[18] The peace of postwar American suburban life belies the violence and war both within and outside the United States that created this sense of security. The "sanctuary" of the suburban home was created through violence: the violence of gender inequality, patriarchy, and abuse that usually saw women assigned the role of caretaker for homes, families, and the nation; the structural violence that offered white Americans the opportunity to own a suburban home at the expense of African Americans; the violence of capitalist restructuring that invested surplus value far from working-class neighborhoods and the Rust Belt; and the violence of war that saw many Americans generously compensated for developing and manufacturing heinous weapons, ranging from land mines to hydrogen bombs. Exploring the creation of Cold War–era suburban bubbles helps us understand how, as many geographers and others have argued, war and violence are not exceptional but are foundational to capitalist economies, the state, and the production of space.[19] In fact, the creation of a clear distinction between war and peace, a division that is integral to the suburban bubble, obscures the original and perpetual violence of liberal peace.[20]

How to Follow Scientists and Engineers through Cold War–Era Pittsburgh

This book explores how a powerful alliance that included Pittsburgh's business and political elites, local corporations, state officials, and engineers and scientists created suburban, technoscientific bubbles in the Pittsburgh region and how those bubbles in turn reproduced the status and privileges of technoscientific workers and their families. It situates these bubbles in relation to broader regional, national, and international processes, such as capitalist restructuring, scientific and technological innovation, and war making. To understand the connections between Pittsburgh and these broader processes, it follows scientists and engineers throughout and beyond the metropolitan region from submarines to suburbs to urban renewal projects. In doing so, it argues that there was a convergence between Pittsburgh's remaking into a postindustrial metropolis, the creation of suburban bubbles, and the global Cold War, and that engineers and scientists were important actors who shaped and were shaped by this convergence.

As I discuss in part I of this book, at the close of World War II, Pittsburgh's corporate and political elites formed a coalition called the Allegheny Conference on Community Development (ACCD) to remake the smoky industrial city into a modern center of the postindustrial economy.[21] They called their widely celebrated and imitated urban remaking the Pittsburgh Renaissance.[22] Pittsburgh's business and political leaders considered scientists and engineers as essential elements of their effort to remake the region from an industrial to a postindustrial center. To borrow from Bruno Latour, Pittsburgh's elite "enrolled" scientists and engineers as "allies" in their effort to remake the region.[23] Not only did local leaders portray scientists and engineers as desirable and fastidious citizens whom they must lure to the region in order to ensure future growth, but scientists and engineers, through their work and everyday lives, contributed to the remaking and suburbanization of Pittsburgh. Engineers and scientists did not exist outside Pittsburgh's remaking and suburbanization; rather, they benefited from and contributed to it.

Scientists' and engineers' ability to socially reproduce themselves and pursue their work is conditioned on the alliances and networks they create and are enrolled in. The understanding that the "construction of facts and machines is a collective process" is fundamental to the work of science and technology studies (STS).[24] Science and technology, according to Latour, are the products of networks of human and nonhuman actors that facilitate the extension of facts and machines across great distances. Scientists and engineers build alliances with "the real world," instruments, laboratories, other scientists, technical journals, funders, and nonscientists in order to make facts and machines. The more diverse and wide-ranging a network, the greater its strength. This emphasis on elaborate extrasocial networks does not mean, as Latour frequently points out, that facts are socially constructed and divorced from "reality." Instead, he argues, "knowledge does not reflect a real world that it resembles via mimesis, but rather a real interior world, the coherence and continuity of which it helps to ensure."[25] This is Latour's central argument: reality exists, but it is the product of networks of human and nonhuman actors whose actions are determined by neither reason nor nature.

Technoscience is the process by which scientists, engineers, and others form heterogeneous networks in order to make facts and machines. Latour is very explicit that this process is not limited to laboratories and that the strongest networks are those with the deepest alliances outside the scientific world.[26] In theory, STS has placed no limits on the domain of technoscience—outside is only that place not already enrolled in a network, where facts and machines are contested. However, in practice STS rarely follows scientists and engineers beyond their laboratory doors to the places where scientists and engineers live, sleep, eat, and recreate. These places are the subject of this book.

Likewise, much of STS has focused very little on the people—usually women, people of color, and the working class—who are excluded from the explicit domains of technoscience. In contrast to Latour, Donna Haraway more carefully considers how objective truth claims are founded in exclusion. Throughout her work, she argues that scientific practice is rooted in a "god trick" in which scientists appear to have developed a disembodied "view from nowhere." She explores how scientists assume the role of "modest witnesses" "whose accounts mirror reality" and how their ability to make objective claims is rooted in the creation of boundaries between the technical and political, and the private and the public. Haraway explores how science in-the-making is also gender-, race-, and class-in-the-making. The space of the early modern laboratory was one where women, the working class, and people of color were epistemologically and physically excluded. The modest witness's ability to make objective claims was premised on his ability to "not be polluted by the body"; the presence of raced, gendered, and classed bodies threatened his legitimacy.[27]

Haraway also argues that Latour, while following the scientist, actually intensifies the "virility" of the modest witness by failing to address the exclusions on which scientific practice is often premised. Contrary to Latour's contention that race, class, and gender are of no explanatory value but can only be explained, Haraway contends that these categories are forged "*through the constitutive practices of technoscience themselves.*" In other words, "both the fact and the witnesses are constituted in the encounters that are technoscientific practice." Race, class, and gender cannot be considered merely the outcome of technoscience; they are also constitutive of it.[28] In place of the "view from no-where," Haraway offers the idea of feminist objectivity, which "is about limited location and situated knowledge, not about transcendence and splitting of subject and object. In this way we might become answerable for what we learn how to see." Feminist objectivity is always heterogeneous, always temporary, and, most important, always located.[29]

Following Haraway and feminist scholarship on social reproduction, this book locates scientists and engineers as class, racial, and gendered subjects whose authority was constituted by and constitutive of Pittsburgh's suburbanization and remaking.[30] Pittsburgh and its suburbs were important nodes in a very wide-ranging network that simultaneously produced facts and machines and reproduced scientists and engineers as privileged actors. Scientists and engineers did not simply create themselves, although they certainly participated, but had the help of a vast network that included universities, professional societies, parents, teachers, spouses, masculinity, neighbors, whiteness, scholarships, inheritances, states, businesses, and many other actors. In Pittsburgh, scientists' and engineers' status as privileged "modest witnesses" incorporated and contributed to a variety of seemingly nonscientific processes, including suburbanization, urban renewal, and war. The formation of scientists and engineers as privileged actors in their labs was inseparable from their formation as privileged actors outside their labs and was also simultaneously a process of making and reproducing the very structures of class, race, and gender that shaped social relations from suburban households to the "renewed" neighborhoods of the city. Scientists and engineers were constituted and reproduced as privileged actors through broad networks that included the places where they worked, lived, worshipped, learned, and recreated. If technoscience includes microbes and atoms as actants, then surely it should also include the spaces, people, and social relations that are essential to the daily existence of scientists and engineers.

In this book, I largely focus on the communities and homes of scientists and engineers rather than their workplaces. I do so for a variety of reasons. First and foremost, there is a massive literature that follows scientists and engineers only in their workplaces. In my university library, there are shelves of books that investigate the historical and contemporary practices of engineers and scientists at work. There are few books that focus on the formation of communities of scientists and engineers and even fewer that focus on their daily experiences outside the workplace. Second, the questions I am interested in—how scientists and engineers were enrolled in the remaking of Pittsburgh and how they were reproduced as racial, class, and gendered subjects—are less visible in their labs than they are in their everyday lives in the city and its suburbs. Third, many of the retired nuclear engineers and scientists who worked on nuclear reactors for the U.S. Navy, whose interviews make up the bulk of the evidence in part III of this book, could not share many details about their classified work. Nuclear scientists and engineers who worked in the commercial nuclear power industry were very happy to speak with me about their work, but these details were rarely relevant to the questions at the heart of this book. For those readers interested in a detailed account of the work of nuclear scientists and engineers, you will not find that in the pages that follow. For those who feel it important to understand how the work of nuclear scientists and engineers shaped and was shaped by the wider world in which they lived, read on.

Throughout this book, unless otherwise noted, I refer to scientists and engineers interchangeably. I do so for several reasons. First, it is in concurrence with the study of technoscience, the development of which was triggered by the "implosion" of science and technology. As a number of scholars have argued, there is no clean boundary between the pursuit of scientific knowledge and technological innovation, and this was certainly the case in many of Pittsburgh's laboratories.[31] Additionally, business and political leaders in Pittsburgh did not differentiate between scientists and engineers in their attempts to boost the region. As far as they were concerned, both scientists and engineers were equally good for Pittsburgh. Likewise, in Pittsburgh's suburbs, where communities of white-collar professionals developed, there was no sense that an engineer was a less preferable neighbor than a scientist, and there was a clear sense that both were superior to a steelworker. Finally, much of this book focuses specifically on nuclear scientists and engineers who, despite some squabbles and differences in approach, usually worked and lived alongside each other, were members of the American Nuclear Society, and identified each other as engaged in a shared project of developing, refining, selling, and advocating for nuclear technology.[32] The broad conditions that allowed for the social reproduction of nuclear scientists and engineers were usually identical.

This book develops five core arguments about scientists and engineers and their role in the remaking and suburbanization of Pittsburgh. First, engineers and scientists were privileged actors, and this privilege was in part the result of class, whiteness, and patriarchy. In other words, the authority and expertise of scientists and engineers was a product not purely of their education, professional status, or abilities but also of their position and power within society. In turn, scientists' and engineers' ability to assume the valorized role of rational and objective actors reinforced existing class, race, and gender divisions.

Second, Pittsburgh's elite portrayed scientists and engineers as crucial to the region's Renaissance. Beginning in the 1940s, Pittsburgh's elite enrolled scientists and engineers as valued allies in their efforts to transform the region from a center of heavy industry to one more focused on coordinating and financing manufacturing that occurred elsewhere. The presence of scientists and engineers bolstered the legitimacy of the corporate-led effort to remake Pittsburgh, and in turn the region's elite actively attempted to make spaces that served the interests of scientists, engineers, and other white-collar workers as well as business.

Third, violence at home and abroad fundamentally contributed to the remaking of Pittsburgh and the creation of technoscientific, suburban bubbles. Whether the violence of deindustrialization that devastated working-class communities, the premature deaths and lower life chances of African Americans in the region, the institutionalized misogyny that shaped laboratories and suburban homes, or the countless deaths and injuries inflicted on people worldwide by the U.S. military with Pittsburgh-made technologies, the events that I explore in this book are violent. Systemic premature death and violence helped form and resulted from Pittsburgh's remaking and the formation of technoscientific, suburban bubbles.

Fourth, many geographers and historians of science have demonstrated the importance of investigating the spaces of science and technology and of disrupting the supposed placelessness of the production of scientific knowledge.[33] This book extends their work by examining the production of spaces where scientists and engineers work as well as the array of spaces that help reproduce their social positions, power, and authority. Because the privileges of engineers and scientists are the product of forces much wider than those that take place within their laboratories and because the actions of scientists and engineers have a significant role in shaping the world around them, in order to understand how they work, we must follow them beyond the most obvious spaces of technoscience.

Finally, during the Cold War, Pittsburgh's Renaissance, with scientists and engineers at its center, became a global symbol of capitalist renewal. Not only did the Renaissance remake Pittsburgh, but it also created a globally deployable myth: Pittsburgh represented the potential for a partnership of state and industry to remake industrial cities into scientific centers that would develop technologies for the benefit of all. This book excavates the Cold War origins of the still-accepted myth that Pittsburgh's remaking into a center of technoscience represents the potential for a more just and equitable capitalist economy.

Plan of the Book

Nuclear Suburbs is broken into three parts that move from an analysis of the Pittsburgh Renaissance, to the creation of suburban spaces for science, to the everyday lives of scientists and engineers in Pittsburgh's suburbs. Part I, "Remaking Postwar Pittsburgh," explores how Pittsburgh's elite installed science and engineering, and scientists and engineers, at the heart of the Renaissance. Part II, "Making Science Suburban," addresses how Pittsburgh-based industry sought out suburban research laboratories as spaces to reproduce distinct class positions for its technoscientific workforce. Part III, "Cold War Community," draws from oral histories in order to examine how nuclear scientists and engineers formed communities and engaged with the Cold War both at home and at work.

Chapter 1 uses the example of the opening of the United States' first nuclear power plant, the Shippingport Atomic Power Station, and its transmission of electricity to Pittsburgh to explore the convergence between technoscience, the Cold War, and the Pittsburgh Renaissance. During the early Cold War, the Pittsburgh region became a key site for the production of both nuclear technology and an aura of American technological progress.

Chapter 2 addresses how Pittsburgh's elite presented the Renaissance as an attempt to make Pittsburgh into a more suitable place for scientists and engineers. It argues that the Allegheny Conference on Community Development, an elite regional alliance, used the figure of the scientist as a mobilizing force for the renewal of the region. The ACCD described scientists as finicky characters who, if satisfied, would contribute disproportionately to Pittsburgh's renewal. Scientists became useful figures in crafting a narrative in which urban renewal was objectively beneficial for the entire region.

Remaking Pittsburgh for scientists legitimated what Roy Lubove described as a "reverse welfare state" and ultimately contributed to growing social inequalities between mill towns, inner-city neighborhoods, and middle-class suburbs.[34]

Chapter 3 looks back to the growth of suburban Pittsburgh as a center of industrial research from the 1890s to World War II. In doing so, it argues that the post–World War II suburbanization of white-collar work continued a much longer process of spatially dividing mental and physical labor that was rooted in and fundamental to industrial capitalism. In Pittsburgh, corporations began striving to create "pure" spaces for research as early as 1916. Corporate and scientific leaders argued that manufacturing contaminated the work of scientists and engineers and that they needed to pursue their research at laboratories located in campus-like atmospheres, insulated from the noxious influence of factories. This chapter argues that industrial firms suburbanized science in order to create a spatial division of labor between conceptualization and execution and a new class of technoscientific worker, whom they named "research man."

Chapter 4 discusses the accelerated suburbanization of industrial research facilities during the postwar period. After World War II, with varying degrees of success, Westinghouse built a succession of research laboratories, corporate offices, testing facilities, and advanced manufacturing plants, all located in the suburbs. This chapter examines why Westinghouse became an increasingly suburban company during the second half of the twentieth century and why it chose to move its facilities away from the industrial center of East Pittsburgh. While business motives and the desire to build on inexpensive land clearly guided these moves, so too did Westinghouse's need to build suburban facilities that suited the needs of scientists and engineers. Like prior periods of industrial decentralization, the suburbanization of research and development during the postwar period was part of the process of forming a distinct spatial division of labor based on the purported needs of scientists and engineers.

Part III shifts focus to a belt of residential suburbs heavily populated by nuclear scientists and engineers located to the south of the Bettis Atomic Power Laboratory. Based largely on oral histories with nuclear engineers and scientists who worked for Westinghouse during the Cold War, it argues that scientific expertise and technological rationality were reproduced in part in the suburbs. Chapter 5 examines how nuclear engineers and scientists found homes in Pittsburgh's southern suburbs during the Cold War. It argues that scientists and engineers took for granted both their decisions to cluster in these particular communities and the racial, class, and gender divisions that resulted.

Chapter 6 follows nuclear engineers and scientists between their suburban homes and workplaces in order to expose the invisibilities of nuclear engineering: essential elements of the field not discussed in any classroom or scientific journal. In particular, it shows how gender, religion, and politics were as important a part of any nuclear reactor as control rods or uranium 235, but nuclear engineers and scientists rarely named them as such.

Chapter 7 returns to the Bettis Laboratory in order to consider how nuclear scientists and engineers thought about their contribution to war making. It argues that in the shift from hot to cold war, the experience of working on weapons that posed unimaginable harm became normalized as work. By coming to see war as work, Westinghouse employees helped cement a divide between the seeming peacefulness of their suburban lives and the violence at home and abroad that reproduced their daily existence.

In the epilogue, I turn to the present, a moment in which Pittsburgh is widely celebrated as a global symbol of how a focus on science and technology can restore an industrial city. As the epilogue makes clear, Pittsburgh's rebirth is yet again rooted in violence and exclusion.

PART I

Remaking Postwar Pittsburgh

1

Going Critical

Technoscience, the Cold War, and the Pittsburgh Renaissance

On February 10, 1958, Walter Cronkite ascended Mount Washington to share a "brief glimpse" of downtown Pittsburgh with national viewers of the Westinghouse-sponsored (and -owned) CBS Studio One. Fred Remington, the media reporter for the *Pittsburgh Press,* described how Pittsburgh "had a magical quality ... its thousands of lights glowing clear and steady through the cold darkness."[1] This was not the first time in recent months that national media had visited Pittsburgh. In December 1957, reporters took a break from their panicked coverage of Sputnik I to celebrate an American triumph in Pittsburgh.[2] Like Cronkite, they too ascended Mount Washington to look down on the city.

What they saw was a city in the midst of its remaking. In the heart of downtown, the new skyscrapers of the city's industrial and financial giants surrounded a newly built park, Mellon Square. On the top floor of the tallest of these buildings was the opulent office of Richard King Mellon, the oligarchical leader of Pittsburgh's Renaissance. From his office, Mellon could look east to where bulldozers demolished thousands of row houses in the predominantly African American Hill District or west to the glimmering stainless-steel office towers of Gateway Center. An emerging network of highways and bridges spanned out from Gateway Center to the suburbs, home to a growing constellation of research centers. Yet in December 1957, the national media was fixated not on the buildings at the heart of Pittsburgh's Renaissance but on the electricity that lit them.

At 4:30 a.m. on December 2, 1957, twenty-five miles northwest of the city on the Ohio River, plant operators raised the control rods in the reactor at the Shippingport Atomic Power Station. In the parlance of the nuclear industry, as neutrons began to collide with uranium-235 atoms and sustain a chain reaction, the plant had "gone critical." The product of an elaborate public-private partnership, Shippingport was funded by the Atomic Energy Commission (AEC), designed by the Naval Reactors Division and Pittsburgh-based Westinghouse, and operated by Duquesne Light Company. On December 18, it began to feed electricity into the power grid, and on December 23, it reached full power of sixty megawatts, enough electricity to power 250,000 homes. Exactly fifteen years after the first self-sustaining nuclear chain reaction at Stagg Field in Chicago, Pittsburgh became the first city in the United States to receive electricity generated by nuclear power.

Shippingport, a relatively small power plant, was the centerpiece of Eisenhower's "Atoms for Peace" program and was intended to demonstrate to the world that atomic energy could be put to peaceful purposes. It was one part of the United States' larger effort to leverage its advantage in nuclear science, technologies, and refined fuels in order to exert political and economic influence around the world.[3] Along with being an "Atom University" for aspiring nuclear engineers from around the world, Shippingport was the first full-scale "commercial" nuclear power plant and the first intended to feed electricity into the United States' domestic power grid.[4]

At Shippingport's dedication in 1958, local and national leaders neatly captured its grandiose promise for the United States and humanity. From the White House, President Dwight D. Eisenhower wielded a neutron wand to restart the reactor, telling the national radio and television audience that the plant "represents what can be done . . . to put the atom to work for the good of mankind." He personally dedicated the plant to "the cause of peace."[5] In Shippingport, luminaries from Washington and Pittsburgh stepped to the stage to wax poetic about the plant's significance. Westinghouse president Mark Cresap likened the plant to the discovery of fire and hoped that it heralded "an era of atomic creation which will fulfill the prayers . . . of men everywhere for peace and for plenty." Pennsylvania congressman and Joint Committee on Atomic Energy (JCAE) member James Van Zandt described it as an answer to Sputnik and proof that private industry gave the United States a decisive advantage over the Soviet Union. The guiding force behind the plant's development, Admiral Hyman Rickover, observed that nuclear power offered man the heavy responsibility to "modify his environment" and "do God's work." During the ceremony, reporters kept an eye on the reaction of "impassive" and "heavy-set, chunky" Soviet diplomat Boris Pavlov, who coyly congratulated American engineers for building a plant that he claimed was similar to one built outside Moscow four years earlier.[6]

"When we consider the power needs of less fortunate nations," the *Saturday Evening Post* told its readership, "our atomic program . . . becomes an implement of—or at least an issue in—foreign policy." The objective of Shippingport was "to stay ahead of Russia in the technology race . . . so that we may win friends by helping them build atomic power plants."[7] This was not Shippingport's only purpose. As Duquesne Light chairman Philip Fleger told a national meeting of electrical utility executives, if the United States was to defeat the Soviets, it would do so through the power of free enterprise. He assured his skeptical audience that "Shippingport is a natural and logical step in an orderly transition from the complete Government monopoly . . . to development of the atom . . . by private business." Because the plant was the result of state and corporate investment, "Shippingport is everyone's story," "everyone's property," and "everyone will own the knowledge that is gained" and "share in the dividends."[8]

In keeping with the overall propaganda value of Atoms for Peace, politicians, corporate leaders, and the media deployed Shippingport and its connection to Renaissance Pittsburgh as an important victory in the broader Cold War. They offered Shippingport as a salvation to the problems of the developed and developing world, as a peaceful response to the militarist Soviet Union, as the latest embodiment of the pioneering destiny of the United States, and as the first step in the privatization of atomic energy. Shippingport and peaceful atomic energy were an alternative to the terrifying destruction of the atomic bomb. At Hiroshima, the atom had terrified the world; at Shippingport, it offered salvation.

At Shippingport's unveiling, national business, political, and military leaders made the plant and Pittsburgh's relationship to the Cold War legible to the public. The Cold War, Matthew Farish argues, was not a fixed, discrete, or exceptional conflict. Nor was it simply a military conflict. Rather, it was part of a long search for security by a variety of actors, from admirals and corporate executives to suburbanites and urban planners. This search for security created multiple "spacings" that connected scales from the globe to the body.[9] Each section of this chapter explores a different Cold War spacing in Pittsburgh. The first examines the most obvious, Pittsburgh's role as a Cold War metropole: the center of a network of laboratories and plants that produced nuclear technologies that helped sustain the economic and military dominance of the United States. The second explores the moment that the high-tech Shippingport plant was connected to Renaissance Pittsburgh. This provided not only electricity but also a global symbol of capitalist renewal that was essential to the Cold War: a new Pittsburgh was modernizing and transcending industrial capitalism. The third section unpacks the Cold War myth that the Pittsburgh Renaissance offered a new form of capitalism that would provide plenty and progress for all residents of the region. The final section punctures this myth and exposes how the Renaissance was an uneven and unjust project that did little to improve the lives of white and Black working-class Pittsburghers.

As this chapter broadly shows, the connections between Shippingport, submarines, and Renaissance Pittsburgh created spacings that instilled an essential Cold War axiom: that technological innovation, produced by private industry, would allow Pittsburgh, the United States, and the world to progress beyond industrial capitalism into a new era of prosperity and security for all. The media, Westinghouse, and various state officials used Shippingport to make the enormity of the Cold War comprehensible to the people of Pittsburgh, the United States, and the world. Using the plant and its connection to America's Renaissance City as an example, they rendered the United States' involvement in the Cold War as a universally beneficial quest for progress and technological advancement.

Cold War Metropole

The Atomic Energy Commission, the Navy, and Westinghouse planned to generate more than just electricity at the Shippingport plant. The centerpiece of Atoms for Peace, Shippingport was a Cold War salvo intended to demonstrate that the United States developed nuclear power for peaceful purposes and that it would supply nuclear power plants—the means of development—to countries worldwide. Westinghouse manufactured the first nuclear power reactor ever exported, the Belgian Reactor-3 (BR3). The United States offered the BR3 to Belgium as a means to maintain access to uranium from the Congo and to encourage the formation of the six-nation Euroatom coalition.[10] The sale of this plant in 1955 marked Westinghouse's entry into the sale and licensing of nuclear reactors worldwide. By 1983 it had supplied 28 percent of worldwide civilian nuclear power plants (ninety-seven reactors), and its licensees Framatone and Mitsubishi developed an additional 23 percent (seventy-one) based on Westinghouse design. Westinghouse produced 49 percent (sixty) of all commercial reactors in the United States and 45 percent (thirty-seven) of exports from the United States.[11] From its offices in Pittsburgh's suburbs, Westinghouse engineers spanned out across the world to develop nuclear reactors throughout Europe and in Brazil, Japan, South Korea, the Philippines, and Taiwan. As the Cold War developed into a battle over political control, resources, influence, and markets, Westinghouse's export of nuclear technology became a key arena of this struggle.

In addition to power plants, Westinghouse produced reactors for naval propulsion. With the exception of the GE-developed U.S.S. *Seawolf* (affectionately nicknamed Dockwolf by Westinghouse engineers), Westinghouse's pressurized water reactor (PWR) technology served as the basis for nearly all the nuclear reactors used by the United States and British Navies during the Cold War. These reactors transformed naval warfare. Prior to their development, most submarines were powered by a combination of diesel engines and batteries and needed to resurface every few hours to recharge and take in oxygen. Nuclear propulsion radically freed submarines from the need to surface. As a result, the Westinghouse-powered U.S.S. *Nautilus* and U.S.S. *Skate*, the world's first and third nuclear submarines, broke a series of records, including being the first submarine to surface at the North Pole and to complete a fully submerged Atlantic crossing.

Because nuclear propulsion required less space for fuel, it also freed greater space for cargo and other materials, such as ballistic missiles. Nuclear submarines' ability to run without surfacing and the quiet of later generations of nuclear propulsion systems made them difficult to detect. As a result, submarines armed with nuclear warheads became vital nuclear deterrents for the Soviet Union and the United States, ensuring that apocalypse awaited either country even if they were able to eliminate all ground- and air-based nuclear weapons. Nuclear-powered vessels also required less frequent refueling than diesel-powered vessels, thereby eliminating one of the key constraints on naval movements.[12] The first use of a nuclear-powered aircraft carrier in combat, the Westinghouse-powered U.S.S. *Enterprise*'s forty-three-day "pounding" of Vietnam, was met with widespread praise. Captain James Holloway, the ship's commander, described its "action in combat" as "magnificent." Rear Admiral Henry Miller argued that the *Enterprise*'s performance proved that the United States needed to "build as many nuclear-powered ships as we can afford." "They're the best and most efficient kind of ships," he said. "The nuclear navy is the navy of the future."[13]

Westinghouse-produced nuclear technology was a means of economic and territorial control during the Cold War. It provided greater freedom of movement to the navy, thereby reducing its reliance on overseas bases.[14] Nuclear submarines became one of the main components of the United States' nuclear deterrent forces. U.S. companies' state-enforced monopoly on the export of nuclear technology and state-led programs to carefully disseminate nuclear technology exerted influence and ensured the existence of a market for U.S.-manufactured nuclear equipment and fuel.[15] As John Krige shows, the United States used its monopoly on nuclear technology, fuel, and expertise as a means of "soft power" and to secure export markets for U.S.-based companies, especially Westinghouse.[16] Finally, the preeminence of U.S. nuclear technology—developed through a partnership between commercial firms, the military, and the state—was used as a marker of the superiority of the United States and the capitalist economic system. Its export was intended to demonstrate that the United States supplied the means of development to the world.

The Pittsburgh region was the key base for the development of nuclear technologies that helped allow the United States to exert influence abroad. As Kanishka Goonewardena and Stefan Kipfer note, "cities have always been crucial to imperialism, given their ability to *centralize* military, political, and economic activities and in doing so draw otherwise disparate social formations into hierarchical and exploitative structural relations."[17] Cities from Boston to Los Angeles and suburbs from Long Island to Palo Alto served as Cold War metropoles—centers for the creation of technologies that would defeat the Soviet Union and exert influence abroad but also bases for the export of the means of progress to the world. Through their work at companies such as Westinghouse, Pittsburghers and their counterparts in cities and suburbs across the United States meaningfully contributed to the Cold War.

Like earlier periods of imperialism, the Cold War incorporated the public in a process of imagining the self and the nation in distinction to an inferior other. As Edward Said wrote, the people of the West have "a commitment" to imperialism and colonialism that

> on one hand, allowed decent men and women to accept the notion that distant territories and their native peoples *should* be subjugated, and, on the other, replenished metropolitan energies so that these decent people could think of

> *imperium* as a protracted, almost metaphysical obligation to rule subordinate, inferior, or less advanced peoples.[18]

As Said repeatedly illustrated, Western powers produce culture at home in order to legitimate imperialism and enlist the public's support. As the Cold War developed into an overt conflict with the Soviet Union that was supposedly over the fate of the world, many Americans came to see their own way of living as superior to those of communist-controlled countries and the Third World. Based on their allegedly superior technology and culture, Americans committed to providing the means of progress to the peoples of the world—from pesticides to medicines to nuclear reactors to the arts—and on the basis of this relationship further cemented their belief that American life was superior. As Christina Klein describes, this was part of a strategy to propagandize the Cold War, "as something that ordinary Americans could take part in, as a set of emotional activities in which they could invest their emotional and intellectual energy."[19] Cold War imperial culture not only justified dominating distant places; it also produced a shared sense of national identity, superiority, and purpose. When the Shippingport nuclear power station was connected to Renaissance Pittsburgh, not only the reactor but also Pittsburgh itself became an important symbol, both at home and abroad, of the superiority and promise of the United States and the capitalist economic system.

The View from Mount Washington

The unveiling of Shippingport was an event of global and national import with implications for U.S.-Soviet relations and international atomic energy policy. It also had major significance for the Pittsburgh region. The ACCD and the region's business and political elite declared that Pittsburgh was now a nuclear city and that its connection to Shippingport was the latest step in their remaking of the region and its economy. They offered the remade city and its connection to Shippingport as an exceptional illustration of how science and engineering would open a new era of progress and modernity for Pittsburgh and the world.

Shippingport's opening unleashed a torrent of commentary in the local press on the exceptional nature of nuclear power. Despite the fact that "atomic electricity" was identical to that generated by burning coal, media commentators described its transmission to ordinary Pittsburgh homes as a historic occasion. Newspaper columnist Inez Robb observed that Pittsburgh housewives would be the first in the world to bake a cherry pie using atomic energy.[20] Similarly, on the day that the plant first fed electricity into the city's power grid, the *Pittsburgh Post-Gazette* proudly told readers that, while they would never know the difference, "the light you read this by may be energized by atomic-powered electricity."[21] Years later, *Pittsburgh Press* journalist William Gill could still vividly remember "the night in December, 1957, when the plant lit the sky of Pittsburgh. It was a prophetic event."[22]

Other commentators noted the convergence between Pittsburgh's bicentennial in 1958, its history as a frontier and industrial center, and its new role as the United States' first nuclear-powered city. A bicentennial pamphlet produced by the Carnegie Library of Pittsburgh proudly noted the inauguration of "A NEW AGE—ATOMIC ENERGY" and reported that "the electric lights which glow in the city are now a symbol as well as a fact of the future of a new power."[23] An "artistic fission" in the *Pittsburgh Press* portrayed two centuries of progress in its foreground from settlers to scientists, while Shippingport and the U.S.S. *Nautilus* loomed in the background.[24] An article that described the "surge in research" in Pittsburgh opened with a photo of the city's new skyline and a caption that encapsulated all the key elements of the Renaissance: "On its 200th Birthday, Pittsburgh faces the space-age frontier with atom-powered lights gleaming in the Golden Triangle's smoke-free dusk." The article focused on the research activities of local firms and noted that Pittsburgh had evolved from "Indian scout to space pioneer."[25] Similarly, a Pittsburgh Chamber of Commerce pamphlet declared that the nuclear industry "opened a new chapter in Pittsburgh's pioneering."[26]

In contrast to modern Pittsburgh, the "historic river packet boat village" of Shippingport, located on "a sleepy bend in the Ohio," was an ideal backdrop for an atomic power plant—a Cold War–era version of Leo Marx's "machine in the garden."[27] Visiting reporters drew an irresistible contrast between the tiny village and its new neighbor, a technologically advanced atomic plant that magically produced electricity without smoke. The *Saturday Evening Post* drew readers' attention to the village's past as "a loading point for beaver pelts" while reminding them that today its "remoteness is more apparent than real."[28] Industry leaders also contrasted the plant to its rural backdrop while noting the parallels between a former frontier town and a "pioneering" scientific effort. According to Duquesne Light chairman Fleger, the plant's location, "near the site of Fort Duquesne, an outpost of freedom for early pioneers," was an apt site for "a great venture . . . destined to mark an historic turning point in the history of the electric power industry, of the United States, and indeed, of the world."[29]

While local and national media described the village of Shippingport as a picturesque, bygone place—a mere backdrop to the plant—they described the Pittsburgh region very differently. The renewed and modern Pittsburgh region was the vibrant business and scientific center out of which the atomic industry grew. The Shippingport plant was the latest sign that Pittsburgh was moving beyond its industrial past. Once synonymous with iron and steel, Pittsburgh was now the "Atomic Capital" of the world. Commentators drew a direct link between Pittsburgh's progressive development into a modern postindustrial region and nuclear power's exceptional nature. As historian Gabrielle Hecht argues, throughout the Cold War the state, industry, and the American public defined nuclear technology as a radical departure from prior forms of energy and the latest realization of a long history of U.S. technological and social superiority. According to Hecht, there are important cultural, economic, and political dimensions of nuclear ontologies—of what is defined as nuclear. Nuclearity is not an objective or inherent condition; it is created within particular contexts. As she writes, nuclearity is "a technopolitical spectrum that shifts in time and space" and "nuclear ontologies have a history, and a geography."[30] The unveiling of Shippingport tied together nuclearity and Pittsburgh's Renaissance to represent the promise of science and technology for Pittsburgh, the United States, and the world.

The Shippingport plant bolstered a wider effort by the region's elite to define Pittsburgh as nuclear. Nuclear energy now powered the region's homes and buildings. At seven different facilities in Pittsburgh's suburbs, more than seven thousand Westinghouse employees worked on a dozen military and civilian nuclear power reactors. This was a greater concentration of private employees in the nuclear industry than in any other region or company on Earth.[31] Its universities not only were engaged in nuclear engineering and physics research but also were educating a new generation of nuclear engineers and scientists for industry. According to the region's boosters, the steel city was being reborn as a research and technology center, and the Shippingport plant was only the latest symbol of this rebirth. Boosters linked the region's newfound nuclearity to their efforts to remake the industrial city.

To this end, prior to Shippingport's completion, Westinghouse president Gwilym Price set out to relabel Pittsburgh as the "Atomic Capital of the Free

World." On February 8, 1956, in a speech to a local chapter of the Society for the Advancement of Management, Price claimed the company's facilities formed an unparalleled concentration of nuclear research and manufacturing. He told those gathered, "There is nothing at all compared to this in any other area of the United States" or anywhere else in the "free world." He doubted there was anything like it in the Soviet Union either.[32] Thus far there had been little "fanfare or publicity," but Pittsburgh was now the "world headquarters for atomic power." The next day, headlines in the city's three daily papers proudly declared: "City A-Power Capital," "City Called Free World 'A' Capital," and "City Proclaimed World A-Center."[33] Two years later, Mayor David Lawrence, the indubitable leader of the city's Democratic machine, seconded Price's assessment, issuing an official proclamation praising Westinghouse for making "Pittsburgh . . . the World's Gateway to the Atomic Age" and enhancing the city's "reputation . . . as a leading technological center in the United States."[34] Westinghouse, local media, and Pittsburgh's promoters grasped the title "Atomic Capital" as a way of moving beyond Pittsburgh's increasingly beleaguered history as the Steel City. Steel represented Pittsburgh's past; nuclear power its future.

On the day of Shippingport's dedication, the *Post-Gazette* once again acclaimed the plant's critical contribution to the Renaissance: "Electricity flowing today from atoms" was symbolic of Pittsburgh's "pioneering spirit." Over the past thirteen years, Pittsburgh's Renaissance had "opened up many avenues of progress." Of these new avenues, none was more important than the "expanding search for knowledge." Due to the "combined forward motion of science and the 'Pittsburgh Renaissance,'" research activities had increased greatly. According to the *Post-Gazette,* the region was now home to 113 research labs that employed 17,200 people and spent $160 million annually.[35] At these labs, "industrial and scientific man has been given the tools, the freedom and encouragement to make his inquisitiveness work for the betterment of not just the Pittsburgh community, but for people everywhere." Pittsburgh's elite had formed a partnership with local government in order to ensure the renewal of the region into a place devoted to progress and modernity. The emergence of the city as "a world leader" in atomic energy—"the newest of industries dependent on research"—symbolized their success.[36] According to Pittsburgh's boosters, they were remaking the Steel City into a postindustrial center, and the Shippingport plant was at the heart of this transformation.

For those who looked down on "radiant" Pittsburgh from Mount Washington in the winter of 1958, the city and its surrounding region had become nuclear. Off in the distance, the city's suburbs were home to an integrated complex of laboratories and plants that produced the nuclear reactor that powered this modern scene. Transmission wires connected glimmering skyscrapers and modern research laboratories to the plant at Shippingport, forming a perfect congruity between the first full-scale atomic power plant and the world's most modern city. Needless to say, the fetish of nuclear technology rendered many of the social relations that produced this scene invisible: the federal funds that paid for the plant, the thousands of workers who labored on it, the elaborate and highly toxic uranium refining process that provided its fuel, and the colonialism on which uranium mining was based.[37] In fact, the very energy itself was equally invisible, no different from the electricity that had lit the city for decades. What had changed was that Pittsburgh had become nuclear. From Mount Washington, Pittsburgh's progress from frontier town to Steel City to Atomic Capital of the World seemed inevitable. The promise of human progress through technology, a vital element of the United States' Cold War arsenal, was instilled in and shaped by the region's Renaissance.

"An Experiment in Survival"

Shippingport's unveiling was not the first time that national media had ascended Mount Washington to make sense of the Cold War.[38] In the winter of 1946, a journalist from *Fortune* looked down on a city that seemed on the brink of collapse. Brought to a standstill by a utility strike, the candle-lit downtown looked as though it had "strayed into some darker century." Pittsburgh, a focal point for a wave of national strikes, "appeared more than ever a city under siege." The "capital of big labor" and of "big industry," Pittsburgh "epitomize[d] the problems of an advanced industrial society and its chances for survival." The problem was not just strikes but also the environment and spirit of the city. The region's rivers flooded frequently; its air was smoky, its neighborhoods "the untidy heritage of nineteenth-century planlessness, a vast slum, a hurt to the eyes." *Fortune* warned that industry was leaving the region, and an accompanying advertisement touting San Diego's plentiful surplus defense plants seemed to prove its point.[39]

Yet not all was doom and gloom, for "Pittsburgh suddenly found itself tired of its dirt, chaos, and congestion." A new generation of business leaders had moved away from "the great, gray chill mansions" of the east end to the "smart country lanes" of the suburbs. Paradoxically, this move corresponded to a new sense of civic responsibility. As Robert Downie, the president of People's First National Bank and vice chairman of the ACCD, told *Fortune,* it was no longer possible to accrue wealth in the "individualistic methods of our grandfathers." In order to retain their wealth, the region's elite needed to remake Pittsburgh and address the needs of the "masses." "If they don't get what they want under our system," Downie cautioned, "they'll be fooled into thinking they can get it under another."[40]

In response to this looming crisis, in 1943 a select group of Pittsburgh's business elite met to form the ACCD: an organization intended to resolve the many crises industry had wrought upon the region. Over the next decade, under the aegis of the ACCD, Pittsburgh's elite, led by financier Richard King Mellon, joined with Democratic mayor David Lawrence to lead the Pittsburgh Renaissance, what *Fortune* called "an experiment in survival" for Pittsburgh.[41] The ACCD, a regional alliance composed of more than twenty corporate leaders from finance and industry and a smattering of university presidents, led the renewal of Pittsburgh's built and natural environment.[42] Its goal, as described by Sherie Mershon, was to "safeguard corporate autonomy" and "replace Pittsburgh's reputation as a grimy, chaotic manufacturing district."[43] The alliance sought to make the region once again conducive for capitalism. It passed pollution control measures that helped clear Pittsburgh's smoky air and built a series of dams that lessened the threat of flooding in the central business district.[44] The ACCD initiated urban renewal projects that cleared swaths of land to make way for skyscrapers, parks, a cultural center, highways, and a shopping mall.[45] Cognizant of the need to diversify the city's economy and ensure future growth, the alliance fostered fields such as higher education, medicine, finance, and research and development. The ACCD collaborated with all levels of government in an attempt to tame industry and ensure that Pittsburgh would remain a successful business center.

In the 1940s, smoky, flooded, strike-prone, economically stagnant Pittsburgh was one of industrial capitalism's most readily cited failures. Through its actions, the ACCD hoped to redeem not only the region but also capitalism as a whole, on the ground and in people's imaginations. Its goal was to clean Pittsburgh's air, clear its slums, tame its rivers, diversify its economy, recover its image as a place of progress, and in turn secure elites' investments in the region. As described by *Fortune,* this was an effort that would be watched with anticipation in "younger industrial centers" around the world, for "Pittsburgh is the test of industrialism everywhere to renew itself, to rebuild upon the ruins of the past a society more equitable, more spacious, more in the human scale."[46] The ACCD created a highly palatable and influential model of regional renewal that was replicated in industrial cities across the United States: a partnership of industry, state, unions, and other organizations that could put aside their interests and remake metropolitan regions for the benefit of all residents.[47] The ACCD created this model, in part, by describing the Renaissance as part of the Cold War.

In the late 1940s, as the Cold War heated up, the ACCD heralded the Renaissance as a modern alternative to communism and industrial capitalism. As it routinely explained, postwar Pittsburgh was plagued with economic, social, and environmental perils. Foremost among these were class antagonism and jealousy that if left unabated would lead to social unrest and economic catastrophe. In response to this imminent threat, business leaders offered to forgo their interests and form a "grand cooperative effort" to remake the region for the collective good.[48] The old Pittsburgh was characterized by inequality and the dominance of the industrial elite; in the new Pittsburgh, all residents would unite under a shared sense of purpose and identity. In the new Pittsburgh, the ACCD offered to supplant class antagonism with cooperation between business, labor, and politicians and a broad sense of civic belonging.

The ACCD's attempts to link the Cold War to the Renaissance were most visible at its annual dinners. At these well-publicized events, held in sumptuous ballrooms, politicians and corporate titans as well as a smattering of union leaders gathered to discuss plans for the region. These plans usually concerned education and culture, urban renewal, and the need to entice high-tech industry to the region, but discussion also turned to the Cold War. At these moments, speakers described the ACCD as a grand democratic partnership that was renewing the region and the capitalist economic system.

In 1951 the ACCD assembled in the gilded foyer of the Carnegie Music Hall for its seventh annual dinner. Arthur B. Van Buskirk, the president of the ACCD, opened the evening. He described the ACCD as "a body of citizens of this community who believe in Democracy and the system of free enterprise." He reminded attendees that inscribed above the doors of the ACCD's offices were the words "The Price of Freedom is Service."[49] He then ceded the dais to two speakers who would reflect on the ACCD's first six years. The first was Mr. P. I. Prentice, the editor of the *Magazine of Building*, who recounted the ACCD's many successes with urban redevelopment and how Pittsburgh had become a model for other cities.[50]

After Prentice spoke, he passed the lectern to a "local diagnostician," the Right Reverend Austin Pardue, bishop of the Episcopal Diocese of Pittsburgh. Pardue's speech focused on the threat that communism posed to the city and described the ACCD as a direct antidote to this threat. He began his speech by telling how when he first arrived in Pittsburgh in 1944, "the blackness outside was hard to believe." Over the past six years, the ACCD had attacked this "blackness," and "human brains, personal sacrifice, and united courage, have wrought a miracle, not only in cleanliness but in literally changing the city's face." Hard work and cooperation helped build this "new city," and he likened Pittsburgh's leaders to those who built the pyramids.[51]

After cataloging Pittsburgh's new assets, Pardue mustered his religiosity and warned, "We must be vigilant because the devil is a roaring lion lurking about seeking whom he may devour." The devil would emerge in one of two forms, "either Communism in one of its hideous Marxist forms" or "a spiritual civic blindness which can be the cause of these plagues." It was the ACCD's responsibility to "integrate" all Pittsburghers "into a sense of full opportunity as offered by the American free enterprise system." If they failed, "the composite citizenry will establish some other system born out of disillusionment, resentment, and hate. That is how Communists are made." He closed his speech to rousing applause, describing how the Renaissance would fulfill the promise of the free enterprise system and America's democratic destiny: "Let Pittsburgh lead in patriotic, economic, social, political, and industrial vision. Let Pittsburgh be the first city in America to so practice the spirit of our Constitution that we will ever keep from our shores the scourges of Communism and all other isms that would deny us our rights as a free people (Applause)."[52] According to Pardue, Pittsburgh's renewal would resolve capitalism's crises and offer community and opportunity to all Pittsburghers, limited only by their willingness to cooperate and work.

The ACCD widely circulated the narrative that the Renaissance was a key battle in the larger Cold War. In 1958, the year of Shippingport's unveiling and seven years after the Right Reverend's speech, Arthur Van Buskirk, the ACCD's past president, traveled to New York to share the story of Pittsburgh's success. Formerly a governor of T. Mellon and Sons, the "inner sanctum of R. K. Mellon's personal interests," Van Buskirk was selected as president in 1945. As Mellon's personal confidant, he exercised considerable control over the ACCD.[53] In his speech to the Committee for Economic Development, titled "What Business Has Learned about Rebuilding a City," he described Pittsburgh's "bleak outlook" after World War II. It was a city with "no civic pride" that stifled the ambitions of the young. In the face of this apathy, "a whole group of younger men" came to power "with new vision and greater social consciousness." He listed their achievements: 25 percent of downtown rebuilt, fifty new buildings, twelve skyscrapers, ninety-five acres of the Hill District "cleared of its slum dwellings," and tens of millions invested in local universities.[54]

The ACCD's success was not only in bricks and mortar. "Its real importance lies in the civic patriotism that has been aroused," Van Buskirk explained. "At the municipal level we have forged a new and stronger democracy of significance to the nation as a whole." In the past, Pittsburgh's industrialists had acted out of a desire for profit and had generated stupendous wealth, but today they aimed for the "common good." Such locally rooted "civic patriotism" was "essential if our nation is to meet the assault of communism." As Van Buskirk described it, business elites' visible participation in the ACCD, a partnership of all Pittsburghers, was of enormous importance for both Pittsburgh and the United States. Communism would triumph as a result not of "widespread war and bloodshed, but rather of apathy on the part of our people."[55]

Van Buskirk did not look far for the "breeding ground" of apathy that he believed gave communism succor.[56] On the edge of Pittsburgh's renewed downtown sat what the ACCD saw as a threat to its investment: the lower Hill District, a largely African American neighborhood that Mindy Fullilove called "pound-for-pound . . . the most generative black community in the United States."[57] Beginning in the early years of the twentieth century, the Hill District was the heart of Pittsburgh's Black community as well as an entry point to Pittsburgh for many immigrants. For immigrants and African American migrants from the south, the Hill District was a place of intense poverty but also of employment, housing, investment, and mutual support.

Van Buskirk and the ACCD, of course, saw something different. Instead of a vibrant community, they saw crowded streets, unkempt housing, unsanitary conditions, and an ever-encroaching threat to their newly redeveloped downtown. As the *National Municipal Review* neatly described it, the Hill District was an "urban jungle"—"105 teeming acres of slum, crime and disease."[58] Thus as Van Buskirk spoke in New York, bulldozers rolled through the lower Hill District, displacing 1,500 families and 400 businesses and preparing the ground for an arena, expressway, luxury housing, and a cultural center.[59]

The ACCD and local political leaders hoped the redevelopment of the Hill District would create a symbol of modern Pittsburgh. In place of the neighborhood, they built a state-of-the-art auditorium where they could attend the opera while gazing out at the city's modern skyline through a retractable roof. Nearby, Pittsburgh-based Alcoa financed a luxury condominium tower where opera-goers could return when the show was over, or they could easily access a ramp to the new Cross-Town Expressway that would take them to the city's growing suburbs.

However, the neighborhood that was destroyed was just as symbolic as the modern buildings that took its place. "How can our democracy be strong," Van Buskirk asked, "when we see central business districts . . . bordered by slums." Slums "are cancers on the body politics of our communities," he said. "The more enterprising residents leave" such neighborhoods, the more "the shiftless and indigent move in, bringing further deterioration." Without further action, he warned, this would become "a breeding ground for communism."[60]

Van Buskirk's claim that slums were "breeding grounds" for communism was not unique. As Samuel Zipp shows, leaders in New York also portrayed urban renewal as a "Cold War bulwark" and a means of "shoring up the nation's internal cultural defenses." The planners of Lincoln Center described it as an effort to clear slums and replace them with a cultural center that countered the notion that the United States was culturally moribund.[61] Van Buskirk was keenly aware of the parallels between Lincoln Center and the ACCD's plans for the lower Hill District. In his speech in New York, he argued that both projects offered the same "lesson": that leaders must band together in the ethos of "imagination, courage, and unselfish public spirit" to remove slums and replace them with amenities befitting the United States.[62]

Conveniently overlooking the blaring racial injustices of the ACCD's work, Van Buskirk told the New York audience that the lesson of Pittsburgh's Renaissance was that business leaders must participate in public life. He cited the example of ancient Greece, where "men struggling for riches, class hatred, political disorder, moral corruption, and waning patriotism" eventually undermined democracy. The dual threat of communism and the obsolescence of industrial cities required a cooperative partnership between business and local government. Such a partnership would eliminate "cancerous areas," halt the spread of communism, and offer an alternative. The cooperative spirit embodied in the ACCD would develop an "urban environment" that "is favorable to the maintenance of personal freedom and democratic self-government." The creation of such a city would "preserve and protect a way of life—the best way of life the world has ever seen."[63]

From Steel City to Atomic Capital

Unsurprisingly the Pittsburgh Renaissance did not initiate a new and more equitable form of capitalism. The decades-long remaking of Pittsburgh's economy and built environment was a deeply unjust and uneven process of investment and redevelopment. From the North Side to the Hill District to East Liberty, the ACCD and its state partners targeted small businesses and white and Black working-class neighborhoods for clearance and redevelopment. In their place, they built new skyscrapers, parks, highways, malls, and cultural, hospital, and university facilities. The ACCD worked to remake Pittsburgh in ways that it believed would appeal to white-collar professionals, investors, and major industrial and financial firms with large offices downtown, such as Mellon Bank, U.S. Steel, and Westinghouse.

The Renaissance did not mark the end of manufacturing in the Pittsburgh region, but it heralded an increasing shift from an industrial to a postindustrial economy. The ACCD and its members, who had been concerned about Pittsburgh's declining role as a manufacturing center for decades, began a concerted effort to diversify the region's economy and ensure its increasing viability as a center for corporate headquarters, banks, hospitals, universities, and research and development centers. As I show in the next chapter, the city's elite believed that visibility of industry and working-class life lessened Pittsburgh's appeal for the key agents of postindustrial modernity who would bring future growth. At the top of ACCD's list of the most desirable people and institutions to attract to Pittsburgh were scientists and engineers and the research facilities where they worked.

As part of the Renaissance and the corporate strategy to shift operations toward areas of future growth, Pittsburgh firms invested heavily in new science and engineering facilities in the suburbs during the 1940s and 1950s. In 1949 Westinghouse opened its first major nuclear facility, the Bettis Atomic Power Laboratory, in a suburb of Pittsburgh. It was here that the company developed the world's first nuclear propulsion system for the submarine U.S.S. *Nautilus*. The PWR technology developed at Bettis served as the basis for the Shippingport plant and the foundation for Westinghouse's entry into the nuclear power industry. Based on this technology, by the 1960s, Westinghouse had secured its position as the world's preeminent developer of nuclear reactors for peace and war. Most of the facilities where engineers, scientists, and other workers designed and manufactured these reactors were located in Pittsburgh's suburbs (see Map 1).

Westinghouse was not the only company to establish research and engineering facilities in the city's suburbs during the Cold War. The city's firms built at least forty new research centers in the suburbs during the postwar period.[64] The largest of these included the research divisions of Gulf Oil, PPG (Pittsburgh Plate Glass), Alcoa, U.S. Steel, Jones and Laughlin Steel, and the federally funded Bituminous Coal Research Laboratory. Political leaders and the ACCD celebrated the region's development as an academic and corporate research center and described it as a needed departure from its industrial

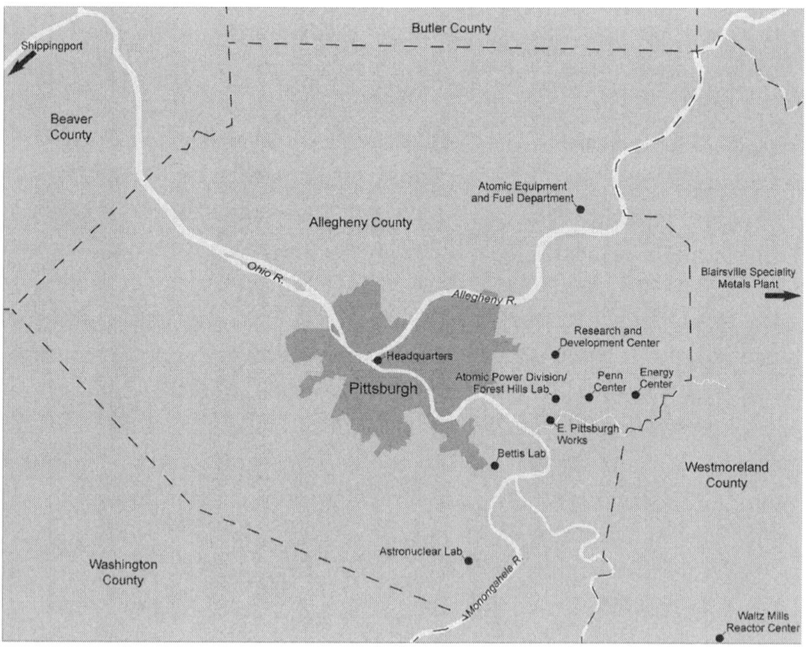

Map 1. "The Atomic Capital of the World": major Cold War–era Westinghouse facilities.

past. They envisioned the growing constellation of research facilities in the suburbs as key to Pittsburgh's reinvention. Science and engineering in the suburbs joined urban renewal, highway construction, and pollution and flood control as central components of the Renaissance.

The growth of research facilities played a significant role in Pittsburgh's suburbanization. Westinghouse and other companies intentionally located laboratories away from the traditional industrial areas along the region's river valleys. They did so for a variety of reasons, including federal tax incentives; the availability of land; a desire to locate proximate to where engineers and scientists lived; and the need to isolate radical labor unions, particularly the United Electrical, Radio, and Machine Workers (UE), which endangered access to defense contracts. Equally important, and inseparable from these structural and political factors, was the widely held belief that firms could create the most suitable place for science and engineering in the suburbs.[65] As I discuss in detail in part II, research directors, executives, architects, the media, and political leaders all considered suburbs, isolated from the immediate demands of manufacturing plants and corporate headquarters, as the optimum work and residential environment for engineers and scientists.

As I explore in part III, scientists and engineers usually moved to racially and socioeconomically exclusive communities that surrounded their suburban workplaces. While working-class suburbs of tract homes lined the region's industrial river valleys, the hills between these valleys increasingly became home to the region's white-collar professionals. Employers, municipal governments, school districts, developers, and suburban residents helped transform suburbs into optimal communities for engineers and scientists. These communities contained the homes, amenities, and school systems that befitted and helped reproduce the race, gender, and class positions of engineers and scientists. Thus the Pittsburgh region's transformation into a center for technoscience was based in the growth of suburban laboratories and office buildings but also in a sprawling profusion of new ranch homes, country clubs, and generously funded suburban school districts that surrounded these facilities.

The makeup of the region's workforce changed alongside its geography. In 1950 southwestern Pennsylvania was still the leading steel manufacturing center in the world, and 49.6 percent of its residents worked in blue-collar occupations. In 1990, after decades of deindustrialization and in the aftermath of devastating rounds of mill closings, the percentage of local residents employed in blue-collar occupations had fallen to 23.6 percent.[66] During the

Table 1. Occupational category (%) of the employed population for the twelve most populated metropolitan areas in the United States in 1950 and change in occupational category by 1990

	1950		1990		Change in percentage points (1950–1990)	
	White-collar %	Blue-collar %	White-collar %	Blue-collar %	White-collar	Blue-collar
United States	36.8	41.0	58.1	26.2	21.3	-14.8
New York	48.0	38.9	70.4	21.7	22.4	-17.2
Chicago	44.4	43.6	64.0	23.7	19.6	-19.9
Los Angeles	48.7	37.7	59.9	26.6	11.2	-11.2
Philadelphia	40.9	45.3	64.5	22.6	23.6	-22.7
Detroit	38.4	50.1	58.8	27.6	20.4	-22.5
Boston	48.4	39.0	70.2	16.9	21.8	-22.0
San Francisco	50.2	35.2	66.6	20.2	16.4	-15.0
Pittsburgh	**38.7**	**49.6**	**61.2**	**23.6**	**22.5**	**-26.0**
St. Louis	42.1	43.6	61.6	24.1	19.5	-19.5
Cleveland	43.2	45.4	61.5	25.3	18.3	-20.1
Washington	57.9	25.3	73.2	14.5	15.3	-10.8

Sources: 1950 *United States Census of Population: Pittsburgh, Pa., Census Tracts,* P-D43 (Washington, D.C.: Bureau of the Census, 1950); 1990 *Census of Population: Social and Economic Characteristics, Metropolitan Areas,* 1990 CP-2-1B (Washington, D.C.: Bureau of the Census, 1990).

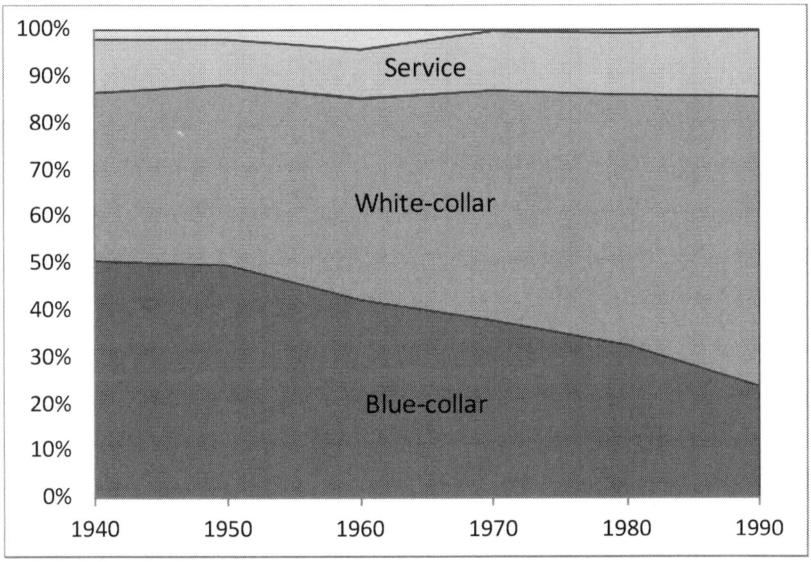

Figure 1. Occupational category (%) of the employed population in the Pittsburgh metropolitan area, 1940–1990.

same time period, the percentage of the region's employed residents working in white-collar occupations grew from 38.7 percent to 61.2 percent. This was a greater shift than that experienced by most major metropolitan regions and of the United States as a whole (see Table 1 and Figure 1).[67]

Engineers and scientists were a small but growing portion of the region's workforce. Between 1950 and 1980, the number of employed engineers grew by 54.1 percent, of natural scientists by 184.7 percent, and of nonmedical technologists and technicians by 964.5 percent. While admittedly a small proportion of the region's overall employment, work in science and engineering was of growing importance (see Table 2).[68] Corresponding to the growth of these and other white-collar fields was an increase in the percentage of local residents who had four-year university degrees, which increased from 4.9 percent in 1940 to 14.6 percent in 1980.

Suburbanization and the growth of this white-collar workforce developed in tandem. As Figure 2 shows, the city of Pittsburgh's population declined precipitously during the second half of the twentieth century, while the metropolitan region's population declined at a much slower rate as it absorbed

Table 2. Engineers and natural scientists by race and gender in the Pittsburgh metropolitan area, 1950–1980

	1950	1960	1970	1980
Total engineers	11,695	14,574	17,945	18,018
Total natural scientists	2,390	2,598	3,277	6,805
Black engineers	42	31	141	336
Black natural scientists	13	18	58	236
Woman engineers	114	62	171	165
Woman natural scientists	252	214	283	155

Sources: 1950 United States Census of Population: Pittsburgh, Pa., Census Tracts, P-D43 (Washington, D.C.: Bureau of the Census, 1950); *U.S. Censuses of Population and Housing: 1960, Pittsburgh, Pa., Standard Metropolitan Statistical Area,* PHC(1)-118 (Washington, D.C.: Bureau of the Census, 1960); *1970 Census of Population and Housing: Pittsburgh, Pa., Standard Metropolitan Statistical Area,* PHC(1)-162 (Washington, D.C.: Bureau of the Census, 1970); *1980 Census of Population and Housing: Pittsburgh, Pa., Standard Metropolitan Statistical Area,* PHC80-2-286 (Washington, D.C.: Bureau of the Census, 1980).

much of the city's population loss.[69] In 1940 the city of Pittsburgh accounted for 35 percent of the region's population; in 1990 it accounted for 16 percent. During these decades, educated, affluent, white-collar, white Pittsburghers increasingly lived in the city's suburbs.[70] They were joined and just as often preceded in the suburbs by research and development centers and office parks.

Increasing suburbanization and the growth of white-collar work resulted in the deepening polarization of the region in terms of place of residence, class, race, gender, income, occupation, and level of education. Areas of growing employment were increasingly concentrated in suburban locations or in downtown Pittsburgh and the neighborhood of Oakland, where most of the region's hospitals and universities were located. Meanwhile, centers of blue-collar employment were largely concentrated in the region's river valleys, which were surrounded by predominantly white working-class suburbs. Pittsburgh's Renaissance helped create and reinforce inequities between these communities. It focused public and private resources in middle-class suburbs and Oakland and downtown. It targeted white-collar professionals, scientists and engineers in particular, as ideal citizens who would bring growth and progress to the region. As a result, the Renaissance was deeply uneven.

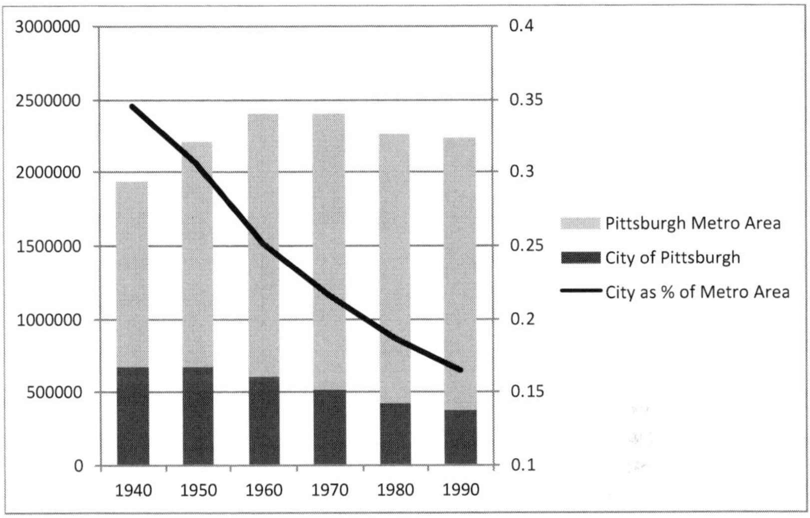

Figure 2. Population of city of Pittsburgh and metropolitan area, 1940–1990.

This unevenness culminated in 1985 when Places Rated Almanac named Pittsburgh "America's Most Livable City"—a widely acclaimed endorsement of the Renaissance—at the exact moment tens of thousands of working-class residents were leaving the region in the wake of plant closings.

In 1957, when Shippingport was connected to Pittsburgh, the region became a nuclear metropole that was intimately connected to the Cold War. The most notable Cold War role of Pittsburgh was as a center of the nuclear industry. It was from Pittsburgh's suburbs that nuclear technology and expertise were exported to Europe, Asia, Africa, and South America. The export of nuclear technology became both a valuable means of political control and an important market for firms such as Westinghouse. Just as important, the United States' export of reactors—then seen as a limitless source of energy that would be "too cheap to meter"—bolstered the Cold War narrative that the United States supplied the means of development to the world.

Pittsburgh-produced reactors not only generated energy for civilian use. They also powered submarines and aircraft carriers. Submarines were a central element of the strategy of the nuclear deterrence that ultimately economically defeated the Soviet Union. Nuclear-powered aircraft carriers have been essential to the United States' ability to launch strikes and occupy foreign ground, from Vietnam to Panama and from Afghanistan to Iraq. Nuclear reactors—designed, maintained, and manufactured in Pittsburgh's suburbs—have been a key element of the United States' military arsenal for more than sixty years.

Pittsburgh's connection to the Cold War was not only through supplying nuclear reactors. The Pittsburgh Renaissance was an elite and business-led effort to remake the economy and built environment of the smoky industrial city. By remaking Pittsburgh, the region's elite hoped not only to secure their investments and ensure future growth but also to create a global symbol of how a benevolent elite and business community could remake capitalist economies for the benefit of all. Pittsburgh's elite identified science and technology as part of Pittsburgh's salvation, a key step down a path from an industrial to a postindustrial economy. In order to achieve this salvation, as I show in the next chapter, they needed to lure scientists, engineers, and other educated workers to the region. To this end, Pittsburgh's Renaissance provided new cultural centers, laboratories, office complexes, and, most important, suburbs that would house and reproduce this privileged class of educated worker.

2

Research and Renaissance

Renewing the City for Scientists

In the 1950s, the Pittsburgh Board of Public Education (PBPE) partnered with the ACCD to publish a series of children's books on Pittsburgh's Renaissance. Funded by the Sarah Mellon Scaife Foundation and taught in local schools, the books described the miracle of Pittsburgh's rebirth and suggested ways that children could contribute. They positioned readers as citizens of a rapidly modernizing metropolis where science, engineering, suburbanization, and urban renewal were essential aspects of everyday life.

One of the books in the PBPE series, *Pittsburgh Is a Good Place to Live,* used the story of Mr. Johnson, an engineer who transfers to Pittsburgh, to narrate the city's remaking. After moving to a "ranch-type home" in the eastern suburbs, the family tours the city, visiting research labs, museums, universities, and redevelopment projects. They marvel at "modern skyscrapers" built on the site of "old warehouses." The book comes to a rousing close with a chapter titled "Rejoicing at Becoming Pittsburghers." The Johnsons reflect on the ease of their new life: "a delightful home," new friends for the children, and many opportunities in "professional, business, and industrial life." "We Johnsons are glad to call ourselves Pittsburghers," they declare.[1]

The Johnsons were not unusual characters. In 1963 the Regional Industrial Development Corporation (RIDC), an ACCD-supported authority that developed office parks, published a guide to Pittsburgh written in verse. It opened with a comparison of Joe and Jon Magarac. Joe is the Paul Bunyan–like steelworker of local lore who is "made to make steel" and throws himself into a furnace in order to make a new mill—"Part Pennsylvania, Legend or Real? / JOE MAGARAC is a symbol of STEEL." On the following page, an illustration of the much less brawny Jon Magarac shows him bending a slide rule, not a steel beam: "His strength can't be measured by muscles or height / His vision, his training, his tools are his might." While Joe throws himself into a ladle of steel, Jon "throws himself into science and math" and "blaze[s] out a path." "Prepared for tomorrow and lighting the way / JON MAGARAC is Pittsburgh today."[2]

The stories of the Johnsons and Jon Magarac reveal how Pittsburgh's elite centered the region's remaking on scientists and engineers during the early Cold War. It is not coincidental that Mr. Johnson is an engineer, not a steelworker. Nor is it coincidental that his family ends up living in the eastern suburbs that were home to many white-collar professionals. Nor is it coincidental that a sixty-three-page book on Pittsburgh spends exactly one page addressing industry and that this page focuses only on pollution control. All the books in the PBPE series share similar characteristics. First, they describe a region that is undergoing renewal for the benefit of all Pittsburghers. Second, they encourage residents to identify with the Renaissance and contribute to creating a well-kept city. Third, they claim that Pittsburgh's renewal represents progress and modernity, the ultimate expression of which is a modern research lab or office tower in a parklike setting easily convenient to a superhighway that whisks white-collar employees to their suburban homes. Fourth, they imply that while the new Pittsburgh is for the benefit of all, the naturalized subject of the region's regeneration narrative is a young, white, suburban family whose college-educated father works in a professional occupation, a family just like the Johnsons. In postwar Pittsburgh, scientists and engineers and their suburban families were the ideal figures around which the region's elite crafted their narrative of renewal.

During the early Cold War, in the PBPE books and many other outlets, the ACCD and its allies reinvented the figure of the scientist as a demanding and peculiar character whose interests they must meet in order to guarantee the region's renewal. Throughout the Renaissance, they deployed the figure of the scientist—whose interests represented growth, objectivity, and modernity—alongside eminent domain and bulldozers. In doing so, they enrolled scientists and engineers in an alliance that linked the remaking of Pittsburgh to the growing prominence of science and engineering during the Cold War.[3]

Scientists and engineers were especially salient figures in the 1950s United States because of the public's burgeoning faith in science and technology and the rapid growth of industrial, medical, and military research. The scarce supply of scientists and engineers and their celebrated character as harbingers of modernity and growth made them powerful allies as businesses and elites undertook the renewal of cities. While scientists and engineers had special symbolic value, the remaking of cities broadly favored all white-collar professionals. Cultural centers, university campuses, office towers, and condominiums replaced blue-collar neighborhoods and factories, as regional alliances remade cities into places for making ideas rather than things. Regional alliances gave hypermobile professionals many names, from scientist to knowledge worker to the creative class, but regardless of its name, they consistently centered the redevelopment of cities on some variant of this figure. For the sake of brevity, in this chapter I use the word *scientist* as shorthand for scientists, engineers, and other Cold War–era knowledge workers. This shorthand captures regional alliances' specific infatuation with scientists during the Cold War and their broad embrace of all white-collar professionals as preferred metropolitan citizens.

The ACCD and its allies portrayed scientists as demanding people who required recreational and cultural facilities, state-of-the-art research centers, and comfortable suburbs in order to effectively pursue their work. They argued that if the region built such amenities, scientists would flock there, ushering in a new era of growth and modernity. They enrolled scientists as allies—as representatives of progress—who added legitimacy to their efforts to renew the region in the interests of business.

By linking scientists to the region's remaking, Pittsburgh's elite constructed scientists as a discrete class subject. They argued that scientists uniquely contributed to transforming the smoky steel city into a center of the post-industrial economy. As I describe in chapter 3, Pittsburgh firms had previously built alliances with scientists in order to transform conditions in their plants, but now they were pursuing a bigger project: scientists would not only develop new technologies and manufacturing techniques that would guarantee future profits; they would also help legitimate the region's renewal. Two spaces played a key role in forging an alliance with scientists: urban renewal sites and suburbs. Violence was at the core of producing both spaces as well as the figure of the scientist. Pittsburgh's elite and businesses steadily remade the region, tearing down Black and white working-class neighborhoods and small businesses while building new amenities intended to appeal to scientists and other professionals. Meanwhile these privileged workers had access to housing in racially and socioeconomically segregated suburbs that provided access to well-functioning schools and steadily escalating property values. Whether they liked it or not, scientists' authority within and outside their laboratories was conditioned on the redevelopment and suburbanization of the region in ways that protected and favored business, white privilege, and the wealthy.

Reinventing Scientists for Urban Growth

In 1946 the ACCD commissioned a report from the Econometric Institute that confirmed its fears about Pittsburgh's decline. Like many similar reports, it documented that the region was too focused on metals manufacturing, which was shifting toward the Midwest.[4] Not mincing words, it deemed Pittsburgh "a declining area." In response, the report called for diversifying the economy, marketing the city's assets, and fostering "a greater Pittsburgh spirit." Most important, the city's elite needed to "rebuild" Pittsburgh from a "place built to work" to "a place in which to live comfortably."[5] While the members of the ACCD disputed many of the claims in the report, they embraced its emphasis on the need to shift Pittsburgh away from heavy industry and toward becoming a more pleasant place to live.

To this end, the ACCD began to promote a narrative that it was transforming Pittsburgh for the good of all its residents.[6] In an array of materials, from planning reports to pamphlets to the aforementioned children's books, the ACCD positioned Pittsburghers as citizens of a modern metropolis in which business-led urban renewal and scientific research were essential aspects of everyday life. The figure of the scientist had two key roles in the ACCD's Renaissance narrative. The ACCD used the figure of the scientist to demonstrate how the Renaissance represented progress that would unify the residents of the region. It also constructed scientists as demanding characters who required a rebuilt city in order to pursue their work.

The ACCD often drew direct connections between the Renaissance and scientific progress. For example, in 1947 the ACCD released "Challenge and Response," a richly illustrated pamphlet celebrating the passage of state legislation that enabled the Renaissance. The pamphlet opened by describing how the ACCD offered a unifying vision, proclaiming, "The conference does not impose. . . . . It unites!" Most of the rest of pamphlet was devoted to pairs of pages, one that darkly depicted a problem of the industrial metropolis and the other the ACCD's solution. After reviewing problems, including smoke, blight, pollution, boredom, and congestion, the pamphlet departed from its "Challenge and Response" structure to conclude with two pages devoted to research and medicine. With numerous images of the region's scientists and laboratories, it described Pittsburgh as a place that "makes continuous research a primary function." From hospitals to universities to industrial research centers, "inquiring minds, backed by ample budgets, push research ahead in Pittsburgh."[7]

It is not accidental that "Challenge and Response" culminated with scientists. The early portions of the pamphlet were devoted to portraying the Renaissance as a unifying project, yet the ACCD's "responses" harmed only working-class, African American, and indigenous communities. Addressing flooding required building dams that flooded rural communities, including the treaty-protected homes of the Seneca Nation.[8] Addressing "blight" resulted in the clearance of poor, African American, and working-class neighborhoods.[9] Even attacks on boredom targeted the cultural and recreational pursuits of the Black and white working class, some of which subverted dominant sexual and cultural norms.[10] The Renaissance devastated the lives of many, but it would benefit Pittsburgh's scientists, who, the ACCD said, would improve the well-being of every resident of Pittsburgh and the world.

Scientists not only served as ideal figures that allowed the ACCD to create a narrative of progress and unity; they also enabled the urban renewal that the ACCD was supposedly pursing in their interests. In his definitive account of the Renaissance, Roy Lubove observed elite Pittsburghers' "ritualistic praise of culture and environmental amenity." Lubove argued that the ACCD's members were driven by their fear that they would not be able to successfully recruit skilled labor to the region, citing the oft-quoted story of "a valuable man" who "quit a Pittsburgh establishment . . . for the sole purpose of securing more pleasant living conditions."[11] The ACCD and its partners repeatedly told this story to argue that they needed to remake the region in order to secure such valuable men.

Influential reports reinforced the belief that scientists were extremely fickle and needed to be lured to the region in order to ensure its growth. In 1954 a study commissioned by the ACCD and the Chamber of Commerce targeted science as key to Pittsburgh's prosperity. This report noted that research facilities were the region's "single greatest asset." From these facilities "will come new ideas for new industries" and "trained, skillful, and imaginative men to establish research-based new companies; if they are impressed with the region their new enterprise will locate here." The report made a number of suggestions to improve the region's hospitableness for scientists, including increasing the stature of universities, providing venture capital, and expanding "cultural, recreational, advanced education, and community convenience facilities . . . because this group is highly sensitive to community amenities."[12]

Nine years later, the most influential study of Pittsburgh's economy in the postwar era characterized scientists in a similar way.

> Research scientists and engineers . . . are highly selective in regard to the kind of area in which they are willing to live. They . . . are generally in such demand that they can indulge their preference for climate, cultural facilities, good schools, and the like. Such factors of personal preference go far to account for the observed tendency of research . . . to concentrate in large metropolitan areas on the West and Northeast Coasts. The conflicting images of Pittsburgh as "the Smoky City" and "the Renaissance City" are both important in determining the Region's success in attracting professional personnel.[13]

The report concluded that in areas such as Southern California and Boston, research had been a significant factor in regional growth. If Pittsburgh wanted to similarly benefit, local leaders needed to create a suitable "research climate."[14]

In order to create this "research climate," the ACCD developed new recreational, educational, and cultural amenities that would supposedly make Pittsburgh more desirable for scientists and other professionals. The largest and most devastating of these projects was the redevelopment of the lower Hill District on the edge of downtown. Climbing the steep hill to the east of downtown, the Hill District was a densely packed neighborhood that was the vibrant heart of Pittsburgh's African American community. While life in the Hill was difficult, it hosted an array of institutions and support systems that allowed African Americans to persevere despite pervasive racism.[15]

In the 1950s, using the federal government's newly created Title I urban renewal program, the ACCD targeted the Hill as the site of a new cultural center. It described the Hill as a "welter of substandard housing" and a "blight upon our community."[16] In the plans for the Lower Hill Cultural Center, the Hill would be crowned with a symphony hall and museum complex that bore an uncanny resemblance to New York's Lincoln Center. The ACCD likened this complex to an "acropolis" or "citadel" rising above downtown. Visitors would look down from the "ramparts" of the complex and "discard the lingering conception of Pittsburgh as a 'milltown' that is bereft of all beauty and grace."[17] New luxury housing would line the edges of the redevelopment site. These new towers and garden apartments would realize "the vision of near town living," be "highly protected and self contained," and have "great appeal to higher income executives and professional people."[18] At the center of the 110-acre site was a state-of-the-art auditorium for the Civic Light Opera, the roof of which would open to reveal the city's skyline to attendees. The new auditorium would "take its place among the wonders of the world" and be "an eloquent expression of the technological advances to which Pittsburgh industry and research have contributed."[19] The ACCD described the Lower Hill Cultural Center as the embodiment of progress that would "shape the sordid world to the likeness of our dreams." It would "replace a slum where men and women now live in misery and degradation" with cultural amenities and housing suited to the tastes of Pittsburgh's white elite and middle class.[20]

The clearance of the Lower Hill was devastating. The project displaced 1,551 families (80 percent of whom were African American) and 416 businesses.[21] The Pittsburgh Urban Redevelopment Authority (PURA) gave residents inadequate compensation for their property and little or no assistance with relocation. In the already harshly segregated region, the displaced crowded into the few neighborhoods open to African Americans. As Mindy Fullilove describes, the effect was not only the loss of housing but also the severing of former residents' intricate social ties, which had supported their daily lives. This "root shock" continued to harm the well-being of former residents for generations.[22]

After clearing the Lower Hill of its residents, only portions of the final project ever materialized. The Civic Auditorium was built, but its roof rarely opened and it proved more appropriate as a site for professional sports than opera. Alcoa and a local industrialist developed luxury apartment towers on the edge of the site that offered far less "near town" living than the neighborhood they replaced. The grand plan for a cultural center remained on the books into the late 1960s, when the ACCD shifted its focus to transforming downtown's red-light area into a cultural district. For decades, the Civic Auditorium sat alone in a sea of parking lots. It may not have appealed to Pittsburgh's scientists, but the need to attract them provided a clear justification for clearing the site. Like similar projects across the United States, the Lower Hill Cultural Center valued the interests and pursuits of middle-class professionals over those of African Americans, the poor, and the working class. The growing emphasis on creating a "research climate" for scientists deepened existing racial and socioeconomic inequality in the region.[23]

In the remainder of this chapter, I address three examples of how Pittsburgh's businesses and elites tried to make the region into a more desirable place for science and engineering. The first is the Westinghouse Electric Corporation's attempts to recruit engineers and scientists to Pittsburgh and its suburbs. Westinghouse and other companies did not just try to lure scientists and engineers; it also, through its partnerships with the state and local universities, worked to remake the region in its interests. In the remaining sections of this chapter, I explore two instances—failed attempts to develop an engineering center and a massive research park—in which Pittsburgh's growth machine worked to make the region into a more fertile place for science and engineering. While local leaders' most prominent attempts to transform Pittsburgh into a center of science and engineering may have failed, through their pursuit of such "unbuilt environments," they succeeded in developing a regional planning framework centered on the figure of the scientist that remains highly influential today.[24]

The Ideal Home of the "Young Man of Industry"

By the 1950s, most Pittsburgh-based industrial firms claimed that suburban locations were vital to the success of their research and engineering activities. While executives argued that such locations were intrinsically important (see part II), they also claimed that attractive suburban facilities and nearby residential communities were vital recruitment tools for highly sought scientists and engineers. Lurking in the background of these arguments was the notion that metropolitan Pittsburgh was less desirable than Boston, San Francisco, or other major centers of high-tech industry. Pittsburgh lacked the scenic and cultural amenities of major coastal cities. Its reputation was tarnished by its industrial past. Local employers and boosters believed that in order to attract scientists, they needed to promote Pittsburgh as a region that was progressing beyond steel into a new era oriented toward the needs of scientists. As a result, they worked diligently to sell the region as both an emerging scientific center and a pleasant place to live.

They hung these claims on Pittsburgh's emergence in the 1950s as the "Renaissance City."

One of the most striking of Westinghouse's recruitment ads ran in the May 1957 issue of the trade magazine *Combustion* (see Figure 3). The ad carried the headline "All This—and a Husband Who's a Westinghouse Engineer" and pictured a woman's head hovering over a model of downtown Pittsburgh—the "Renaissance City of America." It went on to describe how Pittsburgh offered every advantage to the aspiring engineer and his wife. He would be fortunate to secure work with Westinghouse, where he "would enjoy all the advantages of a creative career in *Atomic Power.*" Meanwhile she could "derive all the advantages of living in NEW Pittsburgh." The ad told the engineer's wife that she "need only see the lovely new homes, modern schools, smart shops, and inspiring cultural centers that blanket the city, and you know there is no finer locale for your career as a home-maker, and your husband's career as a *Westinghouse* engineer." According to the ad, Pittsburgh offered an engineer a promising career and his family all the opportunities of a growing, innovative region.

Westinghouse's recruitment materials made a number of assumptions about an engineer's life. The first of these was that engineers were men, that they would be married to women, and that the inevitable outcome of that marriage would be children. The ads often directly addressed engineers' wives, unlikely readers of *Combustion,* in an explicit attempt to convince engineers that metropolitan Pittsburgh would be a satisfying place for their families.[25] The second assumption was that engineers' wives would not work outside the home—this particular advertisement, for example, describes the woman's career as a homemaker, while others directly addressed the wife as they discuss topics such as schools and shopping. The third assumption, building from the former, is that engineers would want to own a home for their families. Westinghouse assumed that engineers would choose to move to the suburban neighborhoods that surrounded its research facilities and provided relocation services that facilitated this move (see chapter 5). The final assumption was that while engineers would surely prefer living in the suburbs, they would also want access to the assets of a major metropolitan region. Thus recruitment ads focused on the proximity of the cultural and educational amenities of the "New Pittsburgh."

In 1957 Westinghouse's Materials Engineering Department published a twenty-five-page recruitment brochure that focused equally on the rebirth

Figure 3. Westinghouse Electric Corporation, employee recruitment advertisement. *Combustion*, May 1957.

of Pittsburgh and career opportunities at Westinghouse. The brochure told potential materials engineers that they would work not alone but in a complex of research centers that the brochure described as the "research and development center of the world." They would have the opportunity to update their credentials at local universities and participate in thirty-five chapters of scientific and professional associations. In short, Pittsburgh offered engineers a lifetime of opportunities for career advancement and the chance to become part of a scientific community. As the brochure declared, "A job with Materials Engineering . . . offers the young man of industry the opportunity . . . to live in a community where scientific advances are a part of daily life."[26]

After reading about the lifelong career opportunities available at Westinghouse, the "young man of industry" could turn the page to find three photos of Pittsburgh: a smoky picture from the past, a current one showing the Gateway Center redevelopment, and a third portraying the future downtown. The text on the opposite page read, "Yesterday Pittsburgh was just another city plagued with many of the same ills common to most large industrial cities," but today Pittsburgh has overcome those ills to become "the most talked about city in the world." It described various aspects of Pittsburgh's Renaissance, including "ultra-modern skyscrapers in a park-like atmosphere," Point State Park, a "dream highway" that "will bring the heart of the city within minutes of . . . Pittsburgh's suburbs," a new cultural center, and many new parking garages. Yet Pittsburgh was not "resting on its hard earned laurels." A "spirit of progress . . . will continue to make Pittsburgh grow." The city was fulfilling its historical destiny; while it once "stood as the Gateway to the West," today it "stands as the gateway to opportunity."[27]

Convinced that Pittsburgh would suit their career needs and desire for greatness, materials engineers could read on to discover that their children would attend schools noted for their "high scholastic standards." When school was out, the region was bursting with recreational and cultural activities to "satisfy the pleasure of everyone young and old." And where would engineers and their families live while they pursued their promising new life? The pamphlet explored this as well.

> Within a ten-mile radius of the "suburban home" of Materials Engineering [based at the Westinghouse Research Laboratories in Churchill], a wide selection of modern metropolitan, suburban, and rural residences are found. Beautiful, individually-styled homes, located conveniently to modern shopping centers

> and stores are available. These new neighborhoods, some of which are set in park-like surroundings, are only a "stone's throw" from Pittsburgh and its bustling shopping metropolis, yet still provide ample outdoor space for the family.[28]

This description and the accompanying photos made clear that the ideal home for a materials engineer was in the suburbs. Wherever they lived, engineers would make a special contribution to the quality of life in their community. They would join other scientists and engineers who throughout the Pittsburgh region "can be found participating in civic affairs and assuming roles of leadership in the social and religious life of the community."[29]

In 1962 a lengthy recruitment booklet for Westinghouse's Research Laboratories addressed many of the same points. The booklet followed the conventional structure used by Westinghouse: first addressing career opportunities, then how the employee would be working with other researchers in one of America's most innovative scientific communities, and finally how Renaissance Pittsburgh and its suburbs were well suited for researchers and their families.

The booklet began with a letter from Westinghouse president Mark Cresap reassuring potential employees that the company not only manufactured electrical products but also contributed to "scientific knowledge" and the "standard of living of the Free World." In an oddly grandiose flourish for such a mundane text, Westinghouse "dedicated" the booklet to "the man who has the urge to create, and has a taste for adventure." It reassured the "professional man" who was reading the booklet that "Westinghouse believes in Research. Westinghouse believes in Professional Man. Because of this we attempt to offer an atmosphere conducive to scientific discovery and professional advancement."[30]

This atmosphere was conducive for research because of its location on a "rolling partially wooded site" in "an attractive area in the midst of fast growing suburban communities." Surrounding the lab, researchers would find not only an array of comfortable housing but also the research facilities of other firms and universities. To illustrate this concentration of facilities, the brochure included a map that labeled seven nearby labs as well as educational and cultural facilities in Pittsburgh. This map was evidence that "the research scientist in Pittsburgh finds himself in a community very much devoted to scientific research." Renaissance Pittsburgh was dedicated to scientists, and the new employee would find that "your professional standing will win you a high regard and immediate welcome in community activities."[31]

Having described Pittsburgh's vibrant scientific community, the pamphlet then suggested the various ways that the region was being remade in the interest of "professional man." Pittsburgh was no longer "a sooty city" but instead a "city reborn" with "clean air," "gleaming skyscrapers," and "new, broad highways." "Proud Pittsburghers" had invested billions in the city, and this had resulted in amenities, including museums, operas, and universities, that would interest scientists. But, the pamphlet continued, while Pittsburgh's status as a center of science and culture was important to the researcher, "the environment of the community is equally important to his family." Researchers could rest easy knowing that the research laboratories were located "in the heart of modern suburban life." While the "caliber" of area schools varied greatly, the pamphlet reassured potential employees that "the areas where a professional . . . would choose to live for general reasons also provide the best schools." From employment at one of the United States' most stable and innovative firms, to a bucolic work environment that offered scientific freedom and a chance to contribute to the progress of mankind, to a region being remade in the interest of scientists and their families, Pittsburgh and its suburbs were the perfect places for the "professional man" to pursue his career and family life.[32]

In Westinghouse's many advertisements and promotional materials, it recruited scientists by offering them not only a promising career but also a secure place within a clearly defined set of heteropatriarchal and white supremacist social relations in the redeveloped city and its suburbs. As I explore in detail in later chapters, industrial firms sited their new laboratories in affluent suburbs that they believed would attract scientists and engineers to the region. Companies also provided relocation services that helped new employees choose appropriate homes. As a result, scientists and engineers settled in communities of predominantly white professionals. They socialized mostly with their neighbors, who often worked at the same lab. Their children attended well-funded school systems that sent the vast majority of graduates to college. Pittsburgh businesses and elites yoked their future prosperity to attracting scientists and engineers to the region. As a result, while deindustrialization, renewal, and racism inflicted uncountable harm on many Pittsburghers, scientists and engineers lived largely contented and comfortable lives in the suburbs and renewal sites of the new Pittsburgh.

The pamphlets discussed here were not unique to Westinghouse or Pittsburgh. Similar job ads were produced by other Pittsburgh-area firms as well as by firms based in other cities such as Boston, Los Angeles, and New York.[33] The recruitment of engineers and scientists was not a trivial matter in the 1950s. There was a tenfold increase in the number of industrial jobs for physicists between 1950 and 1952, and government employment also increased at an extraordinary pace.[34] By the late 1950s, nuclear technology had been replaced by aerospace as the technological cause célèbre, and Westinghouse found itself fiercely competing for recent graduates with more glamorous aerospace firms based in sunnier locations and with more impressive growth prospects. Westinghouse felt compelled to lure engineers and scientists to Pittsburgh by offering them not only stable and rewarding employment but also social standing within a renewed metropolitan region. It described Pittsburgh as a place remade in the interest of scientists and engineers. Westinghouse not only sold Pittsburgh's role as an emerging center of science and engineering to its prospective employees; it also, through its involvement in the ACCD and its investment in its own facilities, participated in its realization.

The ACCD and the Engineering Center

Beginning in the early 1950s, Pittsburgh's business community, led by the ACCD, hatched a variety of plans to lure research and engineering facilities to the Pittsburgh area. In the eyes of business leaders, a Pittsburgh-based national laboratory or major defense contract not only would provide opportunities for their companies but also would improve the region's reputation. These leaders believed that Pittsburgh needed to promote its assets as both a place for scientific research and a community for scientists, engineers, and other professionals. Improving Pittsburgh's standing as a center of science and engineering would support local corporations' efforts to concentrate research labs and headquarters in the region and alleviate the effects of declining manufacturing.

The first of these major efforts came in 1952, when the Engineering Society of Western Pennsylvania (ESWP) and the ACCD began a lengthy attempt to lure the Engineering Center, the Founder Societies' headquarters, to Pittsburgh. The Founder Societies included four major professional societies representing electrical (American Institute of Electrical Engineers, AIEE), mining and metallurgical (American Institute of Mining and Metallurgical Engineers, AIME), civil (American Society of Civil Engineers, ASCE), and mechanical (American Society of Mechanical Engineers, ASME) engineering.[35] In 1903 Andrew Carnegie gave the United Engineering Trust (UET) $1.5 million to finance the construction of the societies' headquarters on West Thirty-Ninth Street in Manhattan.[36] By the 1950s, the building had "become overcrowded and increasingly unsuited to the needs of today," and the neighborhood around Bryant Park had lost its turn-of-the-century luster.[37] The UET appointed a committee to find a new location. The committee narrowed its options to remaining in New York or moving to Chicago, Cleveland, Philadelphia, or Pittsburgh. Sensing a public relations coup and an opportunity to add another piece to the city's Renaissance, the ESWP and the ACCD aggressively courted the Engineering Center.

The ESWP and the ACCD formed committees to raise funds for the Engineering Center and to encourage members of the Founder Societies to choose Pittsburgh as their future headquarters. A. C. Monteith, vice president of engineering at Westinghouse, headed the ESWP subcommittee, and Gwilym Price, president of Westinghouse, headed the ACCD subcommittee, which also included the chief executives of Alcoa, Jones and Laughlin Steel, and U.S. Steel. In 1953 the ACCD created the Pittsburgh Engineering Trust (PET) to raise funds for the Engineering Center.[38] By February 8, 1954, the PET had raised $1,139,250 in pledges, of which $134,750 was on deposit. Of the 130 companies members of the PET contacted, 63 pledged, as did 3 individuals.[39] Donations were based on the size of the company, with the highest promised donations of $200,000 from U.S. Steel and $160,000 from Westinghouse.[40]

The PET raised funds by publicizing the Engineering Center as a key piece of the Renaissance. In a brochure encouraging companies to donate, it noted that the project would bring the staff of the engineering societies—"hundreds of highly educated professional people"—to live in the region. They would make "exceptionally fine citizens" and would help "build the prestige of Pittsburgh across the country." The Engineering Center would also be a "powerful magnet" to lure other technical societies and engineering firms to Pittsburgh. Through their daily activities, the Founder Societies would "provide an automatic flow of constructive dignified publicity to build further the business reputation and technical stature of Pittsburgh." The societies' frequent conferences in the city would also be a boon to the city's hospitality industry and would contribute to further urban renewal.

The "ideal arrangement," according to the Pittsburgh Urban Redevelopment Authority, would be a master planned redevelopment area for the Engineering Center where a hotel, auditorium, and exhibition area would be within easy walking distance.[41] Local leaders sold the Engineering Center to local firms by claiming it would accelerate the region's renewal.

In early September 1953, the UET's search committee visited Pittsburgh to tour potential locations and meet with Mayor David Lawrence, city council, and the ACCD. At a meeting at the exclusive Duquesne Club, speakers presented Pittsburgh's merits and the details of their offer. According to the three speakers, Pittsburgh was a perfect location for the center. Edward Weidlen, president of the Mellon Institute, told the audience that Pittsburgh was "definitely science minded" and relayed several stories of Pittsburgh's engineering fame. He said that not only was "the growing importance of Pittsburgh as a research center . . . one of the brightest and most encouraging developments for this community's future," but the city was "making remarkable progress in the broad field of redevelopment."[42]

Arthur Van Buskirk, president of the ACCD, focused less on the city's prowess as a research center and more on its innovative redevelopment. He described how Richard King Mellon had gathered "some of his closest friends" in 1944 and determined that "something must be done about the community's condition and outlook." They had adopted a "Jeffersonian" perspective and put aside politics and self-interest in order to put "business brains and resources . . . into civic advancement." The results were three-fold: "a cleaner and healthier city," redevelopment that included "wiping out 100 acres of blight in the so-called 'Hill District,'" and "forging new frontiers" in education and culture. Van Buskirk told the committee that if it was looking for nightclubs, then it should stay in New York, but if it wanted progress, then "raise your horizons and dream dreams as we have done." If the committee did so, it would "see a natural relationship between this dynamic and vigorous industrial community with its great technical and scientific research facilities, and the natural aspirations of your organizations."[43]

In the final speech, Westinghouse president Gwilym Price presented Pittsburgh's offer to the UET. He gave the UET its choice of eight prime parcels and held out the promise of other sites. These included a site in Gateway Center immediately adjacent to Point State Park; three locations near the new Civic Arena in the Hill District that would be available following clearance; or three lots in Oakland, one of which was land that was deeded to the city as part of Schenley Park. Depending on the cost of the location chosen (the lots in Oakland were available for no charge), the PET would provide between $1.2 million and $1.5 million for construction and land acquisition. This would cover nearly half the cost of development. In addition, the land would be tax free and Pittsburgh offered substantial savings in terms of construction costs and utilities. Most importantly, the Engineering Center would be moving to "the most progressive city in the United States."[44]

On the days surrounding the search committee's visit to Pittsburgh, the three major local newspapers ran editorials declaring the city the "logical" choice for the Engineering Center and describing it as an opportunity to "make Pittsburgh the engineering and research center of the world."[45] The ACCD printed pamphlets for the Founder Societies that described Pittsburgh's growing scientific stature: 44 major research laboratories, 20,000 engineers, 5,000 scientists, and $85 million spent annually on research. For engineers, "Pittsburgh is a good city in which to work and live." The city's technical assets and redevelopment were often described in the same sentence. As the pamphlet noted, it has "an ever expanding program of civic development, diversified research and engineering, including atomic power. Moreover, Pittsburgh is a clean and healthful city in which to work and live."[46] Pittsburgh was changing rapidly, and this would benefit the Engineering Center. There was 69 percent more sunshine, 25 percent of downtown had been replaced by a "shining city," and "slums . . . are systematically being razed."[47] The Engineering Center would join $1.5 billion of recent redevelopment all made possible by the "dynamic civic leadership" of local executives. The ACCD itself would also be an asset for the Engineering Center—these "cooperative civic leaders" would "help these societies carry forward their good work." In sum, the Engineering Center and its employees would "find our city and the surrounding countryside a good place to make their homes."[48]

In February 1955, the search committee announced its decision to endorse moving the Engineering Center to Pittsburgh.[49] In a letter to the search committee, ACCD president Van Buskirk wrote that the decision "gives due recognition to Pittsburgh's pre-eminence as an industrial center, and to the concentration here of vast . . . research facilities and personnel, all of which afford the kind of professional atmosphere which you are seeking." Again evoking the overlap of Pittsburgh's Renaissance and its scientific community, he foresaw that in the coming years when the Engineering Center's members "mingle with our industrial and scientific leaders a mutual stimulation of ideas is inevitable, with results that could have far-reaching consequences for the entire world."[50]

The board members of the Founder Societies still needed to approve the decision. Monteith sent a letter to the members of the ACCD and ESWP subcommittees with a list of the board members and instructions that "every one of us must help. We must do more than just tell the Pittsburgh story, we must sell this story."[51] In March 1955, Mellon offered the societies an additional $500,000 in research funding if they chose Pittsburgh.[52] Many of the board members were not enamored with the idea of leaving Manhattan. Even as the site committee chose Pittsburgh, other cities continued to make competing offers, and in August the UET asked for a six-month extension of the Pittsburgh Engineering Trust's offer.[53] As debate roiled the societies in 1955, it became apparent that a move to Pittsburgh might tear them apart. In June, the societies decided to hire a "competent firm of consulting engineers" to choose a location. This firm recommended remaining in New York, and in September 1957, the UET announced its decision to relocate to a lot facing the United Nations. Sitting at the edge of the most visible urban renewal site in the world, the building would cost more than twice the one proposed in Pittsburgh but would "add to the stature of engineering in the nation."[54]

While the Engineering Center did not move to Pittsburgh, the attempt to lure it reveals the resources the ACCD and local firms were willing to devote to enhance the region's image as a center of engineering. The ACCD offered the Pittsburgh Renaissance as a perfect complement to the Engineering Center. Pittsburgh was the most progressive city in the world with visionary leadership that was remaking the region specifically for the likes of the Engineering Center.

Urban Renewal for "Educated Man"

In 1956 the ACCD published a recap of its activities over the past decade subtitled "an era of progress and accomplishment." The report first addressed urban renewal and then turned to the ACCD's efforts to foster the growth of research in the region. It highlighted Westinghouse's nuclear research as one of many examples of innovation in Pittsburgh—"a world center of research and technology." In a clear reference to the Renaissance, it noted, "Ideas are best nurtured in an energetic environment, like Pittsburgh, where people are restless and impatient with things wholly as they are. In such an atmosphere, the spirit of adventure is strong and undaunted." The ACCD explicitly included science and technology as key components of its effort to redevelop the region.[55] Following its failure to lure the Engineering Center, the ACCD joined a concerted attempt to redevelop the Oakland neighborhood into a more suitable home for research.

During the 1950s, while corporate laboratories decamped for Pittsburgh's suburbs, the city's universities continued to concentrate in Oakland. Home for the past half century to Carnegie Tech, the University of Pittsburgh, the Mellon Institute, several hospitals, and a smattering of industrial labs, research was hardly new to Oakland. The neighborhood was centered on the gothic forty-two-story Cathedral of Learning, the Mellon Institute, and the block-long Carnegie Institute and Library. Bearing the names Frick, Carnegie, Mellon, and Heinz, the buildings were bestowed by the city's industrialists in an effort to create a cultural and educational center that befitted a great industrial city. Modeled on the broad avenues and Beaux Arts architecture of European cities, Oakland was intended to bring refinement to Pittsburgh—to mellow the coarseness of the immigrant workers who toiled in the neighborhoods below.[56] Yet, while Oakland had served Pittsburgh well during the first half of the twentieth century, by the 1950s, it no longer provided the requisite needs of a major research center. As the region began to take a back seat in the national race for defense and aerospace funding, regional leaders sought to remake City Beautiful Oakland into a space more suited to the needs of big science.

In order to remake Oakland, civic leaders first needed to remake the institution that sat at its heart. In 1955 the Board of Trustees of the University of Pittsburgh (Pitt), chaired by Mellon's brother-in-law Alan Scaife, appointed Edward Litchfield as chancellor. Litchfield, the dean of Cornell's business school, was a rising star in higher education administration. He served on several corporate boards and impressed Pitt's trustees as someone who could navigate a business-dominated city. After accepting his appointment, at what *Science* described as an "academic backwater" in a "dingy industrial city," Litchfield set out a plan to leverage the city's wealth in order to transform Pitt from a commuter school into a research university.[57] At the announcement of Litchfield's appointment at the Duquesne Club, Mellon tasked the chancellor with creating a "great cultural and educational center for the region, a center without which no industrial city can become and remain great."[58]

With the support of Mellon and Pittsburgh's business community, Litchfield launched an ambitious effort to boost the university and Oakland's reputation as a research center. In the words of a colorful retrospective in *Science,* Litchfield sought "to do for the realm of intellect what the bulldozers, architects, and soot filters were doing for downtown Pittsburgh." "If cities can be swiftly rebuilt," *Science* asked, "why not universities?" During his term as chancellor, Litchfield would attempt to do both.[59] He and other regional leaders set out to remake Oakland and its surroundings into a futuristic center of science and academe. None of their efforts succeeded completely, but they nonetheless developed a new model of planning that prioritized attracting scientists and other professionals as essential to the region's future.

Litchfield first contemplated constructing a major research park near Oakland in the late 1950s. He commissioned Paul A. Weinstein, an economist at the Pittsburgh Regional Planning Association (PRPA), to write a report on research parks and the potential to build one in Pittsburgh. Weinstein reviewed how universities in Raleigh-Durham, Boston, and the Bay Area had spurred development through research parks.[60] He documented that while Pittsburgh had a strong concentration of traditional industrial research, it was falling behind in growing fields such as electronics and aerospace. Between 1945 and 1955, industrial research and development (R&D) employment had increased by 350 percent in Boston, 500 percent in Los Angeles, and 14 percent nationwide. In Pittsburgh it had increased by 5.3 percent. Weinstein suggested that the causes of Pittsburgh's failures were threefold: "a reputation as a heavy industry and dirty city," local leaders' "complaisance with the traditional industrial patterns," and "a university complex" that suited the needs of traditional industry "but does not . . . attract new research establishments." However, this pattern was not fixed; using the examples of other universities, he explained that Pitt could take an active role in developing R&D in the region.[61]

In January 1961, Pitt administrators held a retreat in the mountains east of Pittsburgh to discuss campus redevelopment. At this meeting, they produced a crude but revealing map. A white, outlined area in the middle of the map showed Oakland (see Figure 4). Not labeled on the map but in three directions around Oakland, there were clear barriers to further development: to the southeast of Oakland was Schenley Park, to the south the Monongahela River and the Jones and Laughlin steel mill, and to the north the wealthy neighborhood of Shadyside.[62] Immediately to the west of Oakland was the

Hill District, an area that at that time had a growing and crowded population of 21,846 as a result of the displacement of 1,500 families to make way for the Civic Auditorium. According to the 1960 U.S. Census, 95.3 percent of this population was African American. Of the 7,008 employed residents in these census tracts, adjacent to one of the largest complexes of hospitals and universities in the country, only 395 were professional, technical, and kindred workers. This included eight professors, five physicians, and not a single engineer, natural scientist, or chemist. In fact, most of these lived in an affluent, mostly white enclave on the edge of Oakland.[63]

On the map developed during their retreat, university administrators neatly enclosed the unlabeled Hill District with a dotted line and labeled it "Research Park." A more detailed map showed the boundaries of the proposed research park and labeled Oakland, in what was becoming an increasingly popular nomenclature among Pitt administrators, as "The Island."[64] The authors of this map also labeled the white working-class neighborhood of South Oakland as an alternative site for a "research area," no doubt anticipating the

Figure 4. First proposed location for research park. Chancellor of the University of Pittsburgh, Edward H. Litchfield, Administrative Files, 1956–1965, UA.2.10 1956–1965, University Archives, Archives and Special Collections, University of Pittsburgh Library System.

political difficulty of further slum clearance in the Hill District, a neighborhood already crowded as a result of urban renewal and a racially segregated housing market.[65]

In January 1962, executives from Prudential Insurance Company met with a select group of Pittsburgh's elite to discuss financing the construction of a research park in the Hill District. At the meeting were Litchfield; Gwilym Price, former Westinghouse president and current chairman of trustees at Pitt; Mayor Joseph Barr; Richard King Mellon; Frank Denton, vice chairman of Mellon National Bank and Mellon's emissary on Pitt's Board; Frank Magee, president of the ACCD; and Henry Hillman, a wealthy capitalist, donor to the university, and chair of the ACCD. During the meeting, they referred to Oakland as a "Cultural Island" and the Hill District as "ideally suited to the establishment of industrial, scientific, research and development laboratories and similar facilities."[66] They concluded the meeting by discussing the formation of the Oakland Corporation (OakCorp), a private corporation composed of universities, cultural institutions, and foundations that would invest in a research park.

In April 1962, OakCorp revealed its plan to the public, with Litchfield reassuring Hill residents that their removal "would aid the welfare of all persons" and speed "integration."[67] Having already borne the brunt of urban renewal, Hill residents resisted the plan and Mayor Barr announced that while he supported building a research park, OakCorp would have to look elsewhere for a site.[68] The university and local leaders remained committed to building a research park somewhere near Oakland.

Several months after the formation of OakCorp, in a speech to the Pennsylvania Economy League, Chancellor Litchfield explained the importance of a research park for Pittsburgh. He began with the basic thesis that "the way to growth and prosperity for Western Pennsylvania lies through industrial research." Economic diversification was a long-standing concern for Pittsburgh leaders, and Litchfield assured them that a research park would result in "planned innovation" that would translate into "a company's growth, an area's growth, a nation's growth." Litchfield claimed that Pittsburgh already had several assets to attract researchers; most important among these were the "eleven educational research or research-related institutions in what we are now beginning to call the Oakland Island." In what was becoming a pervasive trope in OakCorp's materials, Litchfield described scientists as fastidious people who lived and breathed intellectual and cultural life. In order to grow and innovate, such men need to be near "compatible academic surroundings." This is "no mystery"; researchers "are drawn to the vicinities of large educational institutions where they can find resources, talents and intellectual stimulation." The only way to develop a research park was to attract scientists. The only way to attract scientists was to offer "them the opportunity to associate with scientific, professional and other intellectual people who normally assemble on and around campuses."[69] OakCorp would locate its research park directly between the campuses of Carnegie Tech and the University of Pittsburgh. No other research park in the country would have such an ideal location.

While Oakland already had the amenities to support a successful research park, Litchfield told the Economy League that much work still needed to be done to attract researchers. To do so, OakCorp would loosely follow the Oakland Master Plan created by the PRPA. It called for the wholesale renewal of the neighborhood, including clearing 2,610 dwellings to make way for "completely new residential areas," two new commercial districts, and major hospital and university expansions. The plan would "provide for the private needs of Research Park Personnel" and "add to the character of the Oakland Island, and to its attraction for the scientific personnel." According to Litchfield, two features would differentiate Pittsburgh's research park from others around the country. First, its location was directly adjacent to two major research universities. Second, it was part of a comprehensive program of renewal that would make all of Oakland into a more inviting place for scientific work.[70]

OakCorp's initial plans were modest. It planned to purchase 6.2 acres in the narrow valley between Carnegie Tech and Pitt that it had recently renamed Panther Hollow.[71] It would lease this land to the Gilbane Building Company, which would initially build a 500,000-square-foot building of what would become a larger "scientific-research-office complex." OakCorp was in talks with the architectural firm Charles Zuckerman and Associates, the architects of the Prudential Center in Boston, to design the building. However, in the course of a year, its plan morphed into something much larger.

What began as a modest plan for a research park grew to such a scale that both its architect and the *Pittsburgh Post-Gazette* described it as "one of the architectural wonders of the world."[72] At a press conference on June 5, 1963, OakCorp revealed the plans of its new architect, Max Abramovitz, for the Panther Hollow Research Park. Abramovitz was the favored architect of

Mellon and had designed the downtown headquarters of Alcoa and U.S. Steel as well as Alcoa's new research laboratories in the city's suburbs. He already had a long relationship with Pitt, having worked on its master plan and its new library and professional school quadrangle, both key components of the Oakland Master Plan. He was also very familiar with megaprojects, having contributed to the designs of Rockefeller Center, the UN complex, and Lincoln Center.[73] Abramovitz's plans for the research park called for eventually filling the entirety of Panther Hollow with what he called "the first 21st century structure."[74]

To set the groundwork for renewal, Abramovitz and the university's administrators maligned the hollow as "useless and marginal land"—as "ugly, largely unused," "desolate," a "wasteland," and "a huge and carelessly cut furrow."[75] They shared a photo of the existing hollow that showed a few ramshackle houses and a collapsing hillside.[76] The plans called for eradicating this "scar on the face of Oakland" and replacing it with a sprawling research complex with a park running across its roof.[77] The research park—a "horizontal skyscraper"—would fill the entire hollow. National and local media trumpeted the wonders of the new Panther Hollow. Its unveiling was covered in *Time,* the *New York Times,* the *Wall Street Journal,* and other national and international publications. *National Geographic* described the planned research park as "built out of thin air," *The Observer* of London called it "a subterranean utopia," and the *Christian Science Monitor* evoked "a 150-story building suspended on its side."[78]

The final complex would provide 10.5 million square feet of office and lab space. Running under it would be a "built-in railroad," bus station, parking, and an expressway. The roof of the complex would be a pedestrian-only park. Sunken courtyards would bring light and ventilation into the building and "hanging gardens" would line its edges.[79] All this park space would "create the sort of relaxed atmosphere so important to research work."[80] This would only be the beginning; the research park would eventually fill the entire mile-long hollow. Residential areas would be built on adjacent "marginal land" currently occupied by working-class neighborhoods.[81]

The plans described Panther Hollow as a stylish response to the suburban research park: a carefully composed hybrid of city, country, and suburb perfectly designed for researchers. Knowing the difficulties of "hiring and holding scientific personnel," the designers strove "to create the kind of environment that most researchers seem to prefer."[82] Panther Hollow's design was based on the assumption that scientific personnel were "the kind of people who can go where they wish, people in demand," and that OakCorp must create "a new kind of community, designed to the tastes and needs of these people."[83] Bordered by parks, two universities, and a variety of cultural institutions, "a person could live his whole life within a half-mile radius . . . and an extraordinary rewarding life it would be." Here at last was a city where "people will be the masters of their environment."[84]

OakCorp described Panther Hollow as a partnership between industry, government, educators, and scientists. According to Abramovitz, such a partnership was typical of Pittsburgh, a place where "we see educational, business, and religious leaders resolving to revitalize the economic base of their community." Abramovitz reserved special praise for Litchfield, whom he described as a renaissance man who signified "a return to the role of educators in earlier societies—that of community leaders as well as intellectuals."[85] Under Litchfield's guidance, Pittsburgh would enter a new stage of renewal devoted to "the needs and wants of the educated, cultured, constructive person."[86] Attracting such talented people would diversify Pittsburgh's economy, foster growth, and improve the lives of all its residents.

Industry Follows Educated Man

In 1963 *Pitt Magazine* featured an article by Abramovitz elaborating on how cities must be designed in the wake of "technological revolution." According to the article, which was reprinted in the *Atlanta Journal* and the *Buffalo Evening News,* leaders must reorganize cities around the production of technology rather than manufactured goods. Abramovitz noted that while city leaders used a variety of "lures" such as tax breaks, site development, and "urban face lifts" that "continue to be important," they "too frequently concentrate on removing slums with little thought of putting something innately more beautiful in their place." The problem, Abramovitz argued, is that cities must work to attract both investment and the "Educated Man." He continued: "Technology needs people—trained and talented people: the scholar and his books, the scientist in his laboratory, the technician at his computer. In short, technology needs Educated Man. Where he is, the new industry will follow."[87]

Abramovitz described Educated Man's complicated desires. He enjoys Southern California with its "sunshine, swimming pools, fresh grapefruit, and forty percent of all defense research contracts," but he cannot live on citrus and defense spending alone. Educated Man has "urban inclinations" and "his historic roots are in the city." He "*will* choose urban life," but only if he can "find in it an environment keyed to the enjoyment of his senses and the application of his intellect." This environment is found in a "natural state" around universities. But universities were not enough; local leaders must construct "a community in which Educated Man can produce for the benefit of the region and society." Such a place must include "not just facilities for science, but for . . . the whole panoply of intellectual pursuits attractive to the kinds of people that work in research industries." Panther Hollow was part of a wider effort to create that community. It would combine recreation, culture, housing, museums, and laboratories within the same structure to create "the largest single educational-culture-science center in any U.S. city—a modernized medieval 'university city' within a city." Pittsburgh's former advantages of plentiful coal, cheap labor, and accessible transport had become obsolete. In order to foster the new economy, leaders needed to create conditions to attract scientific talent. A new formula for regional development emerged: "Today . . . Industry must follow people, and people will go where life is most attractive and enjoyable."[88]

Abramovitz's essay was a perfect iteration of what was fast becoming the dominant urban policy regime in Pittsburgh and elsewhere. Earlier in 1963, the *Pittsburgh Press* had editorialized on the need to diversify the region's economy through research. Echoing the same ideas as Abramovitz, it noted, "The planners say that industry—particularly the new, scientifically sophisticated industries—goes to where the talent is. If we assemble the scholars and train the experts . . . the industries will settle nearby."[89] Months later, Congressman William Moorehead told a local Chamber of Commerce that "our economy based upon brawn; must in the space age be based on brains." To foster this new economy, he highlighted the need to create "an environment in which people like to live."[90] Meanwhile Alcoa chairman and ACCD board member Lawrence Litchfield Jr., on receipt of the Western Pennsylvania Industrialist of the Year Award, told the local chapter of the Society of Industrial Realtors that people had replaced geography as Pittsburgh's most important asset.[91] This echoed his statement at the 1962 groundbreaking for Alcoa's Abramovitz-designed research center in Pittsburgh's suburbs, where he noted that "what we are setting out to do here is to equip trained, highly inventive people with the tools and creative surroundings they will require for unparalleled accomplishment."[92] While the idea of planning in the interests of scientists spread through Pittsburgh, Stanford's Frederick Terman, the "Father of Silicon Valley," traveled to Colorado to educate leaders on how to nurture "a community of technical scholars." To encourage them, he warned that similar plans were already under way in Pittsburgh.[93]

While OakCorp told local media of the burgeoning demand for Panther Hollow, in fact few companies showed any interest, and only Pitt committed to occupying significant space. The research park was never built, due to the immense scale of the project, limited business interest, a lack of funding, the collapse of Litchfield's administration, and growing resistance to urban renewal.[94] Yet even in its failure, the Panther Hollow plan reveals how attracting scientists became a core component of urban planning during the postwar period. Today much of Abramovitz and Litchfield's vision has been fulfilled. With the support of the ACCD and Pittsburgh's elite, Carnegie Mellon, Pitt, and the University of Pittsburgh Medical Center are central to the region's economy, and the city is littered with research facilities.[95] At the top of Panther Hollow sits Carnegie Mellon's Mehrabian Collaborative Innovation Center, which hosts on-campus offices of Apple, Intel, and Disney. On the slope above is the Gates-Hillman Center, named for Microsoft founder Bill Gates and Henry Hillman, the industrialist turned venture capitalist and real estate investor who chaired the ACCD for years. For more than seventy years, catering to the figure of the scientist has remained an abiding logic that guides Pittsburgh's ceaseless renewal into a place suited to the needs of large corporations, the wealthy, and the white middle class.

During the Cold War, a coalition of university administrators, business leaders, and politicians launched a series of plans to remake Pittsburgh into a center of research and development. Their dreams of hosting the national headquarters of the major engineering societies and of a valley-filling research park were ambitious. However, these plans, all of them failures, were key examples of what became the dominant framework for regional planning in Pittsburgh and throughout the United States. Through their pursuit of these "unbuilt environments," the ACCD and other regional alliances securely implanted the idea that cities must be redeveloped around the interests of science and scientists.[96] In doing so, they enrolled scientists in their plans to remake cities and helped reinvent them as rational, objective, and highly selective people who would bring progress and prosperity to the regions where they chose to live and work.

The ACCD was the model for numerous other regional alliances that also put research and development at the center of their agendas. In St. Louis, Civic Progress, an organization explicitly modeled on the ACCD, also implemented plans based around the needs of research and researchers.[97] The results in St. Louis, Pittsburgh, Cleveland, Philadelphia, and many other cities were the same: while growth machines had some success revitalizing their regions as centers of white-collar work, these successes came at the expense (often literally) of manufacturing and working-class communities.[98] Planning in the interests of scientists and engineers was premised on and helped reproduce violent divisions of race, class, and gender. It deepened inequality between university-educated white-collar workers and the poor, the working class, and African Americans.

Designing cities around the concerns of the so-called creative class is increasingly a central concern of urban planners and policy makers.[99] This chapter demonstrates that this framework is not new, nor is it based on the need to appeal to the innate character of fast-footed, high-tech workers. Instead, during the 1950s and 1960s, big business and its allies crafted and mobilized the figure of the finicky scientist as a means of advancing their interest in remaking metropolitan regions into centers of corporate administration, finance, and research. In Pittsburgh, planning for the creative class emerged out of the long-standing practice of planning for the needs of private industry. Planning in the interest of science helped pose the Pittsburgh Renaissance as an objective and rational effort that would bring progress and modernity to the Pittsburgh region. By centering the Renaissance on the figure of the scientist, Pittsburgh's elite tried to convince Pittsburghers that the region's remaking was for the benefit of all. Planning in the interests of scientists helped mask the harm and social division that were intrinsic to the Renaissance.

PART II

Making Science Suburban

3

The Invention of Research Man

In 2011 Louise Mozingo authored an op-ed in the *New York Times* titled "To Rethink Sprawl, Start with Offices." Summarizing her recent book *Pastoral Capitalism,* Mozingo argued that one of the main causes of suburban sprawl was the proliferation of suburban office and research parks in the period after World War II. She cited the highly influential Bell Laboratories in Murray Hill, New Jersey, completed in the early 1940s, which "initiated a tide of migration of white-collar workers" into the suburbs. According to Mozingo, this tide, with a few notable exceptions, such as the Nela Park research laboratory outside Cleveland, was largely a post–World War II phenomenon.[1]

There is no doubt that the movement of white-collar workers into the suburbs, including engineers and scientists, accelerated greatly in the period after World War II. However, the suburbanization of research and development and the evolving spatial division of labor and class relations that it represented preceded World War II and its attendant proliferation of defense spending.[2] In fact, industrial research, engineering, and administrative facilities in Pittsburgh, starting with the Westinghouse Research Laboratories in Forest Hills, began to move away from the site of production as early as 1916. Even prior to 1916, the late nineteenth-century movement of research and engineering facilities along with manufacturing into the suburbs was part of a larger process of industrial suburbanization that involved scientists and engineers from the very beginning.

The post–World War II suburbanization of scientific research facilities was rooted in an earlier era of industrialization that resulted in not only new suburban spaces for manufacturing, administration, and research but also a new spatial division of labor and set of class relations that produced industrial scientists and engineers as we know them today. The suburbanization of research labs increasingly separated scientists and engineers from the broader working class. Laboratories and the discourses that circulated through them (re)produced a sociospatial division between technoscientific and manufacturing labor.[3] They helped create enduring, far-flung class, gender, and racial relationships between workers who purportedly work with their minds and those who sell their bodily labor.[4]

This chapter traces the origins of the sociospatial division between mental and physical labor—what Harry Braverman called the conceptualization and execution of work—to the turn of the twentieth century, when industrial firms first institutionalized technoscientific labor as an essential element of production.[5] As I describe in detail, these firms invented, enrolled, and reproduced a class formation of technoscientific workers—what corporate managers and scientists named "research men"—as key allies who would convert science into capital. To help create research men, firms developed research laboratories: exclusive spaces of technoscientific work removed from manufacturing sites. They created spaces devoted exclusively to technoscientific work in order to produce conditions conducive for capital accumulation. These conditions included reproducing the class position of research men, enlisting them in an alliance with industry, and ensuring that they had few other places to work.

The suburbanization of the research laboratory—the separation of laboratories from manufacturing sites—is one of the formative steps in the development of a sociospatial division between mental and physical labor and a corresponding class relationship between research men and other workers. The suburbanization of white-collar work is often associated with the widespread movement of research, defense, and office buildings into the suburbs during the post–World War II era. William Rankin has argued that this movement to the suburbs is indicative of a shift from "monopoly capitalism" to a "flexible knowledge economy."[6] However, industrial research facilities first began to move to the suburbs in the early twentieth century. The suburbanization of industrial research and the invention of research man were overlapping, dialectical processes of producing class and space that were tightly connected to the mechanization of manufacturing, the rise of the corporation and Taylorism, the growth of science-based industry, and the professionalization of science and engineering.[7]

In this and the following chapter, I use a broad definition of research that includes the full gamut of technoscientific work, including product and manufacturing process development, materials testing, and basic research. Much technoscientific work, at Westinghouse or other firms, took place in factories and adjacent offices, not in stand-alone research laboratories. However, regardless of where scientists and engineers worked or what type of work they did, they were invested in the idea that there was a stark difference between mental and physical labor. The building of discrete research labs and the invention of research men helped propagate this widely held notion. Industry actively encouraged research men to assume a shared class position based on the idea that they were different from labor and capitalists. According to scientists and managers, research men selflessly worked to develop new ideas and technologies, but most of their work ultimately boosted corporate profits and lessened workers' control over the labor process.

The invention of research man—like any process of class formation—was fundamentally violent. Industrial firms enlisted research men to develop machines that deskilled labor and to rationalize production processes in order to exert greater control over workers. The technologies and methods that research men installed often made factory work faster, more dangerous, and more demeaning. Meanwhile, the invention of research man starkly differentiated workers based on whether they did mental or physical labor. Industrial firms, universities, the state, and society valorized research men and their labor, while describing manual labor as the basest form of work. As a result, research men accrued greater status and wealth than other workers and usually lived longer and in better circumstances. They also occupied different spaces within and outside plants. Research men were almost always white men, and their status and authority were conditioned on interlocking exclusions of race, gender, and class within and outside their workplaces. Finally, the invention of research man granted an exclusive segment of the workforce greater political, social, and economic authority as experts whose work brought progress and modernity.

This chapter is divided into three sections. The first examines how industrial firms, scientists, and their allies invented research man at the turn of the twentieth century. The next two sections address how Pittsburgh capitalists and industrial firms produced space in order to internalize science and create research men. The first of these sections analyzes the long relationship between the suburbanization of industry, technological change, and class formation in the Pittsburgh region. In the final section, I use the example of Pittsburgh-based Westinghouse's 1916 laboratory to explore how making suburban spaces for science was a vital aspect of the invention of research man. Industrial firms developed laboratories not only as sites of knowledge production but also to reproduce a class formation of technoscientific workers and a socio-spatial division between manual and mental labor that was essential to their ability to dominate production and social life.

The Invention of "Research Man"

More than a half century prior to the invention of research man, Karl Marx and Friedrich Engels observed that capitalists appropriated the "knowledge, judgment, and will" of workers to mechanize production. Capitalists created a division between mental and physical labor and transformed polymath craft production, where workers held some level of intellectual control, into machine-dictated repetitive physical labor.[8] To make machines, capitalists absorbed and refined workers' knowledge and the worker was then "brought face to face with the intellectual potentialities of the material process of production as the property of another and as a property that rules over him."[9] Throughout history, workers' knowledge and tools are foundational to industrialization, even while capitalists present them to workers as alien.[10]

Marx made a somewhat similar argument about scientists. He argued that capitalists appropriated scientists' ideas to develop large-scale industry and that this knowledge was essential to transform nature into machines.[11] Capitalists absorbed science and made it "subservient to capital."[12] However, manual and technoscientific workers developed starkly different relationships to mental labor. Manual workers saw knowledge as alien and imposed upon them, whereas technoscientific workers saw it as core to their work and being.

Marx's writing predated the development of the science-based chemical and electrical industries, the careers of inventors-cum-capitalists such as Thomas Edison, and the emergence of the profession of engineering. He never addressed how capitalists would develop a technoscientific workforce in order to perpetuate the continual process of technological change that was essential to their ability to create new products, control the labor process, and extract surplus value. Marx never considered how, to further accumulation, capitalists had to produce men to mind machines.

In contrast to Marx's limited emphasis on science, by the early twentieth century, the role of research in industry had become an obsession among executives, engineers, and scientists. At this time, as Steven Shapin describes, an earnest and wide-ranging conversation about the character and importance of industrial research and researchers began to appear in technical journals in the United States.[13] This discussion included many of the country's most prominent scientists, including MIT's William Walker, one of the founders of chemical engineering; Noble Prize–winning physicist Robert Millikan; and researchers and managers from pioneering science-based firms.[14] This often casual conversation was not based on careful study but instead consisted of the "hurried jotting down of ideas" about how to incorporate scientists into industry.[15] Leading scientists set out to answer a series of basic questions, including the following: What role should researchers play within business, the state, and society? How should researchers be trained? How should research be organized? What was the difference between pure and applied research? What was the ideal relationship between universities and industry? What "atmosphere" was most conducive to research?

In the midst of this conversation, chemists and chemical engineers invented a new character, research man, who worked within industry but was devoted to the pursuit of knowledge.[16] Research man was soon referenced in electrical engineering, agricultural science, forestry, and other fields. The inventors of research man imagined him as a new type of worker who was neither capital nor labor. Westinghouse research director Perley G. Nutting proposed a three-part class division between "capital," "technical information and skill," and "operating labor."[17] He wrote that the "technical expert" was a new social formation: "a class quite distinct from capital and labor" who "has his own capital invested in his own brain by reason . . . of special education and training."[18] At a time of intense class conflict, scientists and managers cast research man as a new class that existed outside the relationship between capitalists and labor. The invention of research man was an active process of class formation on the part of scientists and their partners in universities, industry, and government. It was a broad effort to expand the presence and status of scientific research in the United States.

The term *research man* had two meanings. On the one hand, it referred simply to a profession: the person employed in research. But it was also used as an indefinite pronoun to signal an emerging type of man who embodied progress, modernity, and expertise. Nearly all authors who used the term implied that research man was a man ("our able young manhood," as one chemist named them).[19] But, in its indefinite though still gendered form, research man represented all of humanity's pursuit of knowledge. Westinghouse's Nutting referenced research man's "racial stock" but also stressed that "men of ability come about equally from all classes."[20] Most scientists agreed that anyone, educated correctly, could become a research man. Nonetheless, during this time, nearly all scientists and engineers, especially those who worked in industry, were white men. Patriarchy and white supremacy buttressed the rise of research man.[21]

The invention of research man began haltingly but accelerated with World War I and the growing concern that American chemical firms were far less innovative than their German counterparts. German companies, first in dyestuffs and later more broadly in the chemical and electrical industries, had led the way in incorporating science into industry. During the war, German superiority in producing fertilizer, explosives, and chemical weapons led to widespread concern that American industry could not compete with the German war machine. The war resulted in increasing collaborative research across industry, the military, and universities and the formation of national bodies, such as the National Research Council, to coordinate scientific work.[22]

As part of these wartime efforts, leading American scientists argued that the United States must embrace research in order to ensure military and economic dominance. Systematic research, they said, was deeply embedded in German character. In contrast, the United States was a "practical nation" with a frontier culture of trial and error.[23] While this frontier culture was still valuable, the ordered pursuit of knowledge must take priority. Much of the wartime discussion of research men focused on the national importance of this class formation. "Create a real research atmosphere," Millikan told his fellow scientists, "and a new generation of research men will quickly be created which will place America in the front ranks in the fields of science."[24]

Scientists and managers deployed the idea that research men were committed not to narrow interests but to the well-being of fellow citizens. They invoked the national importance of research in order to make a political claim for increased resources (from universities, industry, and the state) and for the public to recognize the status and importance of research men. "In the European countries," Millikan argued, "the scientist is held in greater respect."[25] Willis Whitney and C. Alfred Jacobson echoed this common lament, noting that in Germany especially, there was a "useful attitude toward exact knowledge" and "there is public recognition for the research man."[26] In the United States, in contrast, research men were underpaid, unappreciated, and burdened with teaching and other responsibilities. W. D. Richardson, chief chemist at Swift and Company and the founding editor of the *Journal of Industrial and Engineering Chemistry*, wrote that there "is no more important member of our community . . . [and] there is none who feels his importance less."[27] Scientists hoped to increase the social stature of research man so that "men of achievement" and funding would be drawn to the field.[28]

In the earliest statements about research man, authors noted that he was not a genius but could be created through university and industrial education. In 1908 Richardson wrote that research "does not require men of great or special talents" but "can be done . . . by good careful analysts of ordinary skill and common sense."[29] Similar statements suggesting that "research man . . . is a mere average person" were common at the time.[30] The reason for the ubiquity of this opinion was simple: industry "cannot safely depend upon . . . undirected inventive genius" and instead preferred "groups of well-trained thoroughly competent men."[31] The "principal difficulty" was obtaining "a sufficient supply of trained workers" because "we have no plans for producing research men."[32] Research directors and scientists demanded that the state, universities, and industry initiate "a man producing program."[33]

As part of this program, scientists in industry and academia broadly agreed that "the principal function of university research should be to train research men."[34] Universities would undertake research, but primarily for teaching purposes. Academia did not offer professors adequate freedom, equipment, or funding to pursue research.[35] The main role of professors was to ensure a steady supply of well-trained research men for industry. Scientists also warned industrial firms, which paid much higher salaries, that raiding university faculty was "suicidal" and would jeopardize the supply of research men and result in "national scientific bankruptcy."[36]

Large vertically and horizontally organized corporations, such as AT&T, DuPont, GE, and Westinghouse, also helped make research men. They developed close partnerships with universities in order to shape curriculum and gain easy access to graduates. They funded faculty positions and donated equipment to university labs. They sat on the boards of organizations so that they could inform the standardization of these new professions. Disappointed in the abilities of universities to educate scientists and engineers to their liking, they developed training programs to shape new university graduates, as well as skilled workers, to the needs of the corporation.[37]

Modern management techniques were one of the principal skills that research men learned in university and corporate training programs. One of the goals of these programs was to ensure that each student was "surrounded by an 'atmosphere' of manufacturing and business efficiency, where he will learn . . . the modern methods of office and works management."[38] Research men occupied what David Noble called a "double role" that encompassed science and management. Cost and labor time were fundamental variables in their ostensibly technical calculations and experiments.[39] As industrialization intensified the conditions of factory work, research men faced a new dilemma: "the man problem." In tight labor markets, workers were unwilling to conform to the rote forms of manual work that research men often created. Motivated by managerial and progressive inclinations, they took on this "man problem" with the same fervor with which they designed machines. They developed a variety of methods, from time-motion studies to corporate welfare programs, that attempted to encourage workers to conform to carefully designed production processes. As a result, research men increasingly took on management positions and management itself increasingly became a scientific pursuit.[40] Many executives in the 1920s observed that it was "natural" for research men to eventually move from research to managerial positions.[41]

Research men also applied these managerial skills within the laboratory. Edward Weidlen, the research director of the Pittsburgh-based Mellon Institute of Industrial Research, affirmatively cited Frederick Taylor as the best guide to managing laboratories. In the past, he said, research management was done on an ad hoc basis, but today "scientific management" is a "permanent feature of every research laboratory of importance." A successful research director is "an organizationist, a believer in the smoothly operating machinery of management."[42] He recommended that research directors carefully study employees' work, deploy organizational diagrams, and maintain close contact with executives. Research men also managed the work of technicians; craft workers, such as glass blowers and machinists; and fellow scientists.

Much of the literature on research men directly contrasted their labor to that of manual workers. Research directors agreed that they needed to manage research man, but they also emphasized that "the research man . . . needs . . . freedom from restraint and petty annoyances." "As soon as research man becomes tied down by arbitrary rules," Jacobson wrote, "his creative power and effectiveness became diminished."[43] Freedom, scientists argued, was what made research "the most attractive field."[44] Herman Schneider picked up on the contrast between research man's freedom and other workers' lack of freedom in an early textbook on worker education. Schneider was dean of engineering at the University of Cincinnati and the founder of a pathbreaking cooperative education system for engineering students.[45] He argued that there were two broad types of work: enervating and energizing. The "pure absurd repetition" of factory labor was enervating and "the absolute zero of work." In contrast, "the pure research man in science" had "the most energizing work." He added, "Between these two extremes lies the whole range of human labor."[46] Managers and scientists described research men's work in binary opposition to that of fellow workers. A key feature that differentiated research men from other workers was the sense that they were free and had control over their labor. In fact, as Shapin describes, research men were far from free and firms tightly managed their work.[47] Nonetheless, this supposed freedom became one of the main ways that managers and scientists differentiated research men from other workers.

Research men also had different traits than fellow workers. Westinghouse's research director, Charles E. Skinner, emphasized that research men should be judicious, "capable of working with others," and "play the game according to the rules." The ideal research man "should in every sense of the term be a true gentleman."[48] C. E. Kenneth Mees, the director of the Eastman Kodak Research Labs in Rochester, similarly emphasized that research men "must be unselfish and willing to co-operate" and have "moral qualities," "frankness," and "active optimism."[49] Edward R. Weidlein, the research director of the Mellon Institute, described his great skill at "selecting men." First his contacts at universities would inform him about potential employees. Then he would "find out something of his early life, training, home surroundings" and request a photograph. When the prospective research man arrived for an interview, "I can tell almost by the way a man walks in the door, whether he is the type of man I want." Two key traits made a good research man. First, tellingly, he needed "personality," "because these men come in contact with executives."[50] Second, a research man needed to be agreeable and a team player. Weidlein recommended that research directors select research men based on their social character: their ability to adopt the overlapping norms of the corporation and fellow scientists.

If provided with the right training and conditions, research men would benefit not only the United States and its industries but also mankind as a whole. This focus on experts leading society was part of the broader Progressive reform movement.[51] Swift and Company's Richardson claimed chemists' mantle as "the founders of our modern civilization," and GE's Charles Steinmetz noted that "all of our modern civilization, depends on engineering."[52] Westinghouse's Nutting, who made the strongest claim that research man was a distinct class, also argued that research men should increasingly take the lead in governing society. The "best and strongest" democracies, he said, were those that "adopt business methods" and "put [their] ablest experts in control."[53] Once research men assumed their rightful leadership role, they would finally earn the social recognition that they had long lacked. When a scientist succeeds as a research man, the Mellon Institute's Weidlein wrote, he will "find that his knowledge has become power—power to move men and things. He is at last on the highway to an authoritative position, with its prestige, poise, peace and freedom, the highest objectives of professional life and education."[54] By the 1920s, industrial research, which originally involved refining production techniques on the shop floor, became a profession that required a formal university education, accreditation, and learned conformity with corporate and social norms. The trajectory of research men from university to corporate training programs to the industrial laboratory deepened their separation from the world of physical work and workers.

In the 1970s, there was an at-times-tedious debate about whether scientific workers specifically and the professional-managerial class in general constituted a class.[55] Erik Olin Wright helpfully moved beyond this debate by arguing that professionals and managers occupied a "contradictory class location" rather than a discrete class.[56] There are several key features of this contradictory location. Research men avidly adhered to management techniques and economic calculation, developed machinery and production methods that diminished workers' control in their workplaces, assumed management roles inside the lab, and were often promoted to higher managerial positions outside the lab. Research men were often managers, but they also answered to the dictates of research directors and corporate executives.

For the most part, research men, like workers, did not own the means of production. Despite this lack of ultimate control, industry, universities, professional societies, and scientists actively encouraged research men to adopt a consciousness as free and privileged workers. Research men worked with their minds, not their hands; they pursued their passions, not the whims of management; they did not do routinized labor but opened the mysteries of the world. None of these attributes were absolutely true, but all were central to how industry and universities taught research men to perceive their position within the firm and society. Research men's class consciousness subverted solidarity with other workers, drew "talented men" to the field, and reflected how research work was tightly wedded to management prerogatives.

Research men's skills and proclivities reflected their role as allies in industry's pursuit of capital accumulation. One of these proclivities was a sense that research men were loyal to the pursuit of knowledge, not to any other interest. Unlike other class formations, antagonism was not a defining feature of research men.[57] Industry helped produce a consciousness among technoscientific workers that they were distinct from both management and labor and that their work was not narrowly self-interested but benefited the nation and mankind. Industry in part created this sensibility through the production of laboratory spaces that ideologically and physically separated research men from other workers.

The Westinghouse Valley and Industrial Suburbanization

The invention of research man occurred in concert with the development of the corporation and the dispersal of industry at the turn of the century. During the second industrial revolution, industrialists dispersed factories to facilitate mechanization and exert greater control over production. These new suburban factories deepened the sociospatial division of labor between blue-collar workers and those who designed and managed work. The advent of high-speed, continuous flow, and complex manufacturing required increasingly sophisticated levels of administration and greater concentrations of capital, thereby giving rise to scientific management and the modern corporation.[58] The development of a sociospatial division of labor between mental and physical work emerged alongside the rise of the corporation, technological change, and the dispersal of industry.

George Westinghouse established the Westinghouse Electric Company in 1886 in a building it shared with Union Switch & Signal, a railroad equipment manufacturer that he also founded. In its early years, Westinghouse employed about two hundred at this plant located on crowded Garrison Alley in the heart of downtown Pittsburgh.[59] It was a small plant where inventors used "rule of thumb methods" to create machinery on the shop floor.[60] In its earliest years, the demands of production primarily dictated the direction of research.[61] At Garrison Alley, there was no division between the spaces of invention and production; electrical machinery was produced on a batch basis and the inventor labored alongside workers.[62] It was from this plant, along with an off-site laboratory in Great Barrington, Massachusetts, that George Westinghouse created the alternating current (AC) apparatus to light the 1893 Chicago World's Fair, a key victory in his attempt to overtake Edison's direct current (DC) system.[63]

By 1890 this small downtown plant was becoming cramped. Land in downtown Pittsburgh was expensive, crowded, and not suitable for producing the large turbines the company was beginning to manufacture. In 1887 George Westinghouse acquired land along Turtle Creek and the Pennsylvania Railroad's mainline, ten miles to the east of downtown Pittsburgh. He moved the Westinghouse Air Brake Company (WABCO) to Wilmerding in 1889 and a year later formed the East Pittsburgh Improvement Company (EPIC) to coordinate development in Turtle Creek Valley (see Map 2).

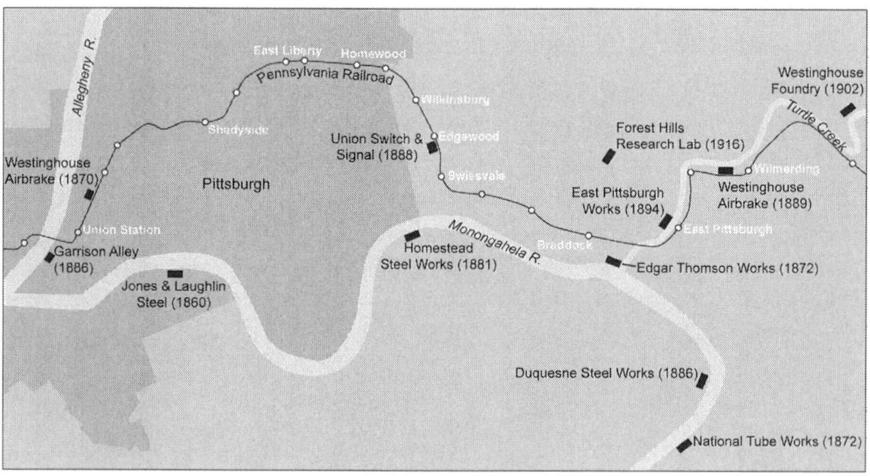

Map 2. The locations of Westinghouse's research laboratory and plants as well as large steel mills along the Monongahela River. The shaded area shows the boundaries of the city of Pittsburgh in 1907. White text labels the names of key stations on the Pennsylvania Railroad. Based on "Map of Pittsburg Showing Location of Westinghouse Interests," n.d., Library of Congress.

In Wilmerding, Westinghouse created a complete company town, including an ornate Romanesque headquarters for WABCO (a building that came to be known as the Castle), a town square, and company-owned housing on tree-lined streets. Wilmerding grew rapidly from a small village to a bustling company town of several thousand.

After his success in Wilmerding, Westinghouse began plans for a larger complex of plants further down Turtle Creek, in East Pittsburgh. In 1894 Westinghouse occupied its first building in East Pittsburgh. Demand for electrical apparatuses was growing steadily, and the company outgrew this building before it opened. It immediately began constructing additional buildings at what would soon become a dense complex of office buildings (including, until the 1940s, the company's headquarters), factories, machine shops, testing laboratories, and rail yards (see Figure 5). This new plant helped create an increasingly stark sociospatial division of labor between manufacturing and other types of work. Workers assembled machinery following plans developed by engineers and scientists in the many office buildings and laboratories

Figure 5. Westinghouse East Pittsburgh Works in 1953. George Westinghouse Museum Collection, Detre Library & Archives, Senator John Heinz History Center.

at the plant. Managers, increasingly removed from the spaces of manufacturing, dictated the conditions and pace of work in the plant.

From the East Pittsburgh plant in the west to smaller satellite plants in Trafford and Irwin to the east, Westinghouse Electric and WABCO dominated life in Turtle Creek Valley. They formed an integrated district of electrical and railroad equipment factories that became known as Westinghouse Valley (see Map 2). By 1899 Pittsburgh accounted for 15.3 percent of national employment in the electrical industry, and Westinghouse Valley ranked alongside GE's main plant in Schenectady, New York, as the largest concentration of the electrical industry in the United States.[64]

Westinghouse's moves to Wilmerding and East Pittsburgh began the company's century-long history of industrial decentralization. It joined numerous other Pittsburgh-based companies in what Edward K. Muller has described as the "centrifugal movement" of industry into the city's outskirts.[65] By 1900 Pittsburgh had become an integrated manufacturing region, stitched together by rail, streetcar, and telegraph and centered on the skyscrapers of downtown Pittsburgh. The metropolitan region's manufacturing was concentrated in four counties, from the coke ovens and glass manufactories of Westmoreland County to the east to the massive steel mills lining the Ohio River in Beaver County to the west, but it also encompassed an even greater hinterland, including much of western Pennsylvania, eastern Ohio, and West Virginia.[66] The vast majority of the region's factories, as well as many of its corporate offices, were located outside Pittsburgh.

As historical geographers have shown for Montreal, Baltimore, San Francisco, and other cities, industrial suburbanization was not unique to the Pittsburgh region.[67] Pittsburgh was prone to industrial decentralization because it was dominated by a small number of oligopoly-sector firms engaged in large-scale, technologically intensive, vertically and horizontally integrated manufacturing and had a challenging hilly topography for large-scale industry. As Pittsburgh firms grew, especially those that produced basic metals, the city's crowded downtown and adjacent neighborhoods no longer provided suitable space for large-scale manufacturing. In Pittsburgh, as elsewhere, industrial suburbanization was driven by industry's imperative to rationalize production, exercise greater control over workers, and develop further outlets for the extraction of surplus value.

New technologies both facilitated and necessitated industrial suburbanization. The advent of technologies such as Bessemer furnaces dramatically increased the scale and speed of production at individual plants, deskilled craftsmen who previously controlled the pace of their work, brought together various manufacturing processes within a single mill and company, and introduced new technologies (in the case of the Bessemer furnaces: steel rails) that enabled further industrial decentralization. Firms such as Carnegie Steel moved to suburban green fields so that they could design plants based around continuous flow, integrated production systems that both increased the scale and rate of production and allowed the company to exert greater control over workers.[68]

The appropriation of scientific knowledge was essential to this dual process of mechanization and suburbanization. Andrew Carnegie attributed his success as an iron- and steelmaker in part to chemistry. In his autobiography, he recounted how a "veritable quack doctor" used instinct to manage his first mill in Pittsburgh. Carnegie decided to dispense with the "rule-of-thumb-intuition manager" and "to find a chemist," something his rivals saw as "extravagant." Integrating the "burning sun of chemical knowledge" gave Carnegie an "entire monopoly of scientific management." Immediately after discussing the importance of science to steel making, Carnegie turned to a subject "constantly in my mind": "the question of location" of his new more-advanced plants.[69] Along with his Presbyterian virtue and work ethic, Carnegie claimed that it was science and the suburbanization of factories that allowed him to gain control of the iron and steel industry.

Industrial decentralization in Pittsburgh was also a key step in dismantling the power of what Francis G. Couvares describes as the "craftsmen's empire," replacing skilled artisans with integrated factories where machines and managers dictated the pace of production.[70] More isolated suburban factories provided distance from the strongholds of craft unions and political machines and gave industrialists greater control over political life.[71] Finally, as firms suburbanized, other firms often followed, whether because they benefited from the externalities created by larger firms or because they supplied or serviced suburban plants. Pittsburgh's industries dispersed outside the city's boundaries, along its river valleys and rail lines, where they formed an integrated network of manufacturing districts devoted to producing basic metals, electrical and railroad equipment, chemicals, and glass.

The decentralization of industry and the mechanization that usually accompanied it was a part of what Marx described as "the appropriation of living labour by objectified labour."[72] In other words, capital—concretized in the form of machines but also as rail lines, utilities, port facilities, and factory buildings—comes to dictate the pace and form of production. All this dead labor was increasingly the product of the living labor of scientists and engineers. Just as Pittsburgh firms created factories that employed the industrial working class, they also made other spaces—universities, research institutes, and industrial research laboratories—in order to reproduce increasingly important technoscientific labor.

Pittsburgh, like many industrial cities, was home to a complex array of institutions whose primary purpose was to educate, accredit, and reproduce engineers and industrial scientists. As factories decentralized, these institutions clustered in the new City Beautiful–inspired cultural and educational district of Oakland. The Carnegie Institute of Technology, founded by Andrew Carnegie, specialized in educating industrial engineers.[73] Likewise, the University of Pittsburgh, which received substantial support from the Mellon family and developed one of the earliest cooperative education programs, where engineering students held temporary positions at local firms, was a training ground for the scientific and engineering talent needed by local industry. Not only did industry rely on these universities for trained employees, but the universities also became reliant on firms to provide funding for professorships, discounted equipment for laboratories, and scholarships for students.[74] Westinghouse even partnered with the University of Pittsburgh to allow professors to spend time in the company's plants so they would be better equipped to teach young engineers.[75]

Sandwiched between the campuses of the University of Pittsburgh and Carnegie Tech, the heavily pillared Mellon Institute for Industrial Research was the United States' first cooperative laboratory providing scientists and engineers on contract to firms from Pittsburgh and across the country.[76] Underneath the master-planned campus of Carnegie Tech, the Federal Bureau of Mines, one of the earliest government-funded research laboratories, developed new technologies to resolve the dangers of underground work. Meanwhile, the city also became home to active chapters of professional societies that accredited engineers, fostered communication, and published journals.[77] Representatives of Pittsburgh-based universities and industrial firms played important roles in developing standardized engineering education, accreditation, and personnel rating systems for engineers, workers, and military conscripts during the early twentieth century.[78] Pittsburgh, with a wide array of industrial firms and two schools of engineering, was one of the most important centers for the development and professionalization of engineering and industrial science in the United States.[79]

Industry, universities, and professional associations created research men and produced the spaces where they would work, learn, and reproduce themselves. At the turn of the century, technological change, suburbanization, the emergence of the corporation, and the professionalization of science and engineering developed in concert. As industry spread into Pittsburgh's suburbs, a growing separation developed between places of physical and mental work. "Technology became a class bound phenomenon" and the research lab furthered and resulted from this class formation.[80]

Making Science Suburban

There are two significant bodies of research on the history of industrial laboratories. The first examined how firms in the early twentieth century internalized scientific research as a key element of corporate strategy. This literature was attentive to the role that research and researchers played within firms but largely did not address the physical setting of laboratories or the broader social and political context in which scientists and engineers worked.[81] More recently, scholars have highlighted how the rapid growth and suburbanization of research laboratories in the post–World War II period was indicative of a shift to the knowledge economy.[82] They identified several features of laboratories that were characteristic of this shift: a campus setting, flexible modular design, and an emphasis on the freedom of technoscientific workers.

These three defining elements of the post–World War II laboratory were already in place at Westinghouse in 1916. Mees, of Eastman Kodak, identified each of these elements in his seminal 1920 book on laboratory design.[83] These attributes, associated with the rise of the knowledge economy, were first adopted by massive industrial oligopolies in the early twentieth century in order to produce research men and create conditions in which they could further capital accumulation.

At the turn of the twentieth century, American industrial firms began to develop stand-alone research laboratories. Many of these early research laboratories, such as GE's laboratory in Schenectady, AT&T's in Manhattan, and Eastman Kodak's in Rochester, were adjacent to existing plants. However, a few firms, most notably DuPont, which opened an experimental station on a campus on the outskirts of Wilmington, Delaware, in 1903, began to locate research facilities away from the site of production.[84]

There were several reasons why industrial firms built stand-alone laboratories. For many companies, a new laboratory was intended to project an image of modernity to consumers and employees. For others, stand-alone laboratories isolated sensitive equipment from the vibration, dirt, and smoke of the factory. Other firms, such as GE, saw the removal of scientists from the shop floor as necessary to provide an appropriate space for scientific reasoning.[85] Still others saw modern laboratories as the best way to recruit scarce scientific talent. Nearly all firms used laboratories as ideal places to invest surplus profits during times of growth. Competition between firms drove the creation of laboratories as they jockeyed to create the image and reality of the most innovative firm.[86] But each of these explanations is only a piece of the story. Another piece is that industrial firms built laboratories in order to create and enlist a technoscientific workforce needed to develop new products, technologies, and managerial techniques that consolidated control over production processes and monopolized new markets.

Firms established laboratories not out of a rarified interest in science but because they understood research as a valuable means to further accumulation, exert managerial control, and monopolize markets. While the federal government provided little funding for research before World War II, it was able, through provisions in patent law, to ensure that marketable innovation would largely be the domain of corporations that had large laboratories and patent law departments.[87] In the early twentieth century, firms increasingly shifted their strategy from purchasing the patents of outside inventors to developing new technologies within their laboratories.[88] Companies pursued industrial research, as David Hounshell describes, because they were "threatened by competition, because they were engaged in a process of rationalizing their organizations . . . and because they saw benefits to internalizing R&D rather than relying on the market."[89] By the 1920s, research alongside sales and production became part of the "triumvirate" of corporate strategy in the United States.[90]

Between 1920, when the National Research Council inaugurated its first directory of industrial laboratories, and 1940, the number of labs in the United States increased from 306 to 3,505. The vast majority of these laboratories were located in the metropolitan regions of the manufacturing belt. In the 1920s, 62 percent of industrial laboratories and more than 70 percent of industrial researchers were located in New York, Illinois, New Jersey, Pennsylvania, and Ohio. By 1940 this regional dominance had fallen slightly to 55 percent of all laboratories and 60 percent of all researchers.[91] Most of these laboratories were small and located within factories, but by the 1920s, many larger and more research-intensive firms had developed stand-alone laboratories within and outside factory sites.

With Westinghouse's move to its massive East Pittsburgh complex, engineers and managers increasingly occupied office buildings and laboratories that were separate from the factory. They conceptualized production systems off-site and then relied on their functionaries on the shop floor to execute these systems. In 1895, a year after its move, Westinghouse opened an engineering department, marking a "shift . . . from cut-and-try methods to an engineering style that emulated science."[92] In 1902 it placed mechanical engineer Charles Skinner in charge of research. In 1906 it formed its first Research Division housed within its Engineering Department, and in 1910 it built a freestanding lab on the grounds of the East Pittsburgh plant.[93] In 1916, claiming that it needed to provide a space for researchers free from the competing demands and disruptions of the factory, the company built a new stand-alone research laboratory on a barren hillside in suburban Forest Hills (see Map 2 and Figures 6 and 7). The research lab was located a mile from the East Pittsburgh Works. This location was intended to be close enough for employees to communicate with management and engineers in East Pittsburgh but far enough away to insulate their work from the direct demands of the plant. In an article titled "Making Research Profitable," lab manager S. M. Kinter described the lab as standing "calmly on a hillside." In relation to the East Pittsburgh plant, it was "far enough to be undisturbed" but "not so far as to lose touch."[94] This tension between the need to be proximate to the plant but far enough away to be "undisturbed" would shape the locations of Westinghouse's research facilities for its entire history. From its inception, the suburban research lab was simultaneously a retreat from and an engagement with industrial capitalism.

For most of the lab's early years, its activities were focused on what Ronald Kline and Thomas Lassman call "engineering research," including material testing, product development, and machine theory, all of which had an immediate effect on work in the East Pittsburgh plant in the valley below.[95] According to Skinner, his staff was not "privileged to study science for the pure love of science, but must become part of the great industrial machine which takes

Figure 6. Westinghouse Research Lab nears completion around 1916. George Westinghouse Museum Collection, Detre Library & Archives, Senator John Heinz History Center.

scientific facts and phenomena and weaves them into a fabric of machines and devices which have to do directly with the commercial advantages of our own times."[96]

In 1920, shortly after the Westinghouse lab opened, Mees, the research director of Eastman Kodak and along with Skinner one of the principal inventors of the term *research man,* published the first guide to industrial laboratory design. In the book, he drew repeatedly from the Westinghouse lab and his extensive correspondence with its research directors. Mees was particularly enthralled with Westinghouse's use of moveable partitions to divide laboratories, a feature that he recommended integrating in all laboratories. The partitions enabled the movement of walls in order "to accommodate any particular type of research." The use of partitions, Mees thought, was the "keynote" of the lab and would allow "for ready changes . . . as the character of the work changes."[97] He added that this flexible design allowed researchers to adapt laboratory spaces for either applied or basic research.

Figure 7. Westinghouse Research Laboratories in the 1940s. Visible at the center of the photo is the Westinghouse Atom Smasher—a piece of research equipment that Westinghouse developed in 1937 to lure prominent academic scientists to the laboratory and bolster the company's image. The lab's suburban surroundings are visible in the background. Westinghouse Electric Corporation Records, Detre Library & Archives, Senator John Heinz History Center.

According to Mees, research directors must offer research men freedom to pursue research that is not immediately profitable, but it was autonomy of a highly managed sort. Like managers at other industrial firms, he advocated the adoption of systems of cost and time accounting, collective administration, and constant contact with "the works" that ensured that researchers did not drift too far from the needs of the company. Ultimate managerial responsibility lay with the research director, and Mees and Skinner both advised fellow directors to offer research men room to pursue their interests but also to be clear about the limits of such exploration.[98]

Mees and Skinner both thought that research should be directly linked to production needs and that labs should maintain close contact with manufacturing divisions. Mees wrote, "It is doubtful whether it is desirable to divorce a research laboratory from the works problems" and that the ultimate success of the lab was determined by whether "the work done in it can be applied." In his correspondence with Mees, Skinner described how the Westinghouse labs were organized within the Engineering Department in order to ensure that researchers attended to factory problems. The research lab, Skinner wrote, "has been so organized that it can be a leader in the development of new things and at the same time keep in the closest possible touch with their application and use." He continued: "Problems for solution come to it from every possible direction and not the least fertile source of theoretical problems is the grist of troubles from the daily routine work in the factory. We believe that the research division should both lead and follow the practical end of the work."[99] Far from autonomous, Mees and Skinner called for research labs that were in constant contact with manufacturing divisions. As Kinter described, the work of the Westinghouse lab was "not spectacular," and most of it was devoted to "improving profit and reducing costs."[100] This focus on developing new products and production processes was typical of industrial labs at this time.

In addition to management's claim that it wanted to separate the research lab from the immediate demands of production, the managers also argued that harsh factory environments had a deleterious effect on the quality of research. In what would become a timeless justification for locating laboratories in suburban locations, research directors said that removing the lab from the factory protected sensitive equipment and research results from smoke, sound, vibration, and electromagnetic interference.[101] As Skinner noted, the company selected a location a mile distant from the plant in order "to secure a site relatively free from vibration, dirt and noise and which would afford a certain amount of isolation."[102] Mees added that building a separate "special building" for a laboratory "under one roof" would ensure "cooperation" among research men.[103] Arthur Percy Morris Fleming, an electrical engineer at Metropolitan Vickers who was trained at Westinghouse, also wrote that a lab should be "separate from but centrally situated in relation" to the factory, a design he followed in Manchester.[104] The area around the Westinghouse lab was mostly undeveloped. The lab, a modest brick colonial structure, described by Skinner as "plain, but substantial," understatedly echoed the look of a college building (see Figures 6 and 7).[105]

In 1927 the lab employed what Kinter called "an elaborate machinery of professional seekers": seventy engineers and scientists who were divided into sections, including mechanics, physics, metallurgy, chemistry, and mathematics. It also employed a support staff of forty, including technicians, clerks, and an array of skilled craft workers. According to Kinter, this "force of expert artisans" was intended "to free the engineer from mere hampering labor and difficulty as to ways and means."[106] Mees reminded fellow managers that it was not economical for highly paid researchers to devote their time to developing research equipment and models.[107] Such equipment should be purchased from suppliers or developed by the shops that most major laboratories had on site. Mees and Skinner both emphasized that while research man was encouraged to make minor adjustments to machinery with his own hands in order to encourage "manual dexterity" and "mental familiarity with the job," he was to protect his time and instead devote it to more exacting intellectual challenges.[108] The detailed division of labor at the lab between technicians and researchers helped maintain the illusion that research man worked in the rarified and pure realm of ideas and deepened the separation between execution and conceptualization.[109] As Stephen R. Barley and Beth A. Beckhy argue, the role of the technician is to "broker the professional's contact with the phenomena over which the profession is reputed to have mastery."[110] Technicians and the laboratory itself created a space where research men could access the material world of manufacturing without having to dirty their hands and status.

While "no race or district, has any clear superiority in producing research men," Kinter observed, there was a predominance of Americans on the staff, most of whom were from the "Middle West." Also included among the engineers were "a Scotsman or two, a few Germans, a Jew, and eight Russian 'intelligentsia' whose presence is due to the Revolution."[111] Based on Kinter's informal census of laboratory employees, the ethnic makeup of the lab differed greatly from the predominantly Eastern and Southern European immigrants who populated the Turtle Creek and Monongahela Valleys. There were no African American research men, and a retired mechanical engineer captured the lab's racially segregated character when he noted the presence of "two black janitors with the unlikely names of White and Paler."[112]

Despite Kinter's earlier statement that no race had an advantage, he had "a feeling that the American tends to be more resourceful." "Idleness" was never a problem among the lab's scientists who were driven to pursue their work. However, sometimes the manager did need to discipline researchers if they were "wandering off the main path into some of the fascinating scientific byways." Employees at the lab were "rather young," and those who were capable and stayed with Westinghouse would eventually follow the "natural movement" to an executive position.[113] After a postsecondary degree and several years working in the lab, research men "make the best of timber from which to select *executives* and high-class *specialists*."[114]

According to R. E. Peterson, a retired laboratory employee, research men at Westinghouse predominantly settled in a string of residential suburbs that lined the streetcar line between Forest Hills and Pittsburgh's affluent East End.[115] There is no listing of laboratory employees' addresses from its early years. However, a 1948 directory confirms that research men largely resided in racially and socioeconomically exclusive communities largely populated by fellow white-collar professionals.[116] Given that little new housing was constructed between 1930 and 1948, this directory provides an approximate sense of the preferred neighborhoods of research men in the 1920s. Most research men lived in affluent parts of Pittsburgh's East End and the suburbs of Wilkinsburg and Forest Hills. By the 1940s, they were also moving into suburbs further to the east, such as Churchill and Penn Hills. They typically lived in this white middle-class milieu for their entire careers. In 1956, when Westinghouse replaced the Forest Hills lab with a new research center in suburban Churchill, executives noted that the most important factor was to find a location in the eastern suburbs that was proximate to its employees' current homes (see chapter 4).[117]

The 1948 directory reveals one more important detail. Few research men settled in East Pittsburgh or the predominantly industrial communities along Monongahela Valley. Based on the directory, I was able to identify some employees who either had a phone listing in the lab's shop or who were women. Because not all women were listed by first name and not all technicians and craft workers worked in the shop, this is an extremely crude way of differentiating research men from other employees. The shop and women employees I was able to identify were far more likely to reside in the industrial areas to the south of the lab. The suburbs that surrounded the laboratory provided patriarchal social relations and racially and socioeconomically segregated school systems and social life that helped reproduce research men and the division between mental and physical labor.

Westinghouse built the Forest Hills lab because research would grant it a monopoly over new technologies and not having a laboratory would cause it to fall behind its rival General Electric. It developed an exclusive space for engineers and scientists, for the same reason that it created office buildings, technical schools, and social clubs for white-collar workers: because these facilities helped differentiate research men from other workers and this would in turn support its pursuit of profits. By creating exclusive suburban spaces for science and engineering, firms sought to create and reinforce research men's loyalty to industry.

Besides Westinghouse, prior to World War II, several of Pittsburgh's largest industrial firms also developed off-site laboratories. These included Gulf Oil, which first contracted the Mellon Institute for Industrial Research in 1927 to investigate oil production and pipelines. This research quickly outgrew the Mellon Institute, and in 1930 it relocated to a newly constructed Art Deco laboratory about ten blocks away on the Boulevard of the Allies. Shifting from a focus on prospecting to an integrated facility that studied all aspects of the petroleum industry, in 1933 it was renamed the Gulf Research and Development Corporation, and in 1935 it relocated to a massive fifty-seven-acre site in Harmarville in Pittsburgh's northern suburbs. One of the largest research facilities in the region, the lab first employed 250 people; by 1948 it employed 1,000 staff.[118] Like Gulf, U.S. Steel also located its first research lab in Oakland and moved to suburban Monroeville in 1953.[119]

In the 1930s, the Aluminum Company of America (Alcoa) opened its first off-site laboratory in the suburban outskirts of New Kensington, where its major manufacturing plant was based. The architects designed the ornate building to showcase the uses of aluminum, and the doors, window casings, grilles, spandrels, chairs, fixtures, and even much of the laboratory equipment itself were all made from the material. Alcoa located the "modern laboratory building" in the "foothills of the Allegheny Mountains" in a campus environment in order "to provide an atmosphere conducive to scientific research." The lab was designed to sell the company's image as a progressive firm, to promote the use of aluminum, and to allow easy expansion and flexibility of research. The company left the rear of the building unadorned in order to allow for additions because "the continual growth of the aluminum industry will surely call for such increased facilities." Like Westinghouse's Forest Hills Laboratory, Alcoa's lab highlighted all the elements historians typically attribute to the postwar laboratory, including flexible design and a suburban location.[120]

The suburban research laboratory existed well before World War II in cities across the manufacturing belt. Such suburban spaces for science were the product of more than just industrial firms' desire to create comfortable, autonomous spaces for scientists and engineers to pursue their work. Industrial firms built research laboratories to reinvest surplus capital, develop and refine technologies that enabled further capital accumulation, and solidify the division between mental and physical labor. The suburban research laboratory was the product of and also contributed to industrialization, the dispersal of industry, and the rise of the corporation.

Regardless of whether laboratories pursued applied or basic research, whether they were located on factory grounds or in the suburbs, whether they drained or boosted corporate profits, or whether they answered to manufacturing divisions or were spaces of pure scientific autonomy, their primary achievement was to create a space that helped reproduce a sociospatial division between conceptualization and execution and created a class formation of skilled workers—research men—to pursue technoscientific work. Industry invested heavily in research laboratories as well as universities, corporate training programs, and amenities in order to ensure that research men became their permanent and needed allies in the pursuit of capital accumulation.

By the start of World War II, industrial firms had helped transform many of Pittsburgh's residential suburbs into spaces devoted to reproducing the class positions of scientists, engineers, and other white-collar professionals. These suburban spaces helped create and solidify the social and geographical divide between mental and physical labor and middle-class and blue-collar workers. As research spending increased during the early Cold War, firms looked again to exclusive suburbs as the only places suited to the social and technical needs of scientists and engineers.

4

The Monroeville Doctrine

How the Suburbs Shaped Cold War Science

In September 1969, the *Times Express,* a newspaper in Pittsburgh's burgeoning suburb of Monroeville, devoted a special issue to the borough's emergence as a research center. The newspaper carried its usual byline, "Serving the nation's research center." In one of the few articles in an issue laden with advertisements, borough manager Carol Pickens surveyed the "diversified development" of Monroeville and described it as "the residential research center of the nation," a claim that also appeared on the municipality's letterhead, signs welcoming visitors, and the Monroeville Chamber of Commerce's promotional materials.[1] In the article, Pickens celebrated the development of "quality industries" that brought a special class of "people who are interested in their community and willing to assist in the efforts to improve the community." Running alongside Pickens's article was a table showing Monroeville's population increase from a rural township of 4,675 in 1940 to a satellite city of 27,701 in 1969, making it Pittsburgh's most populated and fastest-growing suburb.[2] Monroeville was booming, and the *Times Express* and the borough's political leaders attributed the boom to its growing role as a hub of industrial research.

The remainder of the *Times Express* issue was devoted to advertisements from the companies that called Monroeville home. Koppers, the diversified manufacturer of chemicals and machinery, proclaimed its support for "the Monroeville Doctrine," which "stands for growth, prosperity, and progress." Monroeville's government, citizens, and companies shared a commitment to "community advancement," and this was why it had located its research laboratories there in 1961. U.S. Steel's advertisement for its research center, the first developed in Monroeville in 1953, described researchers who developed more than "a beam of high speed electrons." Off the job, U.S. Steel's employees were "busy with civic projects" and serving in local government. The capstone of the special issue was a full-page ad showing a model of the new Westinghouse Energy Center that was scheduled to open in 1970 and would make Monroeville the "NUCLEAR CAPITOL OF THE WORLD." The ad invited residents to visit a temporary Westinghouse display at the Monroeville Mall, where they could learn more about nuclear power and the new energy center.[3]

At first glance, visitors to "the nation's research center" would have seen an unremarkable commercial artery lined with strip malls. However, traveling beyond congested Route 22 into the surrounding hills, they would have

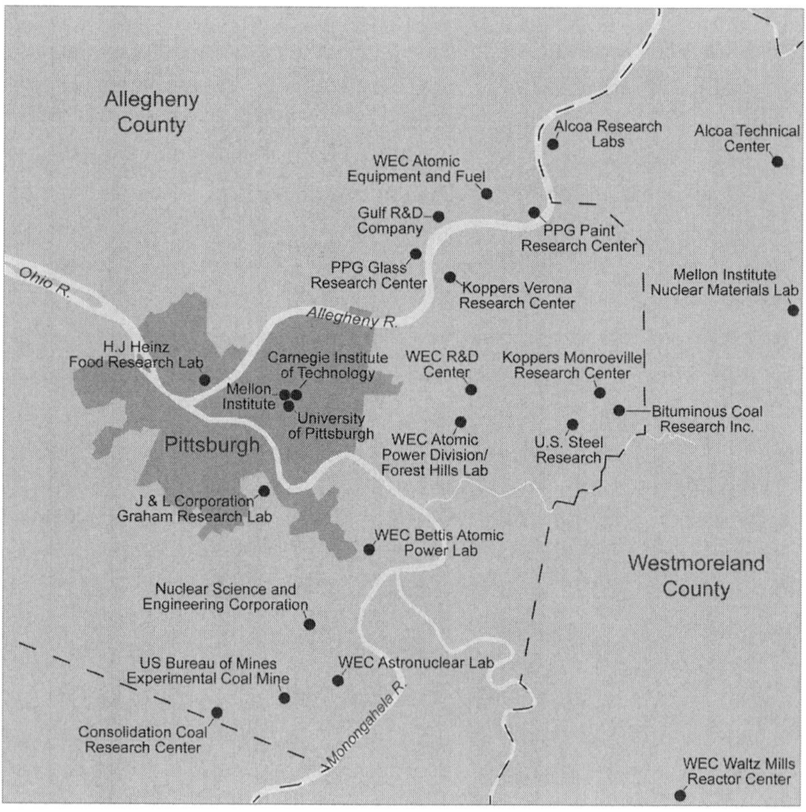

Map 3. Major research facilities in Pittsburgh in 1962. Map based on Lowry, *Portrait of a Region*, 97.

found the research facilities of Pittsburgh's leading industrial firms. Throughout the 1950s and 1960s, numerous companies and private developers created research centers and office buildings in Monroeville and other nearby suburbs. Counts vary, but by 1960 the Pittsburgh region was home to at least forty-one major research facilities and many smaller laboratories. Of these forty-one major facilities, twenty had been built since 1945 and most were located in the suburbs (see Map 3).[4]

During the postwar period, Pittsburgh's eastern suburbs became a location of choice for industrial research laboratories and office complexes that housed engineering services. The growth of research and engineering in Monroeville and other suburbs was facilitated by a number of major changes, including the construction of the Penn Lincoln Parkway in 1953 and its extension to the borough several years later, the availability of inexpensive and flat land, federal tax incentives, and increasing government and private support for industrial research. Industrial firms also pursued the Monroeville Doctrine because they thought suburban space was conducive to research. The Monroeville Doctrine was driven by firms' efforts to build exclusive suburban spaces for science that would help reproduce a technoscientific workforce, open new markets, and capture state funds, which would in turn create new business opportunities. While the Pittsburgh Renaissance ensured that the region and its firms benefited from government spending on urban renewal, its suburban counterpart, the Monroeville Doctrine, attempted to secure their share of federal funds allocated for research and defense.

I begin this chapter with a general discussion of why Pittsburgh firms pursued the Monroeville Doctrine during the Cold War. I then turn to a case study of the move by the Westinghouse Research Laboratories from Forest Hills to Churchill. I use this example to explore how research laboratories and suburban communities built a mutually beneficial relationship based on social exclusion, status, and control. This mutually beneficial relationship was premised on an idealized understanding of research as an exceptional form of mental labor that was radically different from other forms of labor in general and the corporal work of manufacturing in particular. In developing this mutually beneficial relationship, exclusive suburbs and industrial firms enshrined an untenable idea of research that helped maintain racial, class, and gender exclusion in both subdivisions and laboratories. According to local politicians and residents, the only suitable form of employment in residential suburbs was that of highly educated scientists and engineers. In turn, industrial firms agreed to maintain the illusion that research was radically different from other forms of labor in order to access exclusive suburbs that were key to attracting scientists and engineers and defense contracts. During the early Cold War, in the Pittsburgh region and across the United States, industrial research and affluent suburban communities were remade in each other's exclusive image.[5]

The Suburbanization of Research in Postwar Pittsburgh

As in Boston, New York, and many other regions, research centers in Pittsburgh rapidly multiplied and suburbanized in the years following World War II. For corporate executives, modern laboratories presented the cutting-edge character of their firms. For the communities that housed laboratories, they became points of pride. For the region's elite, the expansion of research and development furthered their argument that Pittsburgh was transcending its industrial past.[6] While the image of these pristine suburban labs suggested that they were places of isolated scientific pursuit, in fact they had immediate effects on industrial production, urban development, and local property markets and were an attempt to capture federal spending on defense and research. The typical suburban research lab in Pittsburgh presented an image of scientific autonomy, but the reality was very different.

In 1963 *Region in Transition,* the first volume of the three-volume Ford Foundation–funded *Economic Study of the Pittsburgh Region* (*ESPR*), was released. The study, first proposed in 1958 by the Regional Industrial Development Corporation (RIDC) and the Pittsburgh Regional Planning Association (PRPA), was intended to establish hard facts about Pittsburgh's moribund growth.[7] It was also meant to contribute scientific analysis to the Pittsburgh Renaissance and to serve as a model for the emerging field of regional economic analysis.[8] While the study lamented the region's ominous economic outlook and reliance on the basic metals industry, it also celebrated the presence of industrial research and corporate headquarters in the Pittsburgh region.[9] According to the *ESPR,* only Wilmington, Delaware (12.2 percent) and Detroit (6.9 percent) exceeded Pittsburgh (6.0 percent) in the percentage of its workforce employed in administrative and auxiliary functions. In absolute numbers, Pittsburgh ranked fourth in the United States behind New York City, Detroit, and Chicago. Unsurprisingly, the majority of those employed in these fields in Pittsburgh worked in metals industries, with

32.5 percent in basic metals and 24.6 percent in fabricated metal products, followed by 17.7 percent in electrical equipment and 9.0 percent in petroleum and coal products.[10] In 1960 private research and development employed 13,300, representing an annual growth of 6.5 percent over the previous five years. The third volume of the *ESPR* optimistically projected that by 1985 the region would be home to 51,931 people employed in industrial research and development.[11] Much of that growth, it predicted, would be at Westinghouse.

In a region where there was little hope for economic optimism, the authors of *Region in Transition* highlighted how Pittsburgh's significant concentration of corporate headquarters and research laboratories boded well "in an age when more and more of Man's work involves brain rather than brawn."[12] *Region in Transition* furthered the influential perspective, described in detail in chapter 2, that Pittsburgh's elite must create appealing workplaces, communities, and amenities for scientists, engineers, and other white-collar professionals in order to advance the region's growth. As the *ESPR* described, "a flourishing 'research community'" would "stimulate industrial and other employment," and this "is particularly valuable for a region, like the Pittsburgh Region, which needs a foothold in new growth industries if it is to enjoy even minimal economic growth."[13] While the study projected continued expansion of research and development, it lamented Pittsburgh's lack of specialization in aerospace and electronics, the most promising fields for growth.[14]

Within the region, industrial research was "characteristically suburban."[15] Based on their interviews with local executives and research lab directors, the authors of the *ESPR* outlined several reasons why industrial research facilities exhibited a "virtually unanimous preference . . . for suburban locations." One reason was a deep concern for projecting an innovative image to potential employees and customers. Based on his conversations with research directors, Ira Lowry, the author of the second volume of the *ESPR*, observed that "nearly all respondents stressed the importance of visual appeal" of their research centers. To the research directors, a properly designed research center with "a campus atmosphere helps their recruitment program" and "serve[s] as symbols of progressive management." This "visual appeal" was intended not only to appeal to employees but also to "impress the company's customers and the general public." According to Lowry, the appropriate design of such a research center "call[s] for low sprawling buildings, landscaped grounds, and extensive parking lots."[16]

Firms did not locate their labs based on image alone. Most shared "a vague optimism about future expansion" and projected growth of research for the foreseeable future.[17] Suburban land was less expensive and constrained than land in built-up areas and allowed firms to purchase parcels suitable for expansion. Profit-savvy industrial firms located their research centers in the suburbs with an eye toward growth but also with awareness that suburban land was a good investment that they could always recoup by developing adjacent land.

Many of the research directors Lowry spoke with believed that "isolation" was "advantageous." Like the research directors of the first Westinghouse Research Lab in Forest Hills, they thought that researchers needed to be buffered from the immediate demands of the factory while still remaining in touch with manufacturing divisions. They similarly emphasized that a quasi-isolated location kept staff from becoming "overly involved in production problems at the expense of investigations of longer range." Not only was suburban isolation important for protecting the supposed autonomy of researchers, but the presence of a nearby production site would harm the "visual appeal" of the research center. As Lowry described, "untidy production facilities tend to dominate the environment, damaging the valued image of the research center."[18]

By the early twentieth century, the eastern suburbs of Pittsburgh developed as one of the preferred residential locations for the city's white-collar workforce. By the 1930s, this region, along with the adjacent city neighborhoods of Point Breeze, Shadyside, and Squirrel Hill, contained the residential areas of choice for doctors and academics employed in Oakland as well as engineers, scientists, and managers employed at firms such as Westinghouse. In the 1950s, when firms began to develop plans for new laboratories, they accounted for the current residences of researchers, many of whom could easily find employment elsewhere. As a result, laboratories tended to move even further into the suburbs, where many of their employees already lived.

The authors of the *ESPR* noted that "several respondents mentioned specifically that management had been concerned about the effect of a move on the work force." As a result, before locating a lab, each firm "first investigated the geographical distribution of the residences of the research and auxiliary staff." As firms chose to locate their laboratories in proximity to the suburban neighborhoods where engineers and scientists had always lived, property developers saw the opportunity to develop similar subdivisions. "A move into virgin territory will soon be followed by residential subdividers eager to serve this high-income market," the authors of the *ESPR* observed, and "the development of Churchill and Monroeville as residential communities has been fostered by the cluster of research activities in that area."[19] Firms often promoted the suburbs that surrounded their laboratories to potential and current employees (see chapters 2 and 5).

During the Cold War, research labs may have grown increasingly distant (geographically at least) from manufacturing facilities, but they maintained a close connection to corporate headquarters. The growth of research centers in Pittsburgh's eastern suburbs was facilitated by the construction of the Penn Lincoln Parkway (later known as Parkway East), which provided relatively quick access to downtown Pittsburgh and Oakland. In addition, many firms added little-used helicopter-landing pads in their lab's designs. Such infrastructure fulfilled firms' fanciful modern dreams of researchers and executives whisking from suburban labs to downtown Pittsburgh and the airport.[20]

Research labs clustered in an arc to the east and south of Pittsburgh (see Map 3). This area afforded easy access to the universities and cultural amenities of Oakland as well as to the ring of suburbs that housed Oakland-based professors, doctors, and researchers. With local research and development dominated by large firms, collaboration between laboratories and the creation of spinoff companies was exceedingly rare (disappointingly to the authors of the *ESPR*). In a few cases, labs were intentionally sited in proximity to each other. For example, Westinghouse's research facilities clustered in the eastern and southern suburbs in order to allow easy movement between them. In most instances, though, what research centers shared was their parent firm's faith in the Monroeville Doctrine—that the suburbs offered the most suitable and economical location for industrial research.

The suburbs offered an additional advantage that was unnoticed by the *ESPR*. While it is true that suburban land offered greater flexibility than built-up locations, it also provided compliant local governments that rarely opposed new research facilities. In the 1950s and 1960s, suburban governments were particularly welcoming, especially Monroeville, which prided itself on being a "research capital," and Churchill, whose tax base was dominated by Westinghouse. Growth-friendly municipalities rolled out the red carpet for research laboratories that brought esteemed residents and taxpayers, with few of the side effects of manufacturing. Needless to say, the presence of both significant land developers and the employees of firms on the councils of those municipalities limited the possibility for conflict to emerge. Following a strategy they had pursued since the 1880s, industrial firms sought out and created favorable political and economic conditions in the suburbs.

While these factors all played a role in the growth of research laboratories in Pittsburgh's suburbs, another essential factor was the expansion of state spending on research and defense and favorable federal tax policies. Most local firms developed labs in the hope of netting a share of the Pentagon's largess. Thus the growth in research facilities in Pittsburgh's suburbs during the 1950s corresponded to the massive increase in defense spending that began during the Korean War.

Several federal tax incentives also made it advantageous to develop new research facilities in the suburbs. The Armed Services Procurement Act of 1947 gave the federal government the power to use procurement procedures to encourage industrial dispersal.[21] In October 1950, the Harry S. Truman administration amended the federal tax code to grant facilities given a "certificate of necessity" (attesting that they did defense work) full and accelerated amortization of their new facilities. Geographical dispersal was one basis on which the federal government awarded this new tax status. In 1951 the Truman administration encouraged all federal agencies to adopt measures to encourage firms to locate facilities outside critical defense areas. The most significant federal incentive for industrial dispersal occurred in 1954, when the Department of Commerce adopted a tax policy that granted firms accelerated amortization for *all new* facilities regardless of their location. This broad tax subsidy to new construction, along with federal highway spending, encouraged firms to construct new suburban facilities in Pittsburgh and elsewhere. While generous federal tax write-offs did not ensure decentralization, their combination with high taxes on profits meant that new suburban facilities were often highly affordable investments for businesses.[22] When coupled with subsidies and tax deductions for white suburban homeowners, they accelerated the rush of laboratories and scientists to the suburbs.[23]

A combination of factors contributed to firms' decisions to construct research labs in Pittsburgh's suburbs. Firms moved to the suburbs because they created conditions that would attract and reproduce technoscientific workers, earn public renown, and in doing so, it was hoped, discover new profitable areas of business and attract government-funded research. Despite the complexity of their decision to locate in the suburbs, firms always intended that laboratories pursue three primary goals: the reproduction of a scientific workforce, the opening of new markets, and the capture of federal spending.

Locating the Westinghouse Research Laboratories

In 1956 Westinghouse moved its Research Laboratories from Forest Hills to Churchill.[24] It was one of the largest research centers in the region and at its peak employed more than 2,200 staff.[25] It also had the greatest diversity of researchers (at one point ranging from metallurgists to sociologists), the strongest focus on basic research, and the closest ties to the military. Prominently located along the Penn-Lincoln Parkway, it was also the most visible laboratory in the region. The labs' high visibility and modern design were part of Westinghouse's larger effort in the 1950s to rebrand itself as a firm where scientific innovation was an essential part of business. If the Westinghouse Research Laboratories are any indication, then industry's emphasis on building suburban labs was primarily driven by the prosaic need to retain and reproduce technoscientific workers, invest ballooning profits, earn lucrative tax write-offs, allow for easy expansion, and ensure that the laboratory fit into exclusive suburbs. These factors, as much as the need to develop an ideal place to accommodate research, dictated the design and location of labs.

In 1949, flush with increasing profits from the Korean War and postwar economic growth, Westinghouse's new research director, electrical engineer John A. Hutcheson, began to advocate for a new laboratory. The reasons were simple: the research needs of the company were growing, while the current laboratory could not serve an expanded workforce. The site of the Forest Hills laboratory was bounded on three sides by housing and on a fourth by a steep slope. The company had built additions to the lab many times and had even moved research to off-site buildings, including a nearby shopping plaza and garage. Hutcheson warned that "no significant increase in personnel can be accommodated" at the Forest Hills site. Westinghouse was also entering "new fields of endeavor," particularly electronics, and such fields required increased research. Hutcheson emphasized that "international tensions" were expanding military research that Westinghouse could not accommodate at the current site.[26] If Westinghouse hoped to capture these growing fields, it needed to expand both its workforce and the facilities that housed it.[27] Building such a facility would be affordable because of expanded defense work, "the possibility of short term amortization of a sizeable fraction" of the cost, and "relatively high taxes" on corporate profits.[28]

Convinced by Hutcheson's argument, Westinghouse began to scour Pittsburgh's suburbs for an appropriate site. In a June 29, 1951, letter, Hutcheson listed the key attributes. The parcel of land should be at least fifty acres and flat, in order to keep down expenses. The surrounding land should be "residential rather than industrial" and preferably would allow for additional home construction in the vicinity. It would need to be located "as close to the present site as possible" and no more than thirty minutes from Forest Hills.[29] Throughout the search process, Hutcheson stressed the need for the new lab to be proximate to Forest Hills in order to avoid a "loss of time and personnel." He was especially concerned about the lab's clerical and skilled technical workforce, who he believed lived mostly in Turtle Creek Valley and would be unable to commute a great distance. The loss of this workforce "would inevitably produce a delay in resumption of operations."[30] The site should be accessible to public transit or a highway (but at least a quarter of a mile away to avoid vibration), and there was no need to access rail lines. Finally, the lab used a great deal of electricity, gas, and water; therefore, local utilities needed to be adequate.[31] Water was a particularly pressing concern in Pittsburgh's outer suburbs, where many homes relied on wells that would not meet the needs of a laboratory.

After considering several sites, mostly located in the eastern suburbs, in February 1952, Westinghouse settled on a seventy-one-acre site for $200,000 in the suburban borough of Churchill along the route of the proposed Penn-Lincoln Parkway. Churchill, like most of Pittsburgh's eastern suburbs, was no stranger to "Westinghouse people." In fact, the company's employees had been instrumental in the borough's secession from rural Wilkins Township in 1934. At that time, the land that became Churchill was home to two country clubs and the large estates of corporate executives. Mostly as a result of their belief that the township excessively taxed and obstructed the development of their land, in February 1934, forty-four of forty-five landowners had voted to secede and create "a community to which they could retire and be free of the hustle, bustle, dirt, and factories of the city."[32] Several months after secession, the *Pittsburgh Press* observed that landowners were busy subdividing their estates and creating "restricted" communities. The president of the borough council, H. C. Barton, told the *Press* that they aimed to keep Churchill "highly restricted," in order to ensure "a friendly group of neighbors; people like those residing here who hold responsible positions." Among those people were the borough's seven new councilmen, two of whom were high-level executives at Westinghouse. In the midst of the Depression, the *Press* noted that "the backers of Churchill Borough have built for themselves a community free from the outside world."[33]

Very little had changed by 1952, when Westinghouse moved to acquire land in Churchill. Speckled with country clubs, estates, and new subdivisions, Churchill was growing at the second-fastest rate of any municipality in the Pittsburgh region, quadrupling from 430 residents in 1940 to 1,723 in 1950. Despite this population growth, the borough made no zoning provisions for industrial use and very little provisions for commercial use. As the secretary of the borough proudly stated in 1951, "zoning is so tight your mother-in-law can hardly move in with you."[34] It also remained the home of many Westinghouse executives and researchers, including Charlie Weaver, the vice president of the Atomic Power Division and the former president of the Blackridge Civic Association (a Churchill subdivision); L. W. Chubb, the former director of the Research Lab; Stewart Way, the head of the Combustion Lab; and Daniel Alpert, the current head of the Physics Department and the soon-to-be-appointed associate director of the Research Lab. "Westinghouse people" also played a prominent role in local politics, with Alpert serving on the local school board and two Westinghouse employees—Earl Crawford, a researcher, and Roscoe M. Seybold, Westinghouse vice president and controller—serving on the borough council.[35] Westinghouse employees and their families contributed to Churchill's development as one of Pittsburgh's most affluent and restrictive suburbs. In 1950 "Mrs. L. W. Chubb," the wife of Westinghouse's research director, appeared before the borough council to support a zoning change that would prohibit smaller lot sizes because it was "for the betterment of the Borough" to "maintain zoning high."[36] Ironically, two years later, in order to finalize its land purchase, Westinghouse first had to have the exclusive community rezoned.

On January 7, 1952, Westinghouse submitted a petition to the Churchill council requesting the rezoning of its seventy-one-acre parcel. In the petition, it promised that the new research lab would not produce "dust, dirt, or fumes" and that "no products would be manufactured." It would be "completely landscaped" and would "enhance the appearance of the Borough."[37] Zoning

Ordinance No. 120 created a new zoning district, U-7, that allowed only one additional use within the borough: research laboratories.[38] It defined a research laboratory as

> a building or group of jointly used buildings in which research is conducted by the owner thereof to discover new scientific facts and principles for the sole and exclusive purpose of developing new and improved products to be manufactured by such owner at other locations and in which research laboratory and the land appurtenant thereto no products are manufactured or offered for sale and no services are offered for sale, and in which no operations will be conducted that will constitute a public menace.

The ordinance was very explicit in its intention to not allow any manufacturing within Churchill. It defined nuisances broadly as "odor, dust, smoke, gas, vibration, or noise or interference with radio or television reception" or any other uses that are "incompatible with the primary use of property in this Borough as an essentially residential community." The ordinance restricted building height to seventy-five feet and allowed build-out of only 15 percent of land.[39] These restrictions were intended to ensure that only research occurred on the plot and that the building conformed with the suburban character of the surrounding neighborhoods. The ordinance enshrined a definition of research as mental work removed from sales and manufacturing. This was inaccurate; for example, the laboratory frequently pursued outside contracts and manufactured prototypes, but it did reify a class distinction between research and manufacturing that was essential if the lab was to fit into the exclusive community.

Prior to the public hearing on Ordinance No. 120, residents began to send letters in support of Westinghouse to the Churchill council. E. M. Elkins, who shared the same mailing address as Westinghouse headquarters and owned six acres in the borough, wrote that the proposal "will be of material benefit to the Borough."[40] In a lengthier letter, Charles A. Williams, an employee of the University of Pittsburgh's Business School, encouraged the council to "attract this highly desirable facility." He described Westinghouse's "fine reputation," something, he insinuated, many council members were "more keenly aware than I." He reminded the councilors that "the activities of a research laboratory are a far cry from those of a manufacturing plant" and that the facility would improve the borough's tax base. As if this were not enough, he asked the councilors, "The type of person whom such a laboratory will attract to our community? Is it possible to find a better?"[41] Churchill first reviewed the proposed zoning ordinance at an informal town meeting, where residents heaped more praise on Westinghouse. After a presentation by Westinghouse vice president A. C. Monteith and a discussion among the attendees, 158 Churchill residents voted yes to the proposed ordinance, 14 no, and 9 no opinion.[42]

Support for the ordinance was similarly high when it was presented to the Churchill council the following week. The meeting began with brief presentations from Monteith and Hutcheson, both of whom pledged Westinghouse's appreciation of residents' shared "spirit . . . to maintain a residential atmosphere." Hutcheson presented slides showing the design of the lab. Among the slides was a map of existing employee homes, clustered mostly in Pittsburgh's eastern suburbs. The new location in Churchill "would mean essentially nothing to employees." Consequently, Hutcheson expected no employees would have to move, and this made it "very desirable for us to locate in this general area." Of course, Churchill was more than a central place, and Hutcheson emphasized that "the people in our laboratory are scientists and engineers," and "to these people the atmosphere in which they live is very important." Echoing Westinghouse's employee recruitment materials at the time (see chapter 2), he said that Churchill offered such people comfortable suburbs and easy access to Pittsburgh's "cultural facilities." Hutcheson and his predecessor Chubb, who was a Churchill resident and in attendance, had once considered moving the lab out of the region, but once Pittsburgh was "improving" in terms of "smoke nuisances, and other things," they realized that "every advantage could be retained by staying in this area." Finally, Hutcheson assured the audience, a research laboratory is not a factory. "We are not in the business of producing apparatus," he said. "We are in the business of developing ideas." The lab required no railroad, because "ideas constitute our output" and "our production goes out . . . in the form of reports."[43] Once again Westinghouse reified an absolute distinction between the esteemed mental work of researchers and the labor that took place in its factories.

The vast majority of the residents in attendance were convinced. Each was invited to explain whether they supported or opposed the ordinance. Forty-six spoke in favor and five against. Among those in favor, comments included the following: "we know anything Westinghouse would do they will do right"; "Westinghouse is a firm whose word is as good as its bond"; the lab will have a "stabilizing effect"; and it is "an opportunity we can't afford to pass by." Of those opposed, two residents were concerned that the precedent could open the borough to multifamily homes, "a mental institution," or "a private school . . . say for mental deficient children." Another opponent, A. J. Penshenka, a homeowner adjoining the site, spoke twice about his fear that the borough would be "attacked with the atomic bomb" because of the lab. Hutcheson tried to assure him that the work of the labs took decades to develop and therefore would not be a target, but Penshenka was unconvinced. The most serious complaint came from the Pehna family, who lived next to the site. The Pehnas, represented by their attorney, put forward a formal protest, claiming that "whatever name you call it, it is still industrialization" and would "lower the quality, characteristics and uses of the properties within the Borough."[44] This complaint took nearly a year to resolve, with Hutcheson noting at one point that "we will try to find some way to settle it out of court" and enlisting Gwilym Price Jr., a local judge and the son of the Westinghouse president, to intervene.[45]

The Pehnas' lawsuit was not the last hurdle the lab would face. Westinghouse first became aware of the Defense Production Administration's (DPA) delay in granting a certificate of necessity in the summer of 1952. Such a certificate was necessary in order for the lab to be eligible for accelerated amortization. Hutcheson believed this delay stemmed from the DPA's position that such certificates were granted only to manufacturing-related facilities. He found this absurd, noting the example of a recent GE electronics laboratory in Syracuse, New York, that was granted a certificate. In a statement that he did not share with the residents of Churchill, he argued that the new lab "is as much a part of the . . . manufacturing facility as any laboratory of any kind associated with any other industrial concern."[46] Westinghouse's friends in the Navy and Air Force quickly intervened, and the lab's certificate of necessity was once again presented to the DPA for approval.[47]

At this point, although the DPA was convinced that the lab did critical defense work, it was now concerned that it was located in a critical defense area. In correspondence with the Pittsburgh Area Industrial Dispersion Committee (PAIDC), Hutcheson explained Westinghouse's rationale for selecting the Churchill site. He noted that the company had surveyed six properties and found none suitable except the one chosen. In fact, the one selected was the furthest from downtown Pittsburgh. The reasons for its selection were that "it is actually somewhat closer to the present homes of the laboratory employees" than the present lab and that it had access to utilities. Finally, Hutcheson stressed that since the Forest Hills lab was actually closer to major industrial plants, "the proposed move does not . . . increase the potential of this area as an enemy target."[48] While the PAIDC was convinced and approved the Churchill site, the DPA was not. As the DPA failed to produce a certificate, Hutcheson privately communicated to Monteith that he thought the best course of action was to continue with the Churchill site regardless of the DPA's decision. Among his reasons were a lack of alternative sites that provided utilities and would not result in the loss of "a substantial fraction of our service personnel, and too many of our technical personnel"; the unlikelihood that the company would be able to recoup its $200,000 investment; and its "moral obligation" to Churchill, which had passed Ordinance No. 120 based on Westinghouse's guarantee that it would build its lab on the site.[49]

Monteith and other executives must have agreed, because construction soon began on the site without a certificate of necessity. In September 1954, Hutcheson made a final attempt to convince the DPA to grant a certificate. In a nine-page memo, he explained in detail the rationale behind the site location. He began by arguing, somewhat exaggeratedly, that Westinghouse was building the lab "due entirely to the demand for such facilities in development of information and equipment for the Department of Defense." As a result, there could be no dispute that the research lab was a "critical" facility. He told the DPA that the primary criterion for choosing a site was its proximity to the homes of laboratory personnel. For scientists, he argued, this was important because they often are "individuals who have strong interests of a cultural nature," and therefore they "insist their homes be located so that it will be possible for them to find an outlet for these interests." If Westinghouse located its lab in a remote location, "our scientists would have sought work elsewhere." Nonscientific personnel, on the other hand, "are people of such caliber" that they can find work elsewhere. As usual, Hutcheson mentioned the lab's need for utilities and to consolidate research operations that were scattered across Pittsburgh.[50] Four months after receiving Hutcheson's memo, the DPA issued a certificate for 25 percent of the research lab's value, the portion it deemed related to defense work.[51]

Like many private facilities subsidized by the federal government after World War II, Westinghouse first selected a site that met the company's needs and then advocated for its suitability for defense dispersal. In other words, federal dispersal policy did not induce industrial decentralization; rather, it encouraged and subsidized industries' already established preference for suburban locations. In locating new facilities, private firms and the federal government had to weigh a variety of exigencies, including the ability to attract skilled workers, all of which were considered vital to national defense.

Designing the Westinghouse Research Laboratories

Hutcheson had a clear plan for the design of the Westinghouse Research Labs: it was "a direct copy" of the number 2 building of the Bell Laboratories in Murray Hill, New Jersey.[52] Besides alterations to the ductwork and roof, Hutcheson rejected any major change to Bell's "fundamental plans."[53] The desire to copy Bell Labs is not surprising. According to Mozingo, the 1941 Bell Labs, with its suburban setting and flexible laboratory space, "redefined corporate standards for research and development facilities" and "invented the fundamentals of a corporate campus."[54]

William J. Rankin identifies two features of the Bell Labs that he argues became defining characteristics of postwar research laboratories: "moveable industrial partitions" and "a spacious forested site."[55] In fact, Westinghouse first incorporated moveable partitions in its 1916 laboratory, and C. E. Kenneth Mees had singled it out at that time (see chapter 3). At the new Westinghouse Research Labs, each researcher's laboratory could be customized by moving steel partitions in six-foot increments and was supplied with a full array of gases, vacuums, and various electrical voltages and phases.[56] In the architects' design, they emphasized that the modular concept "provides for the flexibility and adaptability of space arrangement that is required by present research methods." Besides workshops, labs, and office space, the new laboratories also included a cafeteria, lecture hall, and library. The exterior of the building was red brick, selected to "recall the warmth of Colonial Williamsburg." Otherwise there was little ornamentation "in keeping with the entire functional aspect of a great research organization" (see Figure 8).[57] An added advantage of copying Bell's design, Hutcheson pointed out to Westinghouse headquarters, was that it greatly reduced architectural fees.

As for "a spacious forested site," Westinghouse had little choice in the matter. Churchill Borough Ordinance No. 120 allowed it to build on only 15 percent of its land, and Churchill residents were vigilant about the lab's appearance. At the first zoning hearing, residents quizzed Monteith about landscaping. He assured them that Westinghouse would leave most of the

Figure 8. Westinghouse Research Laboratories in Churchill in the 1950s. Westinghouse Electric Corporation Records, Detre Library & Archives, Senator John Heinz History Center.

property "very much as nature has set it down" and the area immediately surrounding the building would be "landscaped . . . the same way as you would around your home."[58]

Westinghouse recruited a laboratory employee, materials engineer Frank Cassel, to design the landscaping. Cassel had frequently published articles in the lab's newsletter on landscape design (including an attack on lawn ornaments and an appreciation of Thomas Church) and had designed the Forest Hills lab's gardens in the "French style."[59] He approached the design of the new site with the same zeal and expertise with which he instructed fellow employees on shade gardening.[60] In the *Research Newsletter,* he introduced his design, emphasizing that he attempted to use plantings to enhance the surrounding community's views. "The landscape about the Center," he wrote, "will not only be a pleasant setting but will be of interest to the personnel and visitors."[61] After the lab's completion, the research director regularly invited Churchill residents and local garden clubs to tour the grounds.[62]

For their own part, residents and the borough council provided frequent feedback on the appearance of the lab. In 1958 the borough council sent an official letter to the lab's staff thanking them for their "efforts in developing and maintaining an attractive site and being an outstanding credit to the Borough."[63] When the company built a fence in 1966, council borough president W. E. Richards wrote to research director William Shoupp to warn him that "irate citizens" bearing a petition attended the last council meeting.[64] The petitioners co-opted the rhetoric that Westinghouse had used to gain the community's approval. Their spokesperson observed that the "unneighborly fence" was "hardly consistent with maintaining the lands 'natural beauty' nor does this contribute to the 'university type appearance' that the laboratories were purported to engender." Moreover, the speaker worried, is Westinghouse "getting first call" in borough government and will this eventually invite an "industrial character"?[65] The residents were right to worry that Westinghouse was receiving special treatment. Richards invited Shoupp to the University Club to discuss the matter and the fence remained.

On June 12, 1953, Westinghouse broke ground on what Hutcheson called "the most modern Research Center in the entire electrical industry." The press release for the groundbreaking emphasized the key components of the lab: its suburban setting, modular design, and location near Renaissance Pittsburgh. The site, described by Hutcheson as "wooded and rolling," would become "a place of beauty as well as efficiency." The generous suburban site would "also provide the necessary space and flexibility" for expansion. John Elder, the president of the Churchill council, welcomed a new neighbor that would bring "beauty and desirability" and "international prestige." Finally, Hutcheson noted that Westinghouse chose Pittsburgh because the region was "acting as well as talking when it comes to progressive community development." It was "a growing area where people not only talk about problems but do something about them."[66]

"The Free World's Industrial Research Capital"

Westinghouse celebrated the opening of its new Research Laboratories with a meticulously orchestrated spectacle that reinforced the exceptional character of the lab and its employees. A month before the lab's unveiling, Hutcheson informed interim director Clarence Zener, a metallurgist, that the dedication was "vitally important" and "must take precedence over everything else." He reminded Zener that the event would "help create the proper image of Westinghouse."[67] In the lead-up to the dedication, the two main planners released almost daily memos to the labs' employees, many of them addressed from "Fates at Bay" and likening the festivities to D-Day.[68] Westinghouse developed a six-day blitz of events, each of which was "aimed at various publics—the general public, the scientific world, important customers, educators, the financial community, civic leaders, and the community in which the laboratories are located."[69] Targeting audiences from the local to the national scale, the dedication impressed upon these multiple "publics" the lab's importance for employees, nearby residents, the Pittsburgh region, and investors as well as for scientific advance, national defense, and human progress.

The first two days were devoted to the national media. Westinghouse chartered planes from Chicago, New York, and Washington to collect reporters and housed them at a hotel in Oakland. A memo instructed employees to be on their best behavior. They were warned to keep the lab clean enough to be eligible for the "Good Housekeeping Seal of Approval," to drink coffee near the dispenser so the "floors won't be stained," to "keep desks . . . and *window sills* clear of clutter," and to remove homemade signs.[70] This was intended to present the lab as mess free while masking many of the problems researchers had discovered when they arrived, hence the homemade signs.[71] The two-day tour was a success. Media coverage, which appeared in all major U.S. publications, was mostly of the sort that claimed that Westinghouse research would "unlock the secrets of the universe."[72] Westinghouse also ran full-page ads touting the Research Labs as the "climax" of "the greatest decade in research and engineering progress in the history of Westinghouse."[73] The company also produced a fifteen-minute television special, "Westinghouse in the World of Research," and two shorter clips. According to Westinghouse, coverage reached 50 million readers and 110 million television viewers.[74]

With media days over, a memo told lab employees to "preserve your strength," because there were still four more days to go. Next up was family night, when employees' families were invited to visit the lab. Again researchers were reminded to keep the lab clean and also asked to leave their blinds at half or full length to "give a neater appearance."[75] Family night was followed by science teachers' day, during which lab employees traded places with local teachers for the day in order to reach the "school public." To ensure an adequate supply of researchers, U.S. Steel, Gulf, and Alcoa also contributed employees to the effort.[76]

Lab employees were required to attend the official dedication on September 20—but were not invited to the VIP reception. Tellingly, for a building that had few women's bathrooms to begin with, most were converted to men's bathrooms for the day. The many guests of honor included "numerous company presidents, Chairmen of Boards, research directors, college deans, editors, vice presidents, chief scientists, 'etc, etc, etc.'"[77] The keynote speakers were MIT president James Killian and Westinghouse president Gwilym Price. Price occupied much of the festivities with a lengthy and characteristically ridiculous speech that was later printed in pamphlet form. He began by noting that the lab was an "epochal step for Westinghouse" and the electrical industry's "most modern research facility." "To Pittsburgh and to Pittsburghers," the lab was "one of three major research installations . . . dedicated in the past eleven months" and one of fifty laboratories within twenty miles of the Golden Triangle. This was, according to Price, who frequently sacrificed accuracy for boosterism, "a concentration of research facilities not paralleled in any other area of the free world." Price noted that six months earlier, he had declared Pittsburgh "the free world's atomic headquarters for atomic power." Today, "after serious deliberation," it was his duty to declare Pittsburgh "the free world's industrial research capital."[78]

Having crowned Pittsburgh the capital of atomic power and industrial research, Price went on to describe recent scientific "revolutions" in the United States. He claimed that these revolutions resulted from the federal government and industry's increasing investment in research. Price emphasized that these two investments were complementary and would continue "so long as Russians keep on acting like Russians" and companies have to "make a profit in order to stay in business."[79] A happy marriage of government and industry would overcome the Soviet Union and many other problems, but to ensure this was the case, Price encouraged the audience to contact their congressmen to "support federal funding for science."[80] Like many an executive, Price was fine with state spending, so long as it was spent at Westinghouse.

Caught up in the gravity of the moment, Price focused very little on the Research Labs itself. When he did, he described it as Westinghouse's gift to scientists and the world: a place where scientists would solve the world's problems, make things "smaller, simpler, cheaper, better," and improve the world's standard of living by at least 50 percent. But this would occur only if Westinghouse granted researchers freedom to pursue their work: "All industry can do is give its scientists the best possible technical facilities, surround them with a pleasant physical environment, honor their status, encourage them to talk about their work in print—and then wait."[81] Price once again recycled the decades-old point that research labs were an exceptional workplace for exceptional and free technoscientific workers.

Price concluded by noting that the lab offered "material growth" to Westinghouse, but it was impossible to "prophecy" at this moment of "revolutionary" change what direction this growth would take. Despite this uncertainty, he was sure that if Westinghouse remained loyal to the principle of freedom enshrined in science, free enterprise, and the United States, then the company would lead the world in scientific innovation. He closed:

> We do know, however, what research *could* mean to us. In pushing back the frontiers of science through organized research, in allowing human ingenuity free play, we could be led to a solution of national and world problems that now beset us. We may learn the basis of human conduct and so end some of our waste of human talent and erosion of the human soul. We may come to understand the nature of matter and the processes of living organisms. We may reach the highest levels of creative thought and ability. We build a new America, and perhaps help to build a new world, richer in spiritual and cultural values as well as in material things.[82]

As researchers returned to their benches and raised their blinds on the manicured grounds, they could be certain that they were special and their work was of enormous import for Westinghouse, the United States, and the world. For Churchill residents and local politicians, they knew that their neighbor was not a manufacturing plant but a modern research facility that would increase the prestige of their community. For Pittsburghers, the lab symbolized the continued renewal of the region, led by benevolent corporate leaders and their firms. For the scientific community, political and military leaders, and the press, Price laid out a vision of how the research of industrial firms was vital to security, prosperity, and scientific advance.

More than a decade earlier, Vannevar Bush had similarly outlined the central place that scientific research would have in the maintenance of postwar prosperity and security. He outlined a vision of how a partnership between the state, universities, the military, and industry would overcome the "endless frontier" of scientific innovation. He described how American prosperity and security resulted from three national characteristics: "the free play of initiative of a vigorous people under democracy, the heritage of great natural wealth, and the advance of science and its application." As it had in the past, "government should foster the opening of new frontiers." If government failed to do so and if scientific advances were not "continuous and substantial," then "the national health would deteriorate," employment opportunities would wane, the standard of living would decrease, and "tyranny" would threaten. Bush proposed that a partnership of state, science, and industry would provide scientists with the freedom *and* financial support to deliver the United States and the world into a new era of endless progress, security, and prosperity.[83]

By 1956, when Price spoke, much of Bush's vision had come to pass.[84] The federal government had created the National Science Foundation and the Atomic Energy Commission and was already funding them at levels well above what Bush called for in 1945. Similarly, with the approval of National Security Council (NSC) Report 68 in 1950, the federal government enshrined the principle that defense spending on research was vitally necessary to preserve national security and economic growth.[85]

The Westinghouse Research Laboratories was part of the company's effort to join and profit from this effort. The labs were one component of a national partnership of industry, scientists, and the state that if successful would deliver progress and prosperity worldwide. The pristine landscaping and modern architectural form of the suburban research lab represented not only the development of scientific solutions to the world's problems but also the place that the private sector would have in creating these solutions. These temples of research, devoted to the uncoerced collaboration of industry, the state, and science, would both answer the threat of communism and provide a capitalist solution.

Research and the Suburbs

Price was right about at least one thing: the Research Labs continued to grow over the coming decades (see Map 4). On the day of the labs' dedication, Westinghouse had already submitted plans for an addition, one-half the size of the existing facility, to house the Materials Engineering Department that was scattered across Pittsburgh.[86] This addition was identical in design to the existing lab, and the Churchill council swiftly approved it.

In 1959 Westinghouse made plans for a major expansion of the labs, now renamed the Westinghouse Research and Development Center. Once again it described the lab as an ideal partnership with the exclusive Churchill community. According to Westinghouse, by supporting the lab, Churchill

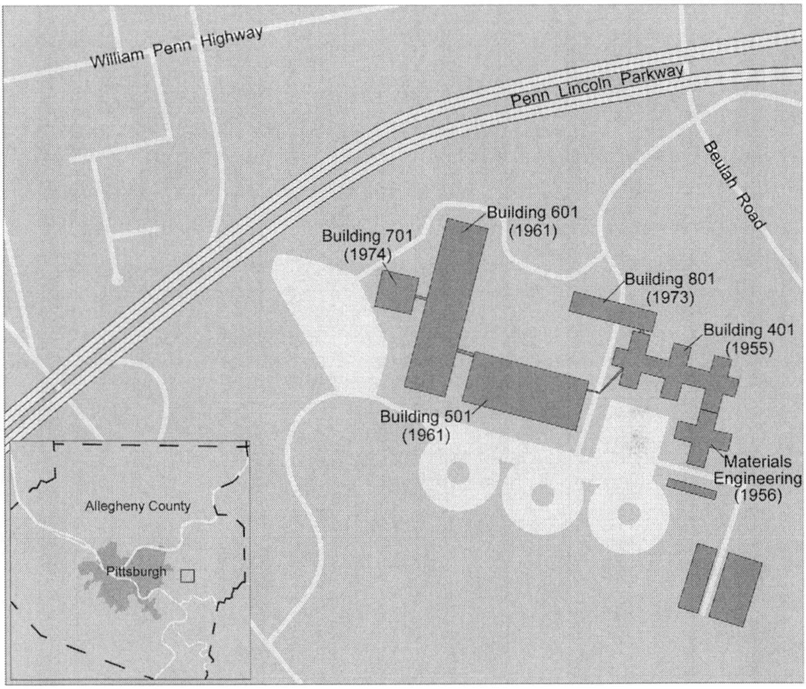

Map 4. Growth of the Westinghouse Research and Development Center from 1956 to 1974.

would contribute to scientific advance, national security, and its tax base and desirability. Westinghouse assured Churchill residents that the "new buildings and associated land areas are designed to fit into the character" of "an area of beautiful homes and natural surroundings."[87] The announcement detailed the features of the modern Skidmore, Owings, and Merrill design, which was a radical departure from the 1956 lab. The design included two long white buildings that formed a "university-type quadrangle" with a courtyard at the center. The proposed research center "not only provides the proper environment for our scientists, but insures an attractive view of the center for the surrounding community." This was sure to be "harmonious and pleasing" to the borough's residents; and the expansion would not involve manufacturing, nor would it produce any "noise, smoke, or odor."[88]

The expansion would also draw more prized professionals to the borough; currently "10 percent of the families in Churchill Borough are Westinghouse people" and "their role in the civic and cultural activities of the borough is well-known." Not only were the lab's employees a credit to the community, but the lab also hosted community events as well as educational activities for local children, and many Churchill gardeners had visited its "beautiful landscape." These opportunities would only expand with the new facility. If residents were still unconvinced, the announcement closed with the coup de grâce: to stand in the way of the new research center was to block the road to economic growth, scientific progress, and "national security." The "new knowledge, new concepts, and new products" created at the center would be vital to the United States' "industrial progress" and "economic and military power." The announcement made explicit the collapsing scales of Cold War militarism and the interlocking relationship between American economic, military, and scientific supremacy. By welcoming the research center, Churchill residents could contribute to economic growth, scientific progress, and national security. The announcement ended with an appeal to residents to "join with us in making our community one of the world's outstanding centers of research and development."[89]

As the research center's design worked its way through the borough's approval process, Westinghouse continued to hit its three main themes: the design of the research center fit into the community; the research center contributed to Churchill; and by supporting the lab, Churchill residents supported the United States scientifically, economically, and militarily.[90] S. W. Herald, vice president of research at Westinghouse, reiterated these points when he spoke to a public hearing on August 18, 1959, about further rezoning of the site. He started off by noting that, "to some degree," if the borough agreed to the proposed expansion, then it was "contributing to this country's research and development progress." Such progress was vital because without it, "our nation's position, both as an economic and military power, is jeopardized." The research center itself would be "a pleasant place to work" and "a place of beauty for our community." He added the usual list of benefits that Westinghouse provided Churchill. It currently paid 13 percent of local school taxes and 25 percent of borough taxes, was a "good neighbor" and laid out the "welcome mat" to local organizations, and hosted science education programs. The biggest benefit the research labs provided was an influx of "Westinghouse people" into Churchill.[91] The zoning amendment passed with five members of the council voting yes and one voting no.

In 1969 Westinghouse made plans for yet another expansion of the research center, this time to house administrative offices. The space that this new building would free was desperately needed as the lab was increasingly oriented toward "division needs," "new product activity," and "cost-price improvement goals." This required more laboratory space in which to test new production processes and products. Likewise, the equipment needed for research was growing, including increasing space devoted to computers. Finally, Westinghouse required larger facilities in order to enter promising new fields of federally financed research, many of them opened up by the urban crisis, including "pollution control, personal services, leisure time activities . . . construction technology, medical and prosthetic devices, power electronics, urban renewal, surveillance systems, and education."[92] Mirroring the growing allocation of federal research funds during the late 1960s, the research center was increasingly organized around "systems research," with a growing focus on "research relevant to social problems."[93]

An added advantage of the proposed addition to the research center was that it dealt with pressing "aesthetic considerations" and improved "the corporate research image." One of Westinghouse's main objectives in 1969 was to block the view of the 1956 Research Labs (renamed Building 401) and thereby "greatly improve the outsider's impression of the R&D Center." Building 401, a symbol of modernity thirteen years earlier, now needed to "be brought into conformity with contemporary Corporate Design policy." Westinghouse had painted Building 401's "warm colonial Williamsburg" brick white in 1968 to make it blend into the 1961 addition, but it nonetheless "does not 'fit' the modern design of the complex." To be blunt, as one Churchill councilor complained, Building 401 looked like a "textile mill out of Lawrence, Massachusetts," and should never have been built.[94] The new addition resolved this problem by blocking the view of Building 401. Improvements to the appearance of the complex were also necessary from a "community relations standpoint" because the research center's location in "Churchill Borough, an exclusive residential area, demands special attention to the architectural beauty of the site."[95]

Throughout the lab's development, Westinghouse derived local benefits from emphasizing the research that took place there. Churchill residents were highly resistant to any indication that it was a manufacturing facility. As a result, at nearly every meeting where Westinghouse presented plans for the site, it emphasized that the laboratory produced ideas, not products. This illusion was necessary to maintain the good graces of the community and compliance with zoning law that explicitly stated that work at the site was limited to the search for "new scientific facts and principles." Borough residents did occasionally contest whether the work taking place at the center was research but usually deferred to Westinghouse, because, as one councilor noted, "once we get into the realm of talking about nuclear energy and nuclear physics, etc., and what goes on at the research lab, we have lost most of us on council."[96] At the same hearing, the council questioned whether a facility to test components for nuclear power plants was research but ultimately accepted an affidavit from Westinghouse stating that it was. At an "exploratory meeting" between Westinghouse and borough representatives in 1964, concerning the rezoning of the property, councilors also expressed skepticism about whether all the work at the research center was research. The resolution of the meeting was Westinghouse executives' promise that they "would not embarrass the borough by manufacturing on the site."[97]

In fact, Westinghouse routinely violated Churchill's zoning ordinance. It was impossible to limit research to the production of ideas, and the lab frequently and openly engaged in sales, the production of prototypes, and activities related to manufacturing. Such activities only increased in the 1960s and 1970s when the company moved away from basic research.[98] Nonetheless, Churchill officials and residents, who saw the lab as part of the exclusive community, ignored these activities in order to maintain the illusion that it was a place where ideas were produced, not products. Churchill residents and politicians and Westinghouse officials imagined the lab as a site of purely mental labor that befitted an exclusive community.

Compared to what occurred in Boston or Los Angeles, the growth of research and development in Pittsburgh's suburbs was relatively small during the Cold War. With the exception of Westinghouse's development of nuclear technology, very few local firms entered the most lucrative fields of defense spending, such as aerospace and electronics. However, even in a region greatly removed from the Gunbelt, the desire to attract government defense and research contracts to the region was irresistible.[99] Firms, from Westinghouse to Alcoa to U.S. Steel, developed laboratories with the hope that they could cash in on the ever-growing spending of the warfare state. Even if they failed, generous tax policies ensured the profitability of their new laboratories. One key component of the Monroeville Doctrine—local firms' belief that research and engineering facilities must suburbanize—was the hope that it would allow them to secure Washington's largess.

But this was only one aspect of the Monroeville Doctrine. Even if these facilities failed to garner government contracts, firms hoped that they would attract scientific and engineering talent who would develop new products and manufacturing processes that would secure future profits. Just as they did prior to World War II, during the Cold War, industrial firms considered building research laboratories as a means to monopolize new technologies and to in turn open and monopolize markets. More often than not, as Scott G. Knowles and Stuart W. Leslie argue, industrial firms' research and development efforts ended up being a financial burden.[100] These facilities succeeded in projecting a high-tech image and attracting qualified scientists and engineers but were a drain on corporate coffers. As industrial decline accelerated in the 1980s and 1990s, many Pittsburgh-based firms began to shutter their laboratories. Today the largest of these facilities are abandoned, relics of the postindustrial age they helped usher in and that ultimately resulted in their destruction.

Throughout history, industry's effort to make and remake the division between mental and physical labor has dominated the Pittsburgh region. The development of industrial research laboratories and their moves to the suburbs played (and still plays) a significant part in this effort. Beginning in the early twentieth century, firms designed these spaces in the hopes that they would attract skilled scientists and engineers who would not only further industry's economic interests but also create a class alliance with such workers. Such spaces had several key results. First, they (re)produced the status and prestige of mental labor in distinction to physical labor. Second, they created a class relationship between scientific and manual workers. As a result, regardless of their role in the production process, scientific workers began to identify with management. The creation of such spaces helped forge a class alliance between scientific workers and industry through which scientists and engineers lent their skills and considerable legitimacy to industry, and industry in turn granted them a unique and privileged position within and outside the firm. Managers not only granted scientists and engineers a special place within the firm; they also welcomed them as neighbors. The privileged role of scientists and engineers was forged in their laboratories and also in the suburbs that they returned to at the end of their workday.

PART III

Cold War Community

5

Finding a Home in the Nuclear Suburbs

In the winter of 1949, construction workers began to quietly transform a small airport in Pittsburgh's suburbs into an atomic laboratory. The Atomic Energy Commission (AEC) and the Naval Nuclear Reactors Division of the Bureau of Ships jointly funded the Bettis Atomic Power Laboratory, and the Westinghouse Electric Corporation operated it under contract. Bordered to the north by the gritty mill towns characteristic of industrial Pittsburgh and to the south by miles of tract homes, strip malls, and boxy manufacturing plants characteristic of postwar suburbs everywhere, the Bettis Laboratory remains an enduring landmark to the ubiquity of the military-industrial complex in the United States.

Little besides barbed wire fencing and an imposing guard shack hint at the work that takes place inside Bettis (see Figure 9). It bears no resemblance to the carefully designed Westinghouse Research and Development Center or other more notable Cold War–era labs. Cars whiz by on busy Pittsburgh McKeesport Boulevard, their occupants scarcely noticing the sprawling laboratory. For those who worked at the Bettis Laboratory, their feelings are different; they know what has taken place and still takes place in this austere jumble of warehouses. They know that at Bettis, Westinghouse designed and developed the world's first "fully engineered" nuclear reactor for naval propulsion.[1] They know that the Mark I pressurized water reactor (PWR) was the basis for the world's first nuclear-powered ship, the submarine U.S.S. *Nautilus,* and served as a model for the majority of the world's nuclear-powered ships and power plants, including the Shippingport Atomic Power Station. The laboratory's employees know—because they continue the work today—that Bettis is responsible for maintaining and improving the U.S. nuclear fleet. Their labor, whether they write manuals, train naval officers, or work to eliminate and anticipate any of thousands of technical problems, contributes to the maintenance of reactors for submarines and aircraft carriers that span the globe. If they stop to consider it, which they usually do not, they know that they maintain submarines that continue to roam the seas with nuclear "deterrents" at the ready and aircraft carriers that have rained death and destruction on the world for more than sixty years, from Vietnam to Afghanistan.

The Bettis Atomic Power Laboratory presents an opportunity to examine what it means to live with the military-industrial complex. Far from the enormous military bases of the southern United States, the defense contractors densely concentrated around Boston and Washington, and the far more storied labs of Los Alamos, Oak Ridge, and Lawrence-Livermore, Bettis did (and does) the humdrum work of maintaining one component, nuclear-powered naval vessels, of the United States' arsenal. It represents the ubiquity of militarization in the United States—the possibility that any suburb might

Figure 9. Bettis Atomic Power Laboratory in the 1950s. George Westinghouse Museum Collection, Detre Library & Archives, Senator John Heinz History Center.

hold a military laboratory. Because the lab and the technologies it produces have nonmilitary applications and seem less warlike than many weapons—nuclear reactors rather than warheads—Bettis allows us to probe the normalization of the violence that results from and contributes to war work. It presents opportunities to consider important questions: How have so many Americans come to accept the presence of military installations right outside their front doors? How have they come to embrace work that has effects that are seemingly impossible to fully understand but present obvious moral dilemmas? How have they learned to live with and even embrace the military-industrial complex?

Many have considered these questions using a range of approaches, but most have addressed the sites where military power is seemingly most immediately produced: bases, labs, factories, missile silos.[2] The third part of this book differs from these studies because it engages directly with an equally formidable site for the production of military power: the suburb. While the suburbs are not a causal entity, embedded and produced within particular Cold War suburbs were social relations of class, gender, and race that were essential to the military-industrial complex, technoscience, and the social reproduction of scientists and engineers.

During the Cold War, as Elaine Tyler May argues, Americans retreated to the suburbs as a refuge from their anxieties about communism and nuclear war.[3] At the same time, as Robert A. Beauregard notes, suburbs became emblematic of and helped produce U.S. global dominance.[4] State-sponsored suburbanization and military spending resolved the postwar crisis of over-accumulation.[5] The postwar suburb and the military-industrial complex developed alongside each other, both the product of unprecedented levels of federal subsidy and investment. Suburbs became the home of choice for the military-industrial complex, while the Departments of State and Housing and Urban Development and their corporate partners offered the suburban home as evidence that in the United States, capitalism provided freedom, security, and prosperity to all.[6] Such rhetoric reached its zenith during the late 1950s when the "Kitchen Debate" between Richard M. Nixon and Nikita Khrushchev took place in a model suburban home and a United States Information Agency (USIA) exhibit toured the world with a U.S. Steel manufactured suburban home. USIA presented the home, identical to those of numerous Pittsburgh suburbanites, as evidence that "People's Capitalism" existed in the United States, capitalism "of the People, by the People, and for the People."[7]

This was more than propaganda; as postwar suburbs swelled with the increasingly prosperous white working and middle class, a variety of commentators from Daniel Bell to Herbert Marcuse declared the end of class antagonism.[8] The extent of this postwar consensus was widely overstated. Somewhat contradictorily, residential suburbs, the products of unprecedented federal largess, became fertile territory for grassroots conservative movements that embraced anticommunism and U.S. militarism, along with white supremacy and opposition to the welfare state.[9] Despite this conservatism, far more suburbanites embraced the Great Society than the John Birch Society. Just as the suburbs became potent ground for conservatism, in northeastern cities such as Boston, New York, and Pittsburgh, they also became the home of liberalism, as suburbanites attempted to grapple with racial disparities and segregation that became increasingly evident in the 1960s.[10] Regardless of partisan political inflection, the suburb became a central site through which Americans produced nationalist identities and understood their relationship to the rest of the world.[11]

While the suburb emerged as a central ideological battlefield during the Cold War, scientists and engineers became key actors. Prominent scientists such as Robert Oppenheimer, Albert Einstein, and Edward Teller became internationally recognizable cultural icons and prominent participants in national and international political debate. In 1960, at the height of the space race, *Time* magazine featured "U.S. Scientists" as its "Men of the Year." Equally celebrated and appearing much more frequently on the cover of *Time* were corporate executives who had helped organize the war effort during both world wars and sat with scientists on advisory panels at the Pentagon, NASA, and the AEC that shaped the postwar military-industrial-academic complex.[12] The tremendous expansion, first of the nuclear weapons program and later of missile and rocket technology, poured trillions of tax dollars into research efforts at universities, state-run laboratories, and industrial firms. This unparalleled federal investment and control, what some conservative critics condemned as "a socialist island," accompanied widespread rhetoric from political and business leaders, such as Gwilym Price, that described an amalgam of free enterprise, liberal democracy, and technological and scientific innovation that would defeat communism.[13] While state funding of scientific research bore much in common with the Soviet Union, it differed according to Teller because of "the traditional spirit of competition" in the United States.[14] According to the dominant public narrative during the early Cold

War, it was this "spirit," not trillions of dollars in federal funds, that would result in human progress and the triumph of the United States over the Soviet Union.

In the postwar decades, there was a convergence between the growing prominence of scientists and engineers; widespread but predominantly white suburbanization; the phenomenal growth of the military-industrial complex; and the U.S. exercise of greater military, economic, and political control around the world. The state's two great postwar projects, the residential suburb and the military-industrial complex, shared more than just a location. The warfare state was materially and ideologically embedded in suburban spaces. These suburban spaces enabled scientists and engineers to develop carefully compartmentalized, scientific worldviews that extended from their laboratories to their homes. In the suburbs, patriarchy provisioned scientists and engineers, white supremacy buffered them from the violence intrinsic to their work, and exclusive school systems and property markets reproduced their class positions. The class, race, and gender relations of the suburbs were essential but always invisible components of Cold War science and engineering.

Using the example of the Bettis Laboratory and the select suburbs that housed its employees, this and the following two chapters explore the convergence between the suburbs, technoscience, and war and how it was (re)produced in the everyday lives of scientists and engineers. By examining the space of the suburb and the defense lab and the social relations embedded within both, these chapters argue that nuclear engineers and scientists normalized a division between peace and violence in their everyday lives. In doing so, they helped obscure and normalize the violence that resulted from their work and that created the racially and socioeconomically exclusive communities where they lived. During the Cold War, defense contractors, the state, and scientists and engineers produced not only weapons but also a race, class, and gender formation whose power was rooted in segregated suburbs. Violence resulted from these engineers and scientists' work and from the production of suburban communities that helped reproduce their power and privilege.

This chapter begins by broadly discussing how to approach the entwined suburban geographies of class and technological rationality and then turns to the question of how nuclear scientists and engineers found homes in Pittsburgh's suburbs. Chapter 6 unpacks the invisibilities of nuclear engineering, the vital components of the profession, including gender and politics, that were never acknowledged in any engineering class or journal. Chapter 7 returns to the Bettis Laboratory in order to analyze how nuclear engineers and scientists experienced war as work. These three chapters intentionally begin with an examination of the residential suburb rather than the laboratory. By subverting scholarly convention that privileges places of work, production, and science over those of social reproduction, I show how the residential suburb was not simply the context in which nuclear science and engineering took place but helped constitute nuclear scientists and engineers' class, race, and gender positions and their privilege and authority. In doing so, I wish to both trouble the too easily drawn boundaries that scholars have traced around spaces of technoscientific work and contribute to the growing literature in geography that defines social reproduction as intrinsic to capitalism.[15]

The Suburban Geography of Cold War Technological Rationality

As I argued in the introduction to this book, scholars in science and technology studies (STS) have largely focused on the immediate sites where science and technology are produced and put to use. These studies portray the lives of scientists and engineers as constrained to the laboratory with occasional forays into corporate and state offices or the fields, mines, factories, and homes where new technologies and facts are extended. If I understood the world only through reading STS, I would be justified in thinking that engineers and scientists do not have families, homes, communities, passions (besides their work), politics, anger, loss, and so on. Oddly, a field that aims to collapse the barrier between scientists and engineers and the wider world portrays them as largely distinct from the things and processes that are so instrumental in shaping the lives and work of the rest of us. The purpose of part III of this book is to show how the privilege and power of scientists and engineers during the Cold War—their ability to appear autonomous—were rooted in the suburbs. It shares the STS goal of breaking down assumed divisions between science and society but does so from the perspective of the suburb, one of many key spaces where this division and the privilege and authority implicit in it are created and reproduced.

Scholars have not always been inattentive to the social worlds of engineers and scientists. The early Cold War, bracketed by James Burnham's *The Managerial Revolution* and Herbert Marcuse's *One-Dimensional Man,* witnessed a proliferation of studies that investigated the growing power of engineers and scientists, bureaucracy, and technological rationality.[16] These were often sweeping sociological examinations of an era defined by expertise, massive corporations, a greatly expanded state, technological and scientific change, and the promise of limitless growth and world annihilation. Whether you called them one-dimensional or organization men, there was a sense that scientists and engineers and the machines and ideas they produced were having a disproportionate effect on the postwar United States and the world. According to C. Wright Mills, William H. Whyte, Marcuse, and others, not only had technologies from nylon to television to the atomic bomb transformed everyday life, but Americans also began to value technical proficiency and well-ordered bureaucracy over all other social forms.

Marcuse opened his influential examination of the ideology of "technological society" with a discussion of the contradictions of the potential for both Cold War destruction and prosperity. How, he wondered, have we learned to live with the atomic bomb and embraced an era where "we submit to the peaceful production of the means of destruction"? How has a "society without opposition" conquered its "centrifugal tendencies" with "technology" rather than "terror," a "society which makes scientific and technical progress into an instrument of domination" and in which technology is synonymous with reason and "logic became the logic of domination"? Marcuse described a prevailing condition he called technological rationality, in which all thought was limited to the domain of the practical. In passing, Marcuse noted that managers, engineers, and scientists will have an important role to play in a society where "domination is transfigured into administration." "Within this vast hierarchy," he explained, "the tangible source of exploitation disappears behind the facade of objectivity." A "technological veil conceals the reproduction of inequality and enslavement" and "unfreedom . . . is perpetuated and intensified in the forms of many liberties and comforts."[17] Marcuse highlights the role of engineers and scientists in creating this unfreedom, but he then moves on, more interested in diagnosing this tendency than uncovering its underpinnings.

In 1977 David Noble picked up where Marcuse left off, arguing that technology and corporate capitalism emerged in concert, bound by "their common medium, modern engineering." Noble, who saw the development of technological rationality as rooted in the second industrial revolution, argued that around the turn of the century, "modern technology became a class-bound phenomenon."[18] But for Noble, the roots of this phenomenon did not extend far beyond the spaces of the corporate laboratory or the engineering school, nor did he give any attention to the geography of an emerging class formation of industrial scientists and engineers. As is typical of scholars who study science and technology, Noble made no mention of where engineers and scientists lived and recreated or of the sociospatial conditions that allowed for the reproduction of their labor. Building on Noble and Marcuse's work, part III of this book excavates the suburban origins of technological rationality and the scientists and engineers who helped create it.

As Whyte aptly put it, the suburbs "were the dormitory of the new generation of organization men."[19] The affluent residential suburbs that first developed in the late nineteenth century and expanded greatly after World War II helped structure a "habitus" for scientists and engineers and other white-collar professionals. Pierre Bourdieu defined habitus as the "mental structures through which [social agents] apprehend the world," "systems of dispositions," and "both the generative principle of objectively definable characteristics and the system of classifications . . . of these practices."[20] Habitus is a "structure structured" and a "structuring structure." According to Bourdieu, it mediates between collective beliefs and individual action as well as between objective structures and subjective constructions. It is the usually taken-for-granted relationship between the world and the knowledge that people develop about it.[21] It produces and reproduces classes and class fractions and is the system by which people often unwittingly learn (and learn to take for granted) their class positions and corresponding "systems of dispositions."

What is the relationship between postwar suburbs and habitus? First, suburbs are one of many key sites where class and other norms are learned and taught. Second, suburbs are not only sites of learning but also objects of knowledge. In other words, part of the learning that takes place in the suburbs is learning to be suburban. Suburbanites adopt particular forms of bodily and neighborly comportment—for example, not hanging your laundry on Sunday or having children play in backyards—that are reflective of both suburban and class norms. Third, Bourdieu argued that class formation was a multiple process that involved the acquisition of different forms of capital in a variety of semiautonomous fields. In the context of Pittsburgh's nuclear suburbs, learning to be suburban often involved learning (and relearning) to be white, a citizen, middle class, a mother, or an engineer. Learning to be suburban is always a process of producing space and subjects that necessarily works through multiplicity and change.

Following the example of Bourdieu and E. P. Thompson, the following chapters evaluate how engineers and scientists and suburbanites (re)produced themselves as a class, race, and gender formation during the Cold War. Like Thompson, it argues that class formation is an active, political process that is not determined exclusively by one's relation to the means of production.[22] People must make and remake their class formations, and this is always necessarily a process of producing space. Thus, while class formation is an unstable process, it is also geographical, meaning that people make their class positions through their participation in the differential production of space.[23] Finally, class formation is a process of making not only space but also subjectivities.

The following three chapters each respectively investigate a different system of disposition that nuclear scientists and engineers created and internalized in Pittsburgh's suburbs. The first is the taken-for-granted assumption that scientists and engineers should live alongside each other in racially segregated neighborhoods of fellow white-collar professionals. The second is that scientists and engineers by dint of their status as educated knowledge makers had a special role to play within and outside their communities. It was broadly assumed that these educated men should lead and that an army of unpaid women should support them. The third system of disposition is that while nuclear scientists and engineers produced weapons that reaped violence and injustice, they imagined their work as being for the benefit of humanity. In sum, these three chapters demonstrate that the technological rationality described by Marcuse and Noble was heavily rooted in gender, race, and class exclusion in the suburbs.

The remainder of this book is based on oral histories with thirty Westinghouse employees who worked for the company between 1945 and 1979. These oral histories ranged from one and a half to three hours and attempted to elicit both a general history of the interviewees' lives and specific details about their move to Pittsburgh, their community, and their feelings about the suburbs, engineering and science, and the Cold War. Of my thirty interviewees, twenty-eight worked as nuclear scientists or engineers (although many later had management roles) and one was employed as a clerical worker and another as a technical writer. All my interviewees were white, and with the exception of a woman who worked as a clerical worker, all were men.[24]

The interviews focused on two overlapping populations of nuclear scientists and engineers who worked at Westinghouse. The first group consists of fifteen engineers and scientists who worked for either Bettis or the Westinghouse Astronuclear Laboratory and mostly lived in the southern suburbs. The second group includes engineers and scientists who predominantly lived in the eastern suburbs and worked for either Westinghouse Research Laboratories or its Commercial Atomic Power Division. With a few exceptions, the evidence in part III is predominantly drawn from interviews with those who worked at Bettis or Astronuclear. However, I do augment this evidence with occasional examples from interviewees who lived in similar conditions in the eastern suburbs and worked in the commercial nuclear power industry.

"Working Man's Heaven"

In its early years, the majority of engineers and scientists at Bettis came from outside the Pittsburgh region. Most had attended elite universities in the Northeast and Midwest, and a significant number were Jewish and had moved from the New York metropolitan area. Despite the promotional efforts of local boosters reviewed in chapter 2, most Bettis employees admitted that they dreaded the prospect of moving to Pittsburgh. Like a "good engineer-scientist," Tim Smith made a matrix of the many job offers he received. In the matrix, "Pittsburgh ranked last in places I wanted to live. *Pitts*—burgh; it had an aura about it that didn't make us want to go there." However, his "hero" Al Henry, the father of space-time kinetics, was based at Bettis. "If you are a disciple of one of the great men of the field, you don't refuse," he told me, and he was drawn to Bettis by its status as one of the two "best places in the world" for the study of reactor physics.[25] Like Smith, most of the engineers and scientists I interviewed were drawn to Pittsburgh by Bettis's reputation as a leading center of nuclear reactor research. As Dan Stein told me, in the 1950s, "if you were interested in reactor physics and developing reactor methods . . . the leading lights were gathered here in Pittsburgh."[26] "Nobody was a native Pittsburgher," and far from being attracted to Pittsburgh, they had to overcome their and their family's aversion to living in what they inevitably described as "that smoky city" or "a filthy old steel town."[27]

The majority of Bettis engineers and scientists settled in an arc of suburbs about four miles to the southwest of the laboratory. The most popular suburbs lined Route 51: Pleasant Hills, Whitehall, and Baldwin (see Map 5). Further to the south and west, Bethel Park, Jefferson Hills, Mount Lebanon, and South Park also attracted Bettis scientists and engineers, and in later years so did the more distant and wealthier suburb of Upper St. Clair. Others resided in Pittsburgh's eastern suburbs, such as Edgewood, Churchill, and Monroeville, which had long been home to Westinghouse engineers and management (see chapters 3 and 4). Before considering how and why Bettis engineers and scientists settled in these particular communities, it is useful to first consider where they did not choose to live.

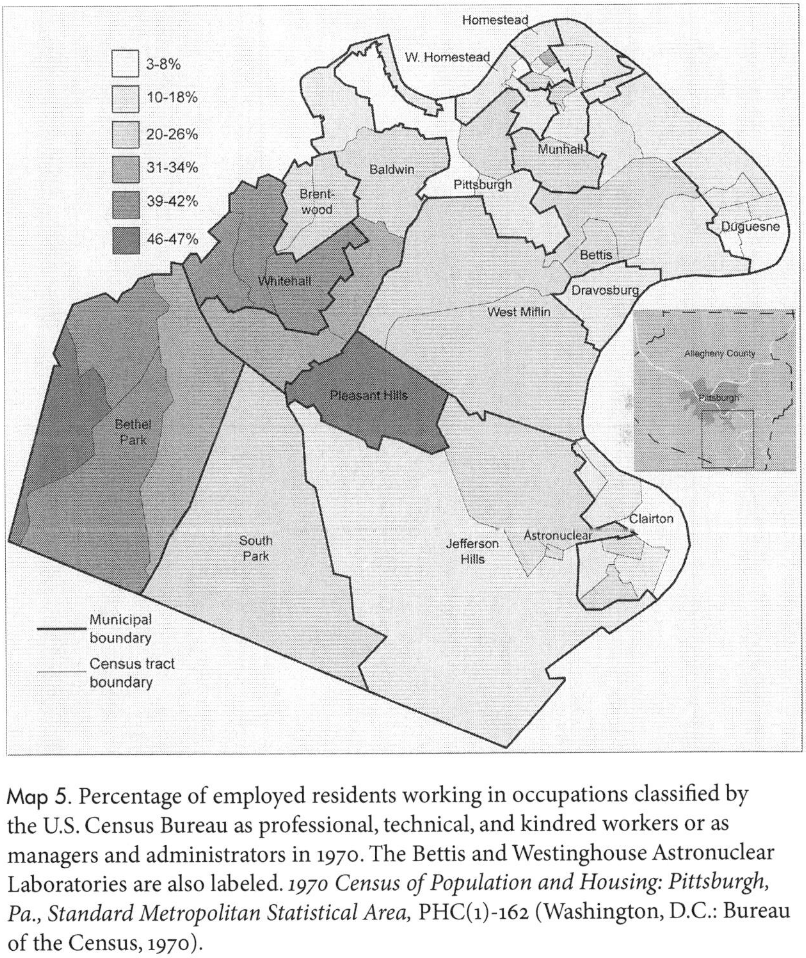

Map 5. Percentage of employed residents working in occupations classified by the U.S. Census Bureau as professional, technical, and kindred workers or as managers and administrators in 1970. The Bettis and Westinghouse Astronuclear Laboratories are also labeled. *1970 Census of Population and Housing: Pittsburgh, Pa., Standard Metropolitan Statistical Area,* PHC(1)-162 (Washington, D.C.: Bureau of the Census, 1970).

Unlike Churchill, West Mifflin was not a bucolic location for a research lab. An industrial and mostly working-class suburb, it was perched on a plateau above four large steel mills and the world's largest coke battery. In 1938 U.S. Steel opened the Irvin Works in the borough, a large rolling mill that processed steel from nearby mills. By 1951 thirteen thousand were employed in a "half-dozen monster plants" in West Mifflin. By this point, Bettis had grown from a workforce of thirty in January 1948 to more than two thousand. At that time, a *Pittsburgh Press* writer singled out West Mifflin as "an industrial 'fat lady' in a suburban dress." "The working men love her," he noted, describing the moves of thousands of steelworkers from "crowded industrial towns" to their "dream house in the country with green grass, picket fence, and all the trimmings" in this "working man's heaven."[28] Driven mostly by working-class suburbanization from nearby mill towns, West Mifflin's population increased from 8,694 in 1940 to 27,829 in 1960.[29] Bettis engineers and scientists did not love West Mifflin, and they commuted to work from the more affluent suburbs to its south.

Nor did many nuclear engineers and scientists settle in the mill towns that lined the Monongahela River in the valley below West Mifflin. As a result of suburbanization and decreasing and erratic employment at the mills, all these communities experienced significant population decline from 1950 to the present.[30] While the white working and middle class sought out new homes in the hilltop suburbs of Monongahela Valley, there was significant Black in-migration in search of industrial employment and affordable housing. At least some of this in-migration can be attributed to displacement from slum clearance projects in Pittsburgh. Just as Thomas Sugrue writes of Detroit, by the 1960s, a familiar dynamic of white suburbanization, Black in-migration, and industrial and urban disinvestment left the mill towns with declining employment and tax bases, limited access to credit for residents and local governments, and a host of social problems, foremost among them stark levels of racial segregation and social polarization.[31]

Very few of Bettis's engineers and scientists lived in Monongahela Valley, but the same could not be said for the hundreds of technicians, maintenance workers, security guards, and administrative staff at the lab. Bill Jones, who spent much of his career in management at Bettis, developed a paternal affection for his employees. Effusive in his praise, he told me that most secretaries and technicians came from Monongahela Valley.

> My secretaries came from McKeesport, we had a lot of technicians from McKeesport and most of them frankly were Polish and wonderful people. I mean hardworking, honest, and they never called in for a day off. . . . They were conscientious and competent. We had a very large number of technicians and secretaries that came out of the Mon Valley. . . . I would give them the highest marks really.[32]

He continued his praise of Polish technicians, calling them "excellent citizens" and singling them out as "reliable, dependable, hardworking, and the salt of the earth."

There is a notable difference between how Jones described technicians and his fellow engineers, whom he called "extremely hyperactive, intelligent, young people." While both earned his friendship and admiration, he characterized engineers as possessing intelligence and a willingness to consider their occupations more than mere work; in contrast, he characterized technicians and secretaries not by their abilities to think creatively but as workers who stood out for their conscientious adherence to workplace discipline. The assumed managerial relationship between the engineers and other employees at Bettis dated to the beginnings of engineering, a profession that developed "as much by the imperatives that propelled the economic system as by the logic and laws of science."[33] Firms such as Westinghouse favored engineers as managers, and even when engineers did not have formal management roles, they assumed an informal one with the feminized, working-class, and less-educated workforce that supported their work (see chapter 6).

Doris MacArthur, a longtime secretary at Bettis, described engineers as "an odd bunch of people." Echoing Noble's argument that economic factors were of primary importance to engineers, she characterized them as detail oriented and "tight." She elaborated that engineers "always wanted to know the price of things" and that whenever employees raised funds for a coworker in need, the engineers always failed to contribute. If the engineers characterized nonengineers as mere workers, MacArthur considered engineers as overeducated, stiff, and socially naive. According to MacArthur, the engineers always "want things to be two plus two equals four. It's like they're geared that way; there's an answer for everything and it has to be the right answer."[34] While there was certainly a great deal of mutual respect across different occupations at the labs, relations were tempered by an overriding assumption that engineers and scientists were different in their class, social norms, motivations, and relationship to management from secretaries, technicians, janitors, and security guards. This division extended not only to their salary grades and whom they sat with in the cafeteria but also to where they lived.

"The Nearest Half-Decent Community"

In 1956 Whyte highlighted "rootlessness" as one of the defining traits of "organization man." He observed that growing numbers of transient white-collar workers always seemed to settle in similar suburbs across the United States.[35] The tendency of "organization men" to cluster together was not simply the product of their cultural tastes; rather, companies such as Westinghouse facilitated the formation of suburban communities of white-collar workers. As I describe in greater detail in chapter 2, Westinghouse sought to counter the appeal of its competitors in sunny and more attractive locales. For example, a 1967 General Dynamics recruitment ad described how its San Diego research facilities offered "a climate of creativity" and "pleasant living throughout the year, excellent academic institutions for graduate work, and extensive cultural and recreational opportunities."[36] Conscious of prospective employees' negative impressions of the industrial Pittsburgh region and their ability to obtain work elsewhere, management at Bettis actively steered new engineers and scientists away from working-class West Mifflin and the mill towns and toward renting and purchasing homes in Pittsburgh's southern suburbs.

Westinghouse frequently attempted to appeal to potential employees by touting the location of its laboratories, "in suburban Pittsburgh close to modern housing, top-level schools and universities, shopping centers, golf courses, ski and lake resort areas."[37] A recruitment brochure from 1956, a period when the laboratory was greatly expanding its workforce, told prospective employees that nearby communities offered "suburban living . . . in a Metropolitan area" and that they would "find plenty of housing at reasonable cost in Pittsburgh's southern suburbs: Mount Lebanon, Brentwood, Whitehall, and Pleasant Hills are all just minutes away."[38] Noticeably absent in this brochure was any mention of West Mifflin or other predominantly working-class suburbs located immediately adjacent to the laboratory. An employee handbook for the Bettis Laboratory in the 1960s described how the lab provided real estate and rental services "to aid employees in establishing homes." The most notable service was "an up-to-date listing of real estate and apartments available in the area" supplied by fellow employees and local real estate offices. The employee handbook also encouraged employees "wishing to buy or sell anything—real estate or otherwise" to advertise for free in the classified section of the plant newsletter.[39] Newsletters at Westinghouse's Astronuclear Division and Research Laboratories also contained classifieds for available homes as well as carpools. These newsletters, relocation services, and carpools reinforced Westinghouse employees' tendency to cluster in particular neighborhoods.

Several, but by no means all, of the engineers and scientists I interviewed availed themselves of the relocation services provided by the laboratory. As one would expect, these services were especially useful to employees who were moving into the Pittsburgh region. These engineers and scientists did not "flee" Pittsburgh but moved directly to its suburbs. As Robert Self argues, white flight is not an entirely accurate description of postwar suburbanization. White suburbanites did not simply flee cities but sought out the "powerful economic and cultural incentives" of the suburbs.[40] This is particularly the case for the millions of suburbanites who moved from one metropolitan region to another during the postwar period.[41]

After he accepted a position at Bettis, Westinghouse flew Herman Schwartz and his wife to Pittsburgh to look for a home. Born and raised in Brooklyn and having spent several years as a postdoc at an Ivy League university, he remembered nearly crying as they approached the southern suburbs through the "disaster" of ramshackle Pittsburgh outskirts along Route 51. "It was a real downer," he remembered. A "very helpful" department at the lab aided them in their housing search by providing a "listing of places to go." When I asked him for more details about the department's assistance, he vaguely recalled, "I can remember going into the office. We sat down. They told us what was there and they said these were the communities." The department "directed" him to look in Pleasant Hills and Whitehall.[42]

Schwartz first rented and later purchased a home in Pleasant Hills because he believed that "Pleasant Hills was the closest, really the closest community." When I pointed out that it was not the closest community to Bettis, he agreed, telling me "nobody told me about Glassport or about McKeesport or Duquesne."[43] Westinghouse systematically shaped the housing decisions of its engineers and scientists. For those moving from out of town, the physical and social geography of the hilly Pittsburgh region, speckled with hundreds of municipalities and school districts, was notoriously confusing. Westinghouse provided helpful aids to ensure that employees chose communities suitable to their stature. Dan Stein, an engineer who first rented an apartment in the southern suburb of Castle Shannon and later purchased a home in Pleasant Hills, recalled that the laboratory "gave me maps and they must have given me a list of houses to rent and apartment complexes to visit."[44]

When I asked Schwartz more about his decision to rent in Pleasant Hills, he admitted that in hindsight his decision was based as much on class as it was proximity. He explained:

> It's interesting. . . . West Mifflin was not, was not really [*long pause*] I don't know why and of course McKeesport is right across the road, but McKeesport is the steel mills; you don't want to live in the steel center. You don't want to live in Glassport. It's right on the [*does not complete thought*], so that's not the place to live for a professional, I would say. So they didn't direct me there. Why they didn't direct me to West Mifflin, I really can't say. But the Pleasant Hills and Whitehall areas were where they directed me to. They may have suggested Upper St. Clair, Mount Lebanon or else out that way, but I probably, I can only recall that I probably said no, I wouldn't go ten miles. I want to be no more than a few miles away. So that's where we went to realtors and we visited some places to rent, in both Whitehall, Brentwood area, and in Pleasant Hills. And we very quickly found a nice little home . . . to rent. It was reasonable, it was a nice house, it had sufficient bedrooms, the community looked nice, and so we just quickly took it. And that's how we settled in Pleasant Hills.[45]

Not everyone looking for a house was as innocent of the class connotations of certain suburban neighborhoods. Many bluntly told me that Pleasant Hills and other middle-class suburbs were the appropriate communities for professionals.

Larry Johnson, Schwartz's neighbor, grew up in Pittsburgh and attended Carnegie Tech (now Carnegie Mellon University). Familiar with the region, he did not use Bettis's relocation services, but the result of his housing search was identical. When looking for a house to move to from his apartment near Carnegie, he thought, "If you're going to work at Bettis you probably want to live in Pleasant Hills." Within two weeks of looking, he ended up buying a house there. Bettis engineers were drawn to Pleasant Hills, he explained, because it was "the nearest half-decent community." There was a "trade-off" between "a longer commute" and living in a "somewhat better community." Johnson first purchased "a small ranch house" in Pleasant Hills that he admitted was "very much like a West Mifflin house." He did not look in West Mifflin because "people with engineering degrees buy houses a step above the average houses in West Mifflin." Like many of his coworkers, after several years Johnson upgraded to a larger house. Learning of a new neighborhood of custom-built homes from a fellow carpooler, he moved to a "parklike" street in Pleasant Hills, "suburbia defined," he called it, that was rapidly filling with the newly built homes of Bettis engineers and scientists.[46]

Like Johnson, Jake Hubert also grew up in Pittsburgh. The son of a steelworker, he was raised in one of the city's oldest public housing projects. After earning a master's degree in physics from the University of Pittsburgh, he purchased a home in Bethel Park, noting that it was affordable and required little down payment. After living there for a few years, he purchased a larger home in Pleasant Hills in order to have more room for his children and shorten his commute. When I asked why he did not move back to Pittsburgh where he had grown up, he explained: "Well the suburbs, the homes were nicer. I was the first person in my family to ever attend college. After we married, we rented an apartment in Brentwood-Whitehall area, the next suburb out is Bethel Park so it was a nice community and that was pretty much the logic."[47] The "logic" that Hubert describes is the seemingly inevitable relationship between where you live and your class position. As he obtained a professional position, he believed that this necessitated a move further into the suburbs.

After earning a PhD from MIT and serving as a nuclear engineer in the military, Tim Smith joined Bettis. For his first six months, he lived in an apartment complex in Baldwin Borough and then teamed up with his coworker Jake Hubert in the "house-hunting process," "spending our noon hours going out and looking for houses." They focused their search on Pleasant Hills, the "nearest bedroom residence to Bettis that had reasonably good schools." Smith ended up purchasing a home on the same street as Hubert. After several years, he "upgrade[d] . . . to a nicer home," purchasing the house of a fellow Bettis engineer before it even went on the market. Like Schwartz, Smith also claimed that Pleasant Hills was the "nearest" community to Bettis. I asked him why he did not consider moving to West Mifflin or Duquesne, both of which were considerably closer to the lab. He explained:

> Well, given the time that we spent and had gotten acquainted with people at Bettis, we understood where people lived. And West Mifflin and Duquesne were largely the lower priced home[s], uh, blue-collar neighborhoods, and as you went west from Bettis you kept moving upscale from Pleasant Hills to Bethel Park to Upper St. Clair/Mount Lebanon to Upper St. Clair. And so it was just kind of a middle choice of saying, well, Pleasant Hills, these are nice neighborhoods, nice homes, not as upscale as Mount Lebanon or Upper St. Clair and they're closer so it's like a fifteen-minute commute so that was—it just seemed like the right place to be.

Offering a careful mixture of proximity to the laboratory and comfortable but not ostentatious "nice" homes, Pleasant Hills seemed just right for engineers and scientists. It was, Smith told me, "the nature of engineers" to be drawn to security, frugality, and comfort, not gaudy communities.[48] Engineers and scientists routinely naturalized their decision to live alongside each other in communities that were explicitly not working class.

Whether because of prudence or lack of funds, most engineers and scientists first rented an apartment before buying a home. When they purchased a home—and all twenty-eight engineers and scientists I interviewed were homeowners—they often determined where to buy based on conversations with fellow employees at the labs. Many Bettis employees, such as Hubert and Smith, even teamed up to search for housing. As a result, certain subdivisions had a remarkable number of Bettis employees, with a short cul-de-sac often housing six or more nuclear engineers.

David Lebowitz, an engineer from New York, first rented an apartment in the southern suburbs. As he settled into the suburbs, he became part of "the Westinghouse community, Bettis community that populated Whitehall, Pleasant Hills, Baldwin." After having children, he decided to buy a house, a decision the native New Yorker described as "traumatic" and "a tremendous undertaking," "but when I looked around I saw other people were doing it and I ended up buying a house on a street with six other Bettis people." He discovered the house for sale during his carpool, and his search was limited only to this house. This street in Baldwin where he moved was "terrific" and like "a little micro-neighborhood" where "my kids could play . . . and we could walk up and down the street."[49]

Peter Copeland joined Bettis in 1954. First living with his wife and kids in an apartment, he told me, "I decided very quickly I got to get out of that place and get a house of my own." His housing search was dictated by his desire to have as short a commute as possible and the information he gleaned from fellow coworkers. "See, there were a lot of people doing the same thing at the same time," he said, and "Pleasant Hills was high on the list." Bettis employees filled much of their free time at work with discussions about home ownership, construction, and renovation. Many interviewees mentioned how these conversations often resulted in their decision to purchase homes on the same streets as their coworkers. Based on his conversations with coworkers, Copeland narrowed his search to Baldwin, Whitehall, and Pleasant Hills. He finally ended up building a house in Pleasant Hills on a street that was "25 percent technical and engineering residents and a mixture of . . . commercial people who worked in downtown Pittsburgh." Despite its close proximity to major steel mills in West Mifflin, Clairton, and McKeesport, he could not remember any steelworkers in the neighborhood. There were, however, "at least a half-dozen" Bettis engineers.[50]

Frank Sampson, a nuclear engineer, has held political office in Pleasant Hills for several decades, is a major booster of the borough, and has thought more thoroughly than most residents about why he loves the community. Like many engineers, he first moved to an apartment, but "I hate apartments so we stayed there for . . . six or seven months." He then purchased a small three-bedroom house in Baldwin that his rapidly expanding family soon outgrew. For their next home, they settled in Pleasant Hills, which he described as a "really convenient location and excellent community with an excellent school system and very fine municipal benefits." When I asked if he considered living in West Mifflin, he told me, "I didn't want to live in West Mifflin," describing it as "a much more industrialized area" that "doesn't have the same level of services or taxes." The only other places he considered living, he told me, were the more affluent suburbs to the south that were too expensive and a much longer commute.[51]

The large pool of "professional people" in Pleasant Hills allowed Sampson to assemble a carpool of engineers that "lasted longer than most marriages," but it also defined the overall character of the community. The borough council, he observed, was "a very well-educated group" composed mostly of college graduates, "people with master's degrees . . . lawyers, scientists, businesspeople." "Education doesn't necessarily equate with morals or good government," he said, "but you can sit down and have an intelligent conversation." He attributed the stability and good government of Pleasant Hills to both the caliber and homogeneity of its residents. Admitting that this was "a difficult subject to get into," he explained that, unlike other municipalities, Pleasant Hills is "pretty much a homogenous grouping of people with more or less the same interests and that leads to more cooperation." He noted that the lack of discord in the borough was evidenced by the rarity of contested elections, and he told me if I attended a council meeting, "you'll be kind of lonesome." There was, according to Sampson, a natural tendency toward homogeneity—for similar people to cluster in similar areas—and Pleasant Hills attracted a homogenous population of well-educated professionals who were better qualified to govern themselves. "We are tribal," he explained. "We have our little community. . . . The outside there is a natural built-in conflict." When I asked whether surrounding communities considered Pleasant Hills snobby, he again resorted to nature, telling me, "People think that way and that's just the way life is." "People are very competitive," he said, "and want to feel that they are better than somebody else."[52]

Two remarkably strong social forces defined Bettis engineers' and scientists' decisions to cluster together in particular suburbs. First, they felt very strongly that they should not live in the same neighborhoods as working-class people. This decision was attributable less to outright snobbery than to more muted and naturalized perceptions that highly educated professionals had different preferences in terms of culture, schools, municipal services, and housing. None of these factors was predominant, but all formed key components of the overall habitus created by engineers, scientists, and fellow professionals in Pittsburgh's southern suburbs. The second force is the assumed naturalness of their decision to live in particular communities. The employees I interviewed were usually taken aback by and struggled to answer my questions about their decades-old housing decisions. The questions disrupted their assumption that it was natural or "tribal" for engineers and scientists to cluster in certain neighborhoods. Like many of the decisions they made daily at the lab, their housing decisions were black boxed. They assumed that certain suburbs delivered the best results, but they did not question the inputs that created them or the segregation and inequality that resulted.

Defendable Suburbs

Nuclear engineers and scientists at Bettis settled predominantly in Pittsburgh's southern suburbs as the product of several factors, including their development of a shared understanding of what were the most suitable communities for professionals and Westinghouse's efforts to steer them toward certain neighborhoods. The communities that developed to the south of Bettis differed greatly from the industrial towns and working-class suburbs of Monongahela Valley.

The communities where Bettis engineers settled were far more racially homogenous than those of Monongahela Valley (see Map 6). In 1970 there was one Black resident among Pleasant Hill's total population of 10,490 and five Black residents among Whitehall's population of 16,551. While both Baldwin Borough and Bethel Park had slightly more sizeable Black populations, respectively numbering 171 of 26,729 and 213 of 34,791, these small populations

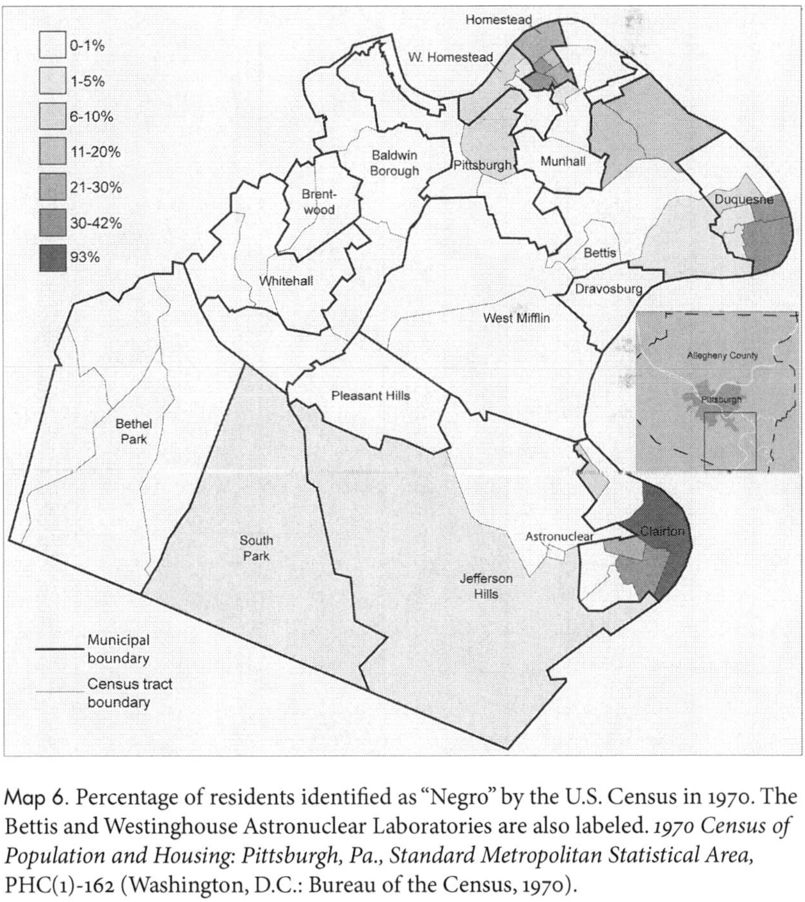

Map 6. Percentage of residents identified as "Negro" by the U.S. Census in 1970. The Bettis and Westinghouse Astronuclear Laboratories are also labeled. *1970 Census of Population and Housing: Pittsburgh, Pa., Standard Metropolitan Statistical Area,* PHC(1)-162 (Washington, D.C.: Bureau of the Census, 1970).

were the result of rural coal-patch and suburban Black communities that predated World War II.[53] Thus, while the population of Baldwin exploded from 1950 to 1970 by 149 percent and Bethel Park's by 207 percent, during the same time, the Black population of Baldwin grew by two residents and Bethel Park's Black population decreased by five.

The whiteness of Pittsburgh's southern suburbs was maintained by a spectrum of racism that most white residents were blissfully unaware of. The federal government, as it did throughout the United States, provided easier access to subsidized home loans for white residents than it did for Black residents. As a result of redlining, it was also difficult for homeowners in nonsegregated communities to sell their homes because of the lack of federally subsidized loans in these communities. Even affluent African Americans had greater difficulty accessing credit and selling existing property, which kept them from moving into newer suburban communities.[54] Likewise, realtors and rental agents throughout the Pittsburgh region actively steered African Americans away from white suburban communities.[55] Equally important was the lack of employment opportunities for African Americans in growing fields such as science and engineering, which were concentrated in the suburbs. In Pittsburgh and across the United States, a very small number of engineers and natural scientists were African American in the period between 1950 and 1970.[56]

Prior to 1948, a few of the southern suburbs, for example Mount Lebanon, had restrictive housing covenants. The wealthy neighborhood of Virginia Manor, which was developed by future governor James Duff, had a restrictive covenant that prevented African Americans and Jews from purchasing homes and limited lot sizes and housing styles.[57] Even after racial covenants were struck down by the Supreme Court in 1948, Virginia Manor residents continued to resist African Americans' efforts to move into the neighborhood. In 1971 Muhammad Ali attempted to purchase a mansion in the neighborhood and was met by active protest on the part of residents. He eventually purchased a home in New Jersey instead.[58]

However, middle-class whites rarely used overt racial restrictions and physical violence to maintain the racial homogeneity of Pittsburgh's white-collar southern suburbs. Rather, affluent, white-collar communities remained racially homogenous largely as a result of residents' ability to purchase a home on the fringes of the city and to move if the neighborhood became desegregated. As Sugrue describes in the case of Detroit, such suburbs were "defended communities whose invisible walls against 'invasions' were far more difficult to breach than the constantly shifting, insecure lines that divided the city."[59] Pittsburgh's southern suburbs remained white because of the advantages afforded to affluent, highly educated white people, including the ability to live in communities that whether because of distance, housing costs, steering by real estate agents, or lack of nearby employment were inaccessible to most African Americans.

As a result, the residents of the defendable southern suburbs faced a contradiction that was common for many middle-class white suburbanites across the United States. They deplored the violence that they attributed to southerners and the white working-class efforts to maintain segregation, but they resided in communities that were even more racially segregated. To work through this contradiction, several interviewees admitted that they were horrified by racial segregation but that the segregation of their community was based on choice and personal taste rather than violence. As David Freund describes, white suburbanites across the United States invoked "immutable and supposedly non-ideological market considerations" as a justification for segregation. In doing so, they "developed a new language about difference, about metropolitan economics, and about the politics of property that justified exclusion by means that seemed genuinely nonracist."[60] In the case of my interviewees, most explained that they settled in the communities that naturally seemed most suitable and that African Americans did not live there, largely because they did not choose to. Segregation was purely the product of choice and differing tastes. The white, affluent residents of Pittsburgh's segregated southern suburbs attributed racism to working-class and southern white communities' efforts to maintain segregation, not their own defendable communities.

During the 1970s, several Westinghouse engineers and their spouses became involved in the South Hills Association for Racial Equality (SHARE). Dan Stein, a Pleasant Hills resident who was peripherally involved in SHARE, told me that it was mostly "the gal next door," the wife of a fellow Bettis employee, who "shamed" him into participating. His involvement included attending a demonstration in Whitehall at the Prospect Park apartments, where management engaged in racially discriminatory rental policies. Yet, while he was clearly opposed to racial discrimination, Stein did not seem to care greatly about the protest. "I don't know that they were guilty," he said, but "we went over and we had signs and we walked around." It was mostly his neighbor's influence that caused him to attend, he added.[61] In 1970, around when Stein picketed the apartment complex in Whitehall, the U.S. Census counted one African American in Pleasant Hills. This was the striking contradiction at the heart of affluent middle-class suburbs. Well-meaning liberals could support the civil rights movement and picket an apartment complex but fail to address or even consider the structures that segregated their own communities.

Nuclear Suburbs

Not only were white-collar suburbs such as Pleasant Hills racially segregated; they were also less socioeconomically diverse than the mill towns of Monongahela Valley. Mill towns contained large working-class neighborhoods and districts that housed managers, storeowners, and professionals. As a result, mill towns were more occupationally diverse than both working-class and white-collar suburbs. Thus Dravosburg, Jefferson, and West Mifflin, all working-class suburbs, had higher percentages of blue-collar workers than Clairton and Duquesne. This was the product of increasing class bifurcation during the post–World War II period, as working-class and middle-class whites moved away from both Pittsburgh and the mill towns but moved to different suburbs.[62] As Table 3 and Map 5 show, the suburbs of choice for Bettis engineers—Bethel Park, Pleasant Hills, and Whitehall—had a high proportion of residents employed in managerial and professional occupations and who had attended four or more years of college and a low proportion employed in blue-collar occupations. Income levels were high and poverty rates low in these three suburbs. In 1970 more than 61 percent of Pleasant Hills families had income higher than $11,999 as opposed to 22.7 percent in Duquesne and 33.7 percent in West Mifflin.

Why did Bettis engineers often end up in the same neighborhoods? Their collective thought process and desire to live in a community with like-minded professionals played a role, but so too did the relationship between the uneven availability of property and the growth of Westinghouse facilities in the southern suburbs. The employment of nuclear engineers and scientists in Pittsburgh's southern suburbs increased significantly from 1949, when Bettis opened, until the early 1970s. After 1949 Westinghouse soon located other facilities in the southern suburbs, including the Plant Apparatus Division (PAD) (which later moved to the eastern suburbs), an office devoted to transferring nuclear submarine technology to the British, and an Astronuclear Laboratory that employed nearly two thousand at its peak.[63]

Given the limited local pool of scientific labor, in the 1950s and 1960s, when Bettis, PAD, and Astronuclear were expanding, large numbers of engineers and scientists moved into the region. This movement coincided with the peak of housing construction in Bethel Park, Pleasant Hills, and Whitehall (see Table 4). This relationship between rapidly expanding employment at Westinghouse, an influx of well-paid young engineers and scientists with growing families, and the development of relatively inexpensive land to the southwest of West Mifflin resulted in communities with unusually large concentrations of nuclear engineers and scientists. Indeed, all the communities popular with Bettis engineers and scientists also had the highest proportion of new occupants from outside the metro area and the lowest levels of stable residence. A similar process played out in Pittsburgh's eastern suburbs, where Westinghouse located its commercial nuclear facilities and U.S. Steel, PPG, Alcoa, and Koppers also had research laboratories. Suburbs very similar to those to the south of Bettis developed near these facilities in Churchill, Monroeville, Plum, and Murrysville.

During the postwar period, suburbanization began to fill nearly all undeveloped land between and along the predominant commuting corridors into Pittsburgh. Developers in turn developed subdivisions that they finely differentiated by housing cost, size, and style. This resulted in a mosaic of suburbs differentiated by class, income, profession, and place of work.[64] While there was certainly a great deal of blurring between different types of white-collar suburbs, by the 1950s, communities centered on commuting to employment centers within the suburbs and housing engineers and scientists had developed to the east and south of Pittsburgh. These resulted from a combination of factors, including the lower value of land in suburban locations, the location of nearby research and engineering facilities in the suburbs, and scientists' and engineers' preference for communities housing fellow white-collar professionals.

The suburbanization of the Pittsburgh region during the post–World War II period was in part, as it has always been, a process of creating class, race, and gender. Throughout the Cold War, nuclear scientists and engineers in Pittsburgh settled alongside each other in suburbs that were almost entirely middle class and white. Scientists, engineers, and other white-collar professionals

Table 3. Population and occupational characteristics, 1970

	Population	Population change 1950–1970 (%)	Black (%)	Four or more years of college (%)	Professional, technical, & kindred and managers & admin. (%)	Clerical (%)	Blue-collar (%)[a]	Median family and unrelated individual income ($)[b]	Families with income below poverty level (%)
Metropolitan Area	2,401,245	N/A	7.1	9.6	23.0	18.1	37.6	9,737	7.2
Pittsburgh	520,117	-23.2	20.2	9.0	21.5	21.1	31.9	8,800	11.1
Mill towns									
Clairton	15,051	-23.4	25.1	3.3	15.0	17.7	44.4	4,674–9,628	10.7
Duquesne	11,410	-35.2	16.2	3.0	15.6	21.6	44.6	5,198–9,565	11.0
Blue-collar suburbs									
Dravosburg	2,916	-23.0	0.2	3.3	11.8	22.7	49.7	7,675	7.9
Jefferson	8,512	53.8	1.9	6.6	17.9	16.4	48.3	10,182–10,293	5.5
West Mifflin	28,070	56.1	5.5	4.8	16.7	18.6	46.3	10,309	4.5
Mixed suburbs									
Baldwin Borough	26,729	148.8	0.6	9.8	25.3	22.0	34.5	10,945	3.3
Brentwood	13,732	9.5	0.0	8.3	21.9	26.2	29.1	8,820–9,342	3.5
South Park	8,187	80.3	5.0	8.6	22.7	21.7	35.1	9,543	5.8

White-collar suburbs									
Bethel Park	34,791	207.2	0.6	21.5	39.7	16.8	22.2	13,235	2.6
Pleasant Hills	10,490	175.5	0.0	27.0	45.7	16.4	19.8	13,178	3.9
Whitehall	16,551	125.4	0.0	20.8	39.6	20.7	19.8	10,621–13,053	2.8

Sources: 1950 United States Census of Population: Pittsburgh, Pa., Census Tracts, P-D43 (Washington, D.C.: Bureau of the Census, 1950); *1970 Census of Population and Housing: Pittsburgh, Pa., Standard Metropolitan Statistical Area,* PHC(1)-162 (Washington, D.C.: Bureau of the Census, 1970).

[a] Blue-collar includes four occupation categories: craftsmen, foremen, and kindred workers; operatives, except transport; transport equipment operatives; and laborers, except farm.

[b] Aggregate median income data are available only for certain municipalities, but tract level is available for all. For those where municipal-level data are not available, I have provided a range of the lowest and highest median incomes for all census tracts in the municipality.

Table 4. Housing characteristics (1970) and housing stability (1960)

	Owner occupied (%)	Housing built prior to 1940 (%)	Housing built b/w 1950 and 1970 (%)	Occupants moved in prior to 1950 (%)	1960 residents residing in same house as in 1955 (%)	1960 residents residing outside metro area in 1955 (%)
Metropolitan Area	65.1	54.4	33.7	21.4	58.9	5.2
Pittsburgh	47.2	74.4	16.4	20.1	57.2	4.1
Mill towns						
Clairton	58.8	64.8	14.6	27.2	61.1	2.4
Duquesne	59.8	74.5	9.2	28.6	65.5	1.9
Blue-collar suburbs						
Dravosburg	65.7	47.6	7.7	29.3	60.2	5.2
Jefferson	82.2	41.5	79.3	24.5	62.7	4.1
West Mifflin	85.8	20.6	52.2	21.9	65.4	2.4
Mixed suburbs						
Baldwin Borough	77.9	14.8	66.4	13.4	50.9	11.2
Brentwood	64.4	43.2	24.1	21.0	55.8	5.4
South Park	78.8	35.9	56.6	19.1	56.2	7.6

White-collar suburbs						
Bethel Park	88.7	13.9	69.6	12.2	50.6	11.8
Pleasant Hills	84.7	5.9	66.0	10.5	40.9	18.4
Whitehall	74.1	9.0	61.1	10.5	49.5	14.0

Sources: 1970 Census of Population and Housing: Pittsburgh, Pa., Standard Metropolitan Statistical Area, PHC(1)-162 (Washington, D.C.: Bureau of the Census, 1970); *U.S. Census of Population and Housing: 1960, Pittsburgh, Pa., Standard Metropolitan Statistical Area*, PHC(1)-118 (Washington, D.C.: Bureau of the Census, 1960).

formed similar communities in other metropolitan regions across the United States, from Boston to Los Angeles.[65] They formed these communities in pursuit of a variety of usually naturalized assumptions: people of the same class shared similar values and should live alongside each other; certain houses and communities were best suited to professionals; racial segregation was the unfortunate and inadvertent outcome of individual choices, not deliberate action or structures; and as the next chapter shows, the primary role of women was to support the work of men. Westinghouse and other companies in high-demand industries, such as aerospace and nuclear power, readily deployed these assumptions and helped develop segregated communities and amenities in order to attract scientists and engineers to their laboratories.

These communities produced and reinforced an array of injustices. Scientists and engineers not only benefited from federal aid to attend postsecondary institutions and depended directly on the federal government for a paycheck; they also accrued wealth through federally subsidized home ownership. Their children attended better-funded school systems than those in more socioeconomically and racially diverse communities and were as a result more likely to attend universities and colleges and become middle class themselves. These racially and class-segregated suburbs helped ensure that the costs and harm of environmental toxicity, industrial decline, and neoliberal austerity were ultimately born by working-class communities of color. The suburbs helped structure radically different experiences for women and men in terms of access to work and community. The result was that each day, a remarkably uniform population of PhD- and master's degree–bearing white men poured from the southern suburbs into the Bettis Laboratory. Their social status as scientists and engineers and their ability to develop reactor technology that powered the American military and economy were reliant upon the class, race, and gender divisions and injustices that these suburbs helped produce.

6

Invisibilities of Nuclear Engineering

In 1960 Bill Minkler, a recent PhD in mechanical engineering from Carnegie Tech, started a job at the Bettis Atomic Power Laboratory. During his early career, he worked as a practicing engineer. In the late 1960s, he discovered a love of teaching at Bettis's Naval Reactor School, and for the next thirty-three years, he taught generations of naval officers who sailed the U.S. nuclear fleet. Minkler was not just well known in the navy; he was also recognized by thousands of nuclear engineers across the United States, not for his technical or teaching skills but for his ability to communicate humorous stories about the everyday lives and work of nuclear engineers.[1]

In 1966 Minkler, who had written for his high school and college newspapers, wrote his first humor column for *Nuclear News,* the monthly magazine of the American Nuclear Society (ANS).[2] That and a follow-up column told the fictitious story of Joe Meshblock, "a young but plodding nuclear analyst trying to cut the red tape so he could attend an ANS meeting."[3] In 1968 Minkler began writing a regular humor column that appeared alongside cartoons, jokes, and occasional poems on "backscatter," the last page of *Nuclear News.* It ran every month for the next fifty years.

For many of the eleven thousand nuclear engineers who subscribed to *Nuclear News,* Minkler's column was the first thing they read. It was so popular that advertisers, including Westinghouse, vied to occupy space on the opposing page.[4] The same fictitious people and places appear again and again in the column: Al the barber, whom engineers seek out for advice; Xenon Labs; Ace Engineering; Nuke University; the Research Foundation; Beta Bar; and Blightsburg, "a fictional town that urban renewal forgot except for its nuclear power plant."[5] Real places and people also sometimes appear, including references to Minkler's suburban home in Bethel Park and moving tributes to coworkers, family members, and the Little Green Machine, a beloved marching band in the southern suburb of South Fayette. Minkler told me that there are "shades of truth" in his column, but it was nonetheless "fictional." He also stressed to me that Blightsburg was not Pittsburgh, because Pittsburgh is "not smoky and blighted" and "all we do now is technological things and hospitals."[6] Similarly, in an introduction to a book of his columns, Minkler writes, "Blightsburg is an imaginary center of industry. . . . Honest. The dysfunctional companies and laboratories in my column are also imaginary. Honest."[7]

Minkler may have filled his columns with "places in my imagination," but a lot of the content was real. He told me his reoccurring accounts of engineers' struggles with copy machines and bureaucracy were "fairly factual" and that many of the people who appear in the column "were maybe based on real human characters." The columns, he said, were generally based on "observations gained from being in that pool of people." He also told me that he got "feedback" from Bettis management "if I touched on anything that was a little too real." Despite the fantasy of Minkler's world, what made it so appealing to nuclear engineers was that it used humor to speak directly to their lives. In the foreword to Minkler's book, the publisher of *Nuclear News* noted that the "humorous vignettes . . . steadily draw us in and tell us something about who we are and where we've been." Likewise, when I asked Minkler what I could learn about nuclear engineering in his columns, he told me, "You could not learn much about nuclear engineering from my columns, no. It's the world we lived in, the world we lived in and worked in that they are about."[8]

Nuclear News is typically dry and unemotive. Content usually includes profiles of prominent engineers, announcements from local ANS chapters, political news about nuclear power, reviews of new technical developments, and advertisements for products and employees. What is often invisible or reduced to caricature in *Nuclear News* is the daily stuff that is essential to nuclear engineers' lives: gender, family, emotions, community, the public (i.e., non-engineers), religion, political beliefs, and the frustrations of their work. Yet all these invisibilities appear consistently in one place in *Nuclear News*: the fantasy world that Minkler created in his columns. For fifty years, Minkler sketched out through humor the contours of "the world we lived in": a world neatly banished from but essential to nuclear engineering.

Using Minkler's columns and interviews with Pittsburgh-based nuclear engineers as a guide, this chapter is also about the world nuclear engineers lived in and how it was often separate from but essential to nuclear engineering. It uses these sources to unpack the invisibilities of nuclear engineering: the people, things, beliefs, and processes that structure the work and lives of nuclear engineers but are often unseen in both scholarly and technical accounts of nuclear engineering. What is most striking about Minkler's columns, along with their popularity, is how they use humor and fantasy to address topics that otherwise are almost never mentioned in *Nuclear News*. The importance of these invisibilities is precisely why Minkler's columns resonated with so many fellow nuclear engineers.

Social Reproduction and the Fraternity of Nuclear Engineers

In the early years of Minkler's columns, he always writes from the perspective of a nuclear engineer and assumes that nuclear engineers are men. Nonetheless, women appear frequently in his columns, and when they do, unlike the assumed male subjects, they are always marked by their gender. Minkler's columns show how patriarchal social relations within and outside the lab were essential but largely unnamed components of nuclear engineering. Gender structured the workforce in the nuclear industry and created the social conditions in the lab, the office, and the home that allowed nuclear engineers to return to work each day. Patriarchal social relations were as essential a part of nuclear reactors as zirconium alloys or steam generators, but they are usually unnamed and invisible on the pages of *Nuclear News*.

In the 1960s and 1970s, Minkler, *Nuclear News*, and its advertisers assumed that their audience was composed entirely of men. The Westinghouse Atomic Power Division, for example, ran a series of ads for new employees that targeted the "Man of Action." The ads included photos of men surfing, golfing, skiing, and carrying a briefcase with over-the-top text, such as "the Westinghouse man is enthusiastic about everything he does . . . primarily his career. Every day is a new experience for him . . . an adventure in living. The man that works for Westinghouse is always thinking . . . learning . . . contributing."[9] While often more subdued, most advertising for employees in *Nuclear News* explained how the nuclear industry offered an upward career trajectory, the company of other successful professional men, and comfortable suburban living for their wives and families (see chapter 2).

It was reasonable to assume that the vast majority of nuclear engineers were men. Despite my efforts to interview women, all thirty nuclear engineers and scientists I interviewed were men. My interviewees confirmed that there were few if any women nuclear engineers in the early years of the industry and very few well into the 1980s. This mirrored the prevalence of women in positions as scientists and engineers throughout the Pittsburgh region during the Cold War (see Table 2 in chapter 1). As a proportion of employed engineers, women hovered between 0.4 percent in 1960 and 1 percent in 1980. As a proportion of employed natural scientists, women decreased from 10.5 percent in 1950 to 2.3 percent in 1980.

Yet if women largely did not occupy technical positions at Bettis and other Westinghouse nuclear facilities, gender nonetheless deeply structured the work and daily lives of nuclear engineers. Most nuclear engineers assumed that it was the role of women to care for their homes and families so they could commit most of their time to their work. Many wives also did essential professional work for their husbands, including relocating households across the world, entertaining, and introducing new coworkers' spouses to the Pittsburgh region. Nuclear engineers also relied on patriarchal relations with single women employed at the lab, not only to complete administrative tasks but also to form heterosexual relationships and families of their own. Finally, the objectification of women was, oddly, a sacrosanct part of nuclear engineering.

There is a rich history of radical feminist work on the role of the home and women's bodies as machines for the reproduction of labor.[10] Historians have also unpacked the varied ways that women's contributions to science and technology have been erased as well as the gendered exclusions and assumed masculinities of various scientific fields.[11] Feminist geographers and other scholars have deepened and complicated our understanding of the varied and shifting divide between production and social reproduction and the role of women's labor in reproducing daily life.[12] They have also reminded us that social reproduction is not a unitary process. Investigating the social reproduction of nuclear engineers during the Cold War gives us insight into the gender divisions that often shaped white middle-class suburban homes at the time as well as the particular ways that patriarchy sustained the expertise, everyday lives, and work of nuclear engineers. The nuclear engineers I interviewed consistently expressed enthusiasm for their homes and did not ever question their implied status as a place of care and refuge.[13] Few regretted moving to Pittsburgh's suburbs, and many lauded their decision. Nuclear scientists' and engineers' shared enthusiasm for their suburban homes and communities reflects the beneficial role of the gendered division of labor in reproducing their privileged positions within and outside their offices and laboratories.

Many nuclear engineers worked long hours and traveled frequently. Their work often intensified during periods when they were bringing a new project online. For example, when Bettis opened the Shippingport plant and later converted it into a breeder reactor, many lived on-site for days at a time. Many of the engineers I interviewed explained that they took very limited responsibility for household tasks or child rearing. Minkler captured this in one column about an engineer who was constantly working and whose wife reminded him "when something important came up," "Like, 'We had a baby last Friday. Her name is Michelle.'"[14] The nuclear engineer I interviewed who expressed the most intense commitment to work was Donald Kruger, who eventually became a high-ranking executive in Westinghouse's Commercial Nuclear Division and likened the company to being "part of my family." As he explained with a tinge of regret: "If I think about my career with Westinghouse—we were family. I mean consider the amount of waking time that you spend with the employees as opposed to your family and then add on all the time you spent traveling.... It made it very simple to think of Westinghouse being your family."[15] Kruger's memories are extreme, but a number of nuclear engineers shared similar stories of their high level of commitment to their work. Peter Copeland, who at one point nearly died from an ulcer, described working at Bettis as "a six-day-a-week job."[16]

Of those nuclear engineers I interviewed who had children—twenty-nine of thirty did—their wives took primary responsibility for child rearing and household work. There was a generalized assumption that women would postpone or give up their own careers in order to raise families. This ingrained belief transcended varied career paths, backgrounds, and political perspectives. For some, such as Frank Sampson, my questions about the household division of labor presented an opportunity to lament the decline of the traditional family. He bluntly explained his belief that unequal power dynamics defined the success of marriages.

> We're [he and his wife] not part of the new age, which I think is the stupidest thing that ever got invented. But [*lightly slaps table and speaks in squeaky*

> *effeminate voice*] "Here's your checkbook, here's my checkbook. You pay the electric bill and I'll pay the grocery bills." No, no. We just [*light slap*], you do what needs to be done and anybody thinks they can get married and have a 50–50 split is going to end up in divorce court. You see it's that simple. It's more like 75–25 depending on the relationship and you can't handle that: don't get married.[17]

Many engineers shared Sampson's thoughts on the gendered division of household work, although they articulated it less forcefully. For the most part, men assumed responsibility for "repairs and maintenance around the home" and women did "all the cleaning" and "all the cooking too."[18] Not only were women largely responsible for childcare and household work, but the spouses of engineers who rose to managerial positions were also expected to support their husbands in a variety of ways, including hosting dinner parties, accompanying them to conferences, and packing up the family for years of work abroad.

The role of gender and family in managing Westinghouse's professional workforce often became most obvious when the company relocated engineers abroad. According to the nuclear engineers I interviewed, Westinghouse's Commercial Nuclear Division often managed the gender and family composition of employees who worked overseas. When he was newly hired as an engineer, Brian Hopkins moved to Paris to work with the company's French licensee. He told me Westinghouse selected him because he was single and that would allow him to "truly get integrated into society there." If he brought a family, he explained, he would spend time with them and not his French coworkers.[19]

For longer projects, Westinghouse often installed entire families and communities overseas in order to ensure the stability of its operations. In the late 1960s, Westinghouse established a permanent office in Brussels to oversee the large number of reactors it was selling in Europe. It hired engineer Otis Holland to take a managerial role in Brussels because, his boss said, he and his wife, Martha, "can go and live anywhere and a lot of people can't." Westinghouse interviewed both Martha and Otis before they offered him any of his numerous foreign assignments. Martha told me that she negotiated with the company about their housing and moving allowance and proudly pointed out the massive marble table she had convinced Westinghouse to move across the Atlantic or Pacific five times. Martha told me her skills at relocating were "well known," and Westinghouse "even asked me one time to write a book about what people should take when they were going overseas and how they should prepare and what they should do, because we adjusted so well. A lot of wives could not adjust and they would have to send the family home and that was expensive." Unlike Hopkins's experience in France, Westinghouse planned to establish a large office of expats in Belgium and intended Martha and Otis to form the heart of that community. They described their Westinghouse coworkers in Belgium as "like a family."[20] Their coworker Clarence Carter agreed, noting his time in Brussels "was a really close family thing of maybe ten to twelve American families" who shopped and socialized together and whose children attended the same school.[21]

Westinghouse used patriarchal relations not only to stabilize its workforce of engineers abroad but also to supply labor to its office and labs. With the exception of a short period during the 1950s when women mathematicians programmed Fortran computers, nearly all women at Bettis and at Westinghouse's Commercial Nuclear Division worked in administrative and secretarial positions. This workforce of women was a frequent topic in Bill Minkler's columns, and the "backword" (a play on *foreword*) to his 2002 book acknowledges the outdated "gender language and attitudes" that he often used.[22] Typically women appear in Minkler's columns as magical characters who carry out the calculations, editing, and copying that allowed engineers to do their work. An October 1968 column introduced a recurring character, Lois Brawnski the Computress. As engineers at the Xenon Nuclear Laboratory struggle to deal with the layers of forms and complex relationships that define "Big R&D," they turn to Brawnski, who, in her "husky female voice," briskly completes a basic calculation for fuel element cladding thickness that teams of engineers cannot determine.[23] In a later column, when engineers at the neighboring Research Foundation are struggling to use a computer, they "borrow" Lois from Xenon. Before she arrived, "The young bachelors looked forward to the flirting, and even the old dogs anticipated tutoring a sweet young thing in the Ways of Science." When Lois appeared, "six feet, 195 pounds of muscle," with a "subtle quality . . . that made you want to snap to attention," "these visions evaporated." Lois entered the computer room and "barred the door"; the engineers listened to the "thumps, screams, sparks," and when she emerged, smoke poured from the computer and henceforth there were no errors and all calculations were completed in twelve minutes max.[24] In a later column, we meet Connie, "a thin brunette typist" who impeccably produces a constant stream of pointless technical reports while answering phones and dealing with engineers' requests. In the case of Connie, like Lois, there is a strong sense that women's work is vital and overlooked at the lab. Connie's reports, typed on a thirty-year-old typewriter, are "beautiful," but, Minkler jokes, this must be the result of her "boss's keen analytical mind."[25] By the 1980s, women administrative workers were less visible in Minkler's columns; they had been replaced by a computer that automated the writing of "Meaningless Technical Reports."[26]

Sexism was rampant and a rarely contested aspect of work in the nuclear industry. As Doris MacArthur, a longtime administrative worker at Bettis, described, "In the early years . . . you know, the men were the bosses and we were the servants, so to speak." From her perspective, many of these men exercised managerial and technical authority to create patriarchal relations that were more dominating than those at home. She explained, "Some of the women would say when a boss would say, um, 'Get me a cup of coffee,' it's because he couldn't say that to his wife."[27] Even in the 1960s, when women engineers began to enter the field in greater numbers, this challenge was not easily surmounted, and according to MacArthur, many had to struggle against men's efforts to relegate them to secretarial tasks.

PoWeR Lines, a short-lived newsletter from the fuel element subdivision at Bettis, lends further credence to MacArthur's observations. Authored by men and typed by women, it featured hand-drawn cartoons and satirical writing and was ostensibly designed to "create a friendly intershop relationship and make friends of strangers."[28] The newsletter's unstated purpose was to document the movements, activities, and marital status of women who worked at the lab. *PoWeR Lines* was often outright degrading. The introduction of new vending machines had one employee "roaming the halls looking for a girl dispenser," and in another issue the authors observed that "Girls in the G-Building" were frequently eating out and this could lead to weight gain.[29] *PoWeR Lines* published a "Female Formula" modeled on a description of an element. It described Female's physical properties as "boils at nothing. Freezes every minute. Melts when treated with sugar. Bitter if ill used." Female also "possesses great affinity for Au [gold]," "turns green when exposed to a superior specimen," and is the "most effective income tax reducing agent known."[30]

Rewriting technical terms with sexist meanings was a timeless activity, and *Nuclear News* also gave it a try. In 1969 Kermit Garlid, a chemical engineering professor at the University of Washington who eventually helped found the Department of Nuclear Engineering and served as vice provost, submitted a glossary to *Nuclear News* that offered new meaning for twenty-four reactor physics terms based on sexual reproduction. In his glossary, men were neutrons seeking "reactions" with women who were inert nuclei. He defined upscattering as man's encounter with a "young, energetic women" that leaves him feeling younger. Downscattering was an "equilibrium stage reaction" reached when a "sluggish partner . . . drains more energy out of the man" and often "occurs with older, less energetic women." Light nuclei were "fickle, attractive women," and an absorption reaction was "a barren, but faithful marriage."[31] Minkler also wrote a less misogynist glossary of terms that included definitions for "free body (human relations) a contemporary coed" and "ion pair (anatomy) common occurrence for a girl watcher."[32] Minkler also wrote several columns lamenting the declining hemlines of women and calling for a "fight to save the Mini and preserve the female thigh as a National Historical Sight."[33]

Using humor as a largely ineffective means to mask chauvinism, *Po WeR Lines* and *Nuclear News* cemented the role of the nuclear lab as a place that helped realize heteronormative relationships between engineers and administrative workers. One employee authored a poem in *Po WeR Lines* recounting the story of a fire at the lab.

> The engineers were nestled all snug in their chairs,
> While visions of girlies danced in their heads;
> The secretary in her see-more, and I in her lap
> Had just settled our brains for a CENSORED[34]

Other poems documented the vacant feelings of a wife as she eagerly awaited her husband's return from the lab or explained that women's only faults were "Everything they say / And everything they do."[35]

Far from benign, *Po WeR Lines* reflected and helped structure gender relations at the lab. Several marriage announcements in the newsletter noted that the newlyweds were both Bettis employees and met at the lab. When a new secretary was hired to replace a newlywed, her marital status was also announced: "sorry fellas, she's married."[36] The arrival of new secretarial staff was greeted with headlines such as "New Girls Everywhere!!"[37] Thus, while the reference to a "girl dispenser" vending machine was intended as a joke, there are few reasons to take it seriously. As young unmarried engineers poured into the region, they often found a spouse at the lab. *PoWeR Lines* claimed that both men and women enjoyed participating in the lab's marriage market. They published the following request from "female readers":

> With the rapid influx of new personnel, the secretarial grapevine is having trouble keeping up with the marital status of the newcomers. Therefore the *PoWeR Lines* should come to the rescue. We in turn suggest that management could asterisk the names of all single personnel in the telephone listings.[38]

In fact, several of the engineers I interviewed married secretaries they met at work. Larry Goldblatt, an engineer who arrived at Westinghouse's Commercial Nuclear Division fresh from the university, described the office as a "happy hunting ground" and a logical place to meet a spouse.[39] Paul O'Connor, who worked with Goldblatt, also married a coworker. He had an informal rule with fellow bachelors not to date coworkers because "if you break up, you got them there: you're looking at them and they're looking at you." O'Connor broke the rule and began to date a secretary in secret because he was "getting a little long here . . . and I might not catch another one." When they decided to get married, he insisted she quit her job, and she did a week before their wedding. His reasoning was that he "didn't want her working" and they "didn't need the money," but also her presence would contaminate his work. He explained to me, "I didn't think it was a good idea for the two of us to be working in the same place because . . . she was working with the manager of nuclear engineering and I interreacted with him a great deal at the time."[40] O'Connor internalized a widely institutionalized logic among the white middle class and their employers that single women were desirable as employees and partners but that those roles must not overlap and that partnered women would interfere with work and did not belong in the office or the lab.[41]

There is one remarkable moment in *Nuclear News* where the underlying misogyny of nuclear engineering was named, and the response is telling. In the early 1970s, Columbia Labs regularly included photos of bikini-clad women alongside its advertisements for sensors used in nuclear reactors. In November 1972, two readers of *Nuclear News* wrote letters denouncing the ads. Robert Dennig of Cincinnati condemned the "blatant misogynic attitude" and added that using a woman as "bait" was "inexcusable in an ad directed at a supposedly skilled and educated group such as engineers." Margaret Mlynczak, the chair of the ANS student branch at Northwestern, asked why *Nuclear News* "publish[es] ads defiling women in general and insulting every women engineer, scientist, and technician who opens the magazine." The editor of *Nuclear News* offered a lukewarm apology and passively agreed that the ad "could well be considered in poor taste."[42]

In the following two months, *Nuclear News* published six letters that aggressively attacked and ridiculed Dennig and Mlynczak. For a magazine where letters usually focused on technical disagreements or shared ire for antinuclear activists, this was unusual. Paul Gast of Argonne National Laboratory wrote that if *Nuclear News* removed the photos, then "a lot of us guys might not notice any ads at all." R. S. Stone of Oak Ridge mocked the "frenzied disapproval" and "misuse" of words in the earlier letters. J. P. Davis wrote that "ads with good looking human beings" were an appreciated "break from . . . tubing, turbine generators, scintillation detectors, etc." As a "female," she offered "unsolicited advice" to Mlynczak: "If you're going to enter this 99 percent male field, you'd better develop a bit of tolerance for the cute little foibles of male persons, and respond with humor and not indignation."[43] The most aggressive letter came from J. W. Jacox of Mine Safety Appliances in Pittsburgh, who "bitterly resented" the letters, derided their "ludicrous points of view," called the writers a "fanatic . . . and frivolously silly minority," and wrote that *Nuclear News* should not "waste space," when the nuclear industry faced many "critical problems." He suggested that the letter writers "remove themselves from the American Nuclear Society, the Engineering Fraternity, and preferably industry in general."[44] Misogyny was evidently an important part of being a nuclear engineer. Jacox would not have the last word, and both Davis and Gast called directly on Minkler, the spokesperson for nuclear engineers on such matters, to "write a funny column on this subject."

In his column devoted to the swimsuit controversy, Minkler noted that *Nuclear News* was mostly devoted to "technical details" and it was his role to "keep you abreast of Truly Great Issues." To get to the heart of the swimsuit debate, he spoke with fictional coworker Yvonne LeLeur, a manager at the Research Foundation.[45] LeLeur had desired an "engineering career since kindergarten," but when she tried to enter the industry, "interviewers would ignore her straight-A academic credentials, seeing only long, wavy black hair, and 36-18-36 aspect ratio." Instead of hiring her as an engineer, interviewers suggested secretarial work, "where people can see you," and asked what LeLeur was doing on Friday night. Minkler's column continued, "To focus attention on her mind, Yvonne covered her physical assets—with a white lab coat . . . and later an asbestos welding suit." By obscuring her body, she rose through the ranks, but her coworkers could still recognize that "she was . . . well-constructed," and the American Society of Mechanical Engineers (ASME) awarded her an "'N' stamp,'" the technical certification used for reactor pressure vessels. LeLeur eventually began to deploy her femininity for professional gain and found if she wore less, "men are even more attentive at staff meetings." She told Minkler she was concerned about different photos in *Nuclear News*: there were eighty-two men and four women pictured in the last issue. She would like to see equal representation across the magazine with women wearing whatever they like, and then "while the men are ogling the pictures, we girls will move in on the top jobs."[46] Minkler's columns, which often included women as both heroic workers and objects of interest, subtly resisted the virulent misogyny of his coworkers and named the real problem of sexism among nuclear engineers. But Minkler's humor was too subtle. No one responded angrily to his column about LeLeur because it was, of course, a joke.

Sexism was at the core of nuclear engineering and every bit as important as calculating the efficiency of nuclear fuel or ensuring reactor safety. When I asked Clarence Carter whether he ever discussed politics with coworkers in the cafeteria, he told me it was too divisive. Instead they talked about, "you know . . . what do you think about this part of the strategic plan . . . ? Or you would fall back on sports . . . because it's nonthreatening and people in this area are on the same side most of the time. Occasionally a girl walks by with a short skirt and you say, hmm, that's interesting."[47] Carter casually identified objectifying women in the workplace as a nonthreatening activity that united the "fraternity" of nuclear engineers.

From the lab to the home, Pittsburgh's suburbs facilitated patriarchal social-spatial relations that were essential if nuclear engineers were to pursue the long work hours and frequent travel that Westinghouse often required of them. Engineers moved to Pittsburgh's suburbs because they believed they would be a refuge from work. They developed a gendered division of labor that extended from these suburbs to the laboratory itself. At both home and at work, engineers were largely reliant on women to care for children, clean homes, prepare meals, and organize social life in the community. The suburban home and the lab developed as places that helped structure patriarchal social relations and reproduce the standing and class positions of engineers.

Jewish Nuclear Engineers at Bettis

Bill Minkler rarely mentioned religion in his columns, and many nuclear engineers told me it was a topic, along with politics, that they studiously avoided discussing with their coworkers. Nonetheless, religion structured the workforce at Bettis and was an important part of life within and outside the lab. In the 1950s and 1960s, a large number of Jewish nuclear engineers worked at Bettis, and many of them formed a small community centered on Pleasant Hills that provided fellowship and allowed them to maintain their religious practice. Prior to World War II, antisemitism was common at both Westinghouse and GE, and Jewish engineers were relatively rare at both firms.[48] Donald Kruger claimed that "it was almost unheard of" for Jews to be hired as engineers. "It was hard to break into an existing organization being Jewish," he said, "but in new fields like nuclear you didn't have those impediments."[49]

Westinghouse actively recruited Jewish nuclear engineers, and many stressed that the lack of antisemitism among management at Bettis and the Commercial Nuclear Division was key to the company's early dominance of the nuclear industry. In 1952 Bettis hired Fred Forscher, an émigré from Vienna and a mechanical metallurgist with degrees from Princeton and Columbia. He described the lab's technical director Bill Shoupp as "not Jewish, but very friendly to Jewish scientists." Possessing a skill set that was highly in demand, Forscher had offers from GE's Knolls Atomic Power Laboratory and Bettis. As he recalled, "Bettis did such a good job inviting my wife and taking a day off and showing her all the goodies in Pittsburgh and the kosher delicatessen and kosher butcher on Murray Avenue. So then we decided to come to Pittsburgh."[50] Far from seeing the lab as antisemitic, Jewish engineers saw it as a place that embraced them. When I asked Dan Stein whether he ever encountered antisemitism at the lab, he insisted that he did not and that it was "full of very talented Jewish guys."[51] Likewise, David Lebowitz told me there was "absolutely no hint" of antisemitism at Bettis.[52] Some engineers even believed that a lack of antisemitism among Bettis management helped the company form a lasting relationship with Admiral Hyman Rickover, a Jewish immigrant who led the nuclear navy for decades and had experienced intense antisemitism as a student at the Naval Academy.

Herman Schwartz, a physicist who grew up in an Orthodox tradition in Brooklyn and joined Bettis in the 1960s, confirmed that there were "a lot of Jewish people at Bettis." He claimed that "everyone I interacted with was

Jewish" and "there was just a large number of Jewish managers, engineers, scientists, in the physics areas, there was just a lot of Jewish people." Schwartz attended high school and college in Brooklyn and rarely strayed from his neighborhood until he was in his twenties. After working for a year at GE, where he encountered discrimination against African Americans, which "was a shocker to me," he enrolled at a rural university for a PhD and was deeply impacted when a landlord refused to rent him an apartment because of his Jewish last name. "I was still, I was shaking, I was ready to run out, I was afraid to speak," he told me. While he had read about discrimination, "I hadn't experienced it."[53]

Schwartz's experience in Pittsburgh's suburbs was very different. When he arrived, he found a small but active Jewish community in the southern suburbs and at Bettis. When his wife was hospitalized shortly after their arrival in Pittsburgh, a Jewish coworker volunteered his wife to help care for their four children. Unlike many engineers who socialized mostly with the Westinghouse community in the southern suburbs, Schwartz claimed that the Jewish community in Pleasant Hills "became my second family." However, there was pronounced overlap between these two communities. When a parent of a coworker died, Schwartz joined a minyan at Bettis. For a year, every day at noon, these ten men "would go into someone's office . . . and we used to say afternoon service."[54] They were often joined by the head of the Naval Reactors Physics Division, Doctor Radkowski, an Orthodox Jew who Schwartz remembered bringing his own kosher food to the lab whenever he visited from Washington.

While many Jewish engineers chose to settle in the affluent Pittsburgh neighborhood of Squirrel Hill, where there was a large and established Jewish community, several of the engineers I interviewed chose instead to live in the southern suburbs. To Schwartz, who lived in Pleasant Hills and attempted to balance a secular and Jewish life, living in Squirrel Hill "was far from my mind." He explained his decision not to move to a place more like Brooklyn in terms of Jewish culture as intentional: "I didn't have that same . . . even though I grew up with a lot of Jewishness, I was very, 'Hey, I can interact with anyone—what's the difference.' I just never felt any need to live in a Jewish community because we're all equals; that was my general feeling."[55]

Despite his desire not to live in Squirrel Hill, Schwartz associated largely with the approximately one hundred families that made up the Jewish community in Pleasant Hills.[56] Without a nearby place of worship, in 1958 Bettis engineers established Beth Israel, a small conservative synagogue. PhDs were so prevalent at Beth Israel, Lebowitz joked, that when he encountered someone from a Squirrel Hill synagogue who "would say, 'Oh yes, so and so belongs, he has a PhD in engineering,' we'd go, 'Big deal. At our synagogue if you don't have a PhD, we're not sure we're going to let you in.'"[57] A labor of love for its small congregation, Beth Israel members devoted countless hours to its maintenance and operation. To Schwartz, Beth Israel was vital because it ensured that "my children had to interact with other children of the Jewish faith."[58] He and fellow engineers and scientists created a Jewish community in Pittsburgh's southern suburbs that extended from Bettis to their neighborhood to the synagogue. This religious community, an important but mostly overlooked part of the nuclear industry, provided fellowship to Jewish engineers while allowing them to maintain their religious practice and identity.

Engineering Politics

Engineers at Bettis were a carefully selected group by virtue of their education and their need to pass a security clearance. The process of obtaining a security clearance functioned as a ritual that initiated engineers into a privileged, segregated, and rationalist elite.[59] As Dan Stein noted, this exclusivity shaped not only who could access the lab but also the character of his wider social network. After telling me that almost all his friends "were people from Bettis," he explained the beneficial secondary effect of security clearances.

> Bettis was a wonderful place in the sense that the people were absolutely exceptional. I mean some of the brightest people that I've contacted. And of course it was a bit self-selecting. You had to have a security clearance so certain kinds of problems are immediately eliminated. You weren't going to have a druggie. . . . We had some very responsible people.[60]

Like Stein, many nuclear engineers embraced being a member of overlapping suburban and professional communities that they defined as distinct from the broader public. Nuclear engineers described themselves and their colleagues as independent, responsible, and self-reliant, often integrating key racist tropes. They characterized nuclear engineers as having loyalties to objectivism and science that they opposed to radicalism and politics in general.[61]

Some Westinghouse engineers, especially those who entered management, were intensely invested in their work and did not have active social lives outside work, but for those who socialized or were more broadly involved in the community, most of their friendships were with fellow engineers and their wives. Because many Bettis engineers were neighbors, these friendships encompassed both the lab and the neighborhood. For example, Larry Johnson, a Pleasant Hills resident who lived in a neighborhood crammed with nuclear engineers, told me, "Socially we mainly hung out with Bettis people."[62] Stein, who lived in the same neighborhood, described it as a "close community," and Tim Smith, who also lived there, told me, "A lot of our friends were Bettis friends."[63] Sometimes they even chose social activities because of their supposed appeal for engineers. Many nuclear engineers and their wives rotated between suburban houses for weekly games of bridge, which has "a logic that is related to the engineering mind."[64] Nuclear engineers and their wives also became involved in local school and municipal politics, library boards, and organizations, including women's and garden's clubs. In their communities and laboratories, engineers developed an insular technopolitics that merged their shared commitment to the suburbs, their profession, and the Cold War.

Scholarly and popular discourse frequently cast Cold War–era suburbanites as politically complacent and conservative.[65] Some historians have contested this caricature, arguing that suburban women were often politically active and that the suburbs should be seen as much as a base for liberalism as for conservatism.[66] Other scholars have argued that an active metropolitan politics focused on race and suburban homeownership was the crucible out of which a revived populist conservativism developed during the 1960s and 1970s.[67] In the following section, I complicate this picture by arguing that engineers played a particular role in the formation of metropolitan and national politics during the Cold War. Just as they did during the Progressive Era (see chapter 3), engineers during the Cold War expressed political positions that emphasized their faith in meritocracy, science, and rationality.[68] These positions aligned with their investment in their ability to make objective truth claims both inside and outside their labs.

According to many engineers I interviewed, they always took objectively derived positions that transcended partisan and self-interested politics. Because of the authority of their profession, they frequently offered technical solutions to a number of unrelated problems, from racial segregation to public education to conflicts in the Middle East. Running across all these different political acts was engineers' disposition to see themselves as nonpolitical rational actors who could separate themselves from an otherwise disorderly world. The defining trait of nuclear engineers' technopolitics was their belief that their attempts to shape the world were nonpolitical. Politics was a visible and important part of nuclear engineering, but it was rarely named as such. Technopolitics—the tendency to reinscribe political questions as questions of scientific and technical expertise—took root in and shaped the suburbs.[69] Pittsburgh's nuclear suburbs not only helped nuclear engineers embrace identities as apolitical actors but also served as bases from which they could readily apply their expertise to the world around them.

There was not a predominant partisan political affiliation among nuclear engineers. Some nuclear engineers suggested that their coworkers favored Democrats, while others argued that connections to management made them more inclined to support Republicans. Regardless of party position, most agreed that engineers were socially conservative as a result of their education and worldview. Engineers, I was consistently told, were concerned with objective facts and rigorous analysis inside and outside the lab. As Lebowitz explained, "engineers in general like to make sure things work" and "the one thing engineers like to do is see the numbers, see the calculations."[70] Minkler agreed, telling me that engineers "deal with nuts and bolts and neutrons . . . and try to design something and make it work and get a job done." There are "lots of controversial issues going on in the world," he explained, but these were not discussed in engineering school, where instead "you would write a differential equation and solve it: the answer is six. And there is your answer right there." Engineers, he continued, were ill equipped for "dealing with people and feelings and things like that" and politics was not what they were trained to do.[71] Nuclear engineers had a faith in what William Whyte called "scientism," "that questions of policy can be made somewhat non-partisan by the application of science."[72] Their political positions were rooted in their professional adherence to broad principles of reliability, accountability, and rationality. They believed that such skills were not distributed evenly across the population and that as a result they had an important role to play in politics at all scales.

Quite a few interviewees argued that it was engineers' nature and training to be conservative. For some, this did not necessarily mean politically conservative. Hopkins ruefully explained that he was conservative "to a fault" and that this often manifested on the ski slopes, when his "liberal" wife would speed down hills and he was left at the top cautiously studying the map. To Hopkins, this cautiousness was "an engineering type thing" that he compared to "anticipating safety in a plant."[73] For other nuclear engineers, their conservativism was outwardly political. Roger Thompson, a longtime employee of Westinghouse's Commercial Nuclear Division who eventually rose to the rank of vice president, was adamant that engineers were intrinsically conservative. He explained that this conservativism extended from their concern about double-checking calculations to their commitments to monogamy and the nuclear family. As he told me:

> I think that engineers are basically conservative. We didn't, uh, we weren't party-goers and drinkers and playing around. I mean it was a very stable society. I often remark that through most of my career as I associated with engineers . . . there were very few divorces among the group. It was just really good family people. Just basically what engineers were back then: nerds with a pocket protector.[74]

Later in the interview, Thompson expanded on his belief that engineers' values were rooted in their allegiance to individualism and self-reliance. When I asked whether conservativism was the predominant political mindset among nuclear engineers, he explained:

> THOMPSON: I think so; maybe it's just the kind people I tend to associate with that thought like me. Again I think [conservativism]'s an engineering kind of a bent, a conservative, uh, self-reliant kind of attitude.
>
> VITALE: But what would be self-reliant about engineers? I mean, they're like the rest of us, fairly dependent on a bunch of other people to get where they get.
>
> THOMPSON: Sure they are, but you accomplish things because of what you did, you were responsible for what you did, you were accountable for what you did, there were certain expectations about how you should behave and operate and that's the way you did it. You weren't dependent on other people, looking to other people to bail you out; you didn't have a victim kind of attitude. It was, what you got was what you worked for.
>
> VITALE: So you really think there is something intrinsic to engineering that is conservative?
>
> THOMPSON: I do, I do. I don't know why I say, but I mean . . . it would be interesting if you checked the divorce statistics and those sorts of things for

> engineers. We're very logical, we're very, we're not far out, we don't tend to be artistic [*laughs*]. We're just a different breed.[75]

Thompson's comments seamlessly blend his faith in the rationality of engineers with many of the key markers of the late twentieth-century culture wars. While invoking the logic of engineers, he also references engineers having a nuclear family and being "self-reliant," "accountable," and without "a victim kind of attitude." These are, of course, the opposite of those traits ascribed to the apocryphal welfare queen and the Black family.[76] Thompson constructs the objectivity and independence of the engineer in contrast to the supposed dependency of those reliant on the welfare state. His comments draw an easy equation between technopolitics rooted in rationality and expertise and the broader politics of conservatism based in faith in individualism, the market, and "traditional" values.[77] Importantly, both reinforce and legitimate the other.

Few engineers evoked racist catch phrases of the culture wars as Thompson did, but many others also referenced the objectivity of engineers and how it extended to their political views and actions. Ralph Murphy, who was educated as a naval engineer and worked as a technical writer, told me that he "always admired" engineers and scientists because "they were mostly independent thinkers." He elaborated:

> They seldom would come down hard on anything without looking at it carefully and studying both sides of the issue. I think most engineers and scientists are well informed because of the nature of their mind. They are devotees of the scientific process and as a result I think they apply it either knowingly or unknowingly to the rest of other things in their life.[78]

The comments of Thompson and Murphy are ideological in the most pernicious way. They cast scientists and engineers as objective, not political, actors. According to this way of thinking, this is either the outcome of their training or their natural orientation. Either way, their status as objective actors is not worthy of evaluation. It is a given. In addition, they suggest that engineers are people *who do something.* They work, and this work is contrasted to others *who do not.* This casual conflation of scientific objectivity and independence binds Cold War–era scientific expertise—the "technological veil"—to the racial politics of suburban homeownership and conservatism.[79]

More than any other issue, nuclear engineers shared a commitment to nuclear power both out of a need to defend their livelihoods and because of their firm belief that it was a superior means of generating electricity. Every nuclear engineer I spoke to held this view, from Tim Smith, who described himself as "an advocate and a missionary" for nuclear power, to Frank Sampson, who was not "out there with the banner running around" but nonetheless strongly supported nuclear power.[80] Such support often extended to their voting behavior. Sampson said that he voted for politicians who "vote[d] for the Navy contracts." Likewise, Stein told me, "I jokingly say I vote the straight nuclear ticket."[81] For most engineers and scientists, their advocacy for nuclear power extended far beyond voting. Particularly on the commercial side of Westinghouse, engineers made frequent visits to community organizations and schools to explain the merits of nuclear energy. By the 1970s, with the reputation of the industry fading, Westinghouse formalized this public relations work through its Campus America program, which trained young engineers and gave them time off to advocate for nuclear power on university campuses.

Part of nuclear engineers' political perspective was developed through their struggle with the supposedly inexpert advocacy of antinuclear activists. At best, engineers were willing to differentiate between scientifically trained activists who worked in the realm of objective truth and the irrational masses who objected to nuclear power without resort to science. At worst, they disparaged all antinuclear activists and described the public as misinformed and uneducated. Johnson described those who opposed the Yucca Mountain nuclear waste repository as "religious driven."[82] An otherwise reserved O'Connor told me that he and fellow nuclear engineers saw people opposed to nuclear power as "a bunch of nuts . . . and extremists" who had "no solutions themselves; just against any form of progress."[83] Martin Robinson, who testified at numerous public hearings on nuclear power, shared this opinion, telling me that antinuclear activists were "idiots" and "obstructionists" who were "trying to scare the public and I was trying my best to educate the public."[84] Thompson, who was involved in the development of numerous nuclear plants, described encountering "little old ladies with tennis shoes picketing." "A lot of them," he explained, "didn't want to understand." When he spoke to the public, "I was trying very hard to do the right thing and be responsible." But the public "didn't really care," "they just wanted to kill the project."[85] Similarly, Phil Thomas explained that he was frustrated by the objections of people "who talk about energy and energy policy who have almost no understanding of the real world." He advocated leaving decisions about energy policy to those who "have an understanding of how you actually get something done."[86]

Minkler often lampooned opponents of nuclear power and described how obstructionism and regulation would lead to inevitable decline. He fired off several columns on the subject in 1980, the year after the Three Mile Island accident. One asked if the government should begin to regulate mountains, given the recent eruption of Mount St. Helens. Another entered the dream state of an engineer living in a future United States where the "antinukes" had won. The dream follows two boys and their nuclear engineer father to a Nuclear Nostalgia Center, where they learn about objects that are no longer used, including a washing machine and a car. In a locked room, they find "an old rag with red and white stripes on it," but then the father quickly rushes them out of the room before they "get in trouble with the Commissar."[87]

The more nuclear power became embattled, the more the industry attempted to address its diminished public opinion, the greater engineers embraced their positions as experts in relation to the uneducated public. This reached new heights after Three Mile Island when Westinghouse developed a series of training videos on how to deal with the public. In one training video, John Yasinsky, a Westinghouse vice president and former Bettis employee, appears on a news program opposite an actress playing Leda Lounds, a caricature of an angry and irrational activist. Yasinsky politely listens while Lounds declares that Westinghouse is building a breeder reactor that could explode with the force of two hundred tons of dynamite. He calmly responds that Westinghouse is only trying to create "electricity made in America" and that career activists "appear to put most of their effort into fighting and opposing something as opposed to promoting and doing something." Some activists "don't have all of the facts," he says, but others are careerists whose only interest is in obtaining more publicity.[88] By the 1970s, Westinghouse and the trade association Atomic Industrial Forum were spending tens of millions of dollars declaring the reliability and safety of nuclear power and the irrationality of its critics. Nuclear engineers, who had faith in the technologies they built, felt that the public's opposition to nuclear power must be the product of self-promoting activists and misinformation. There could be no objective reason to challenge nuclear power.

Outside their advocacy for nuclear power, the most common arena where nuclear engineers exercised their authority as experts was in local schools. The legacy of the quilt of hundreds of municipalities that overlay the Pittsburgh region, public schools in southwestern Pennsylvania are fragmented into numerous small districts, including forty-two school districts in Allegheny County alone. These districts are funded in large part through local property taxes and as a result have wildly divergent levels of funding and performance. This has led to frequent bankruptcy, state takeover, and sometimes closure of underperforming school districts in former mill towns. Meanwhile, "high-performing" school districts in municipalities where nuclear engineers lived—such as Bethel Park, Murrysville, Pleasant Hills, Upper St. Clair, and Mount Lebanon—sent the vast majority of their graduating classes to college or university. If education reproduces and inculcates class norms, then the multitude of varied and unequal school districts in the Pittsburgh region took on the task of differentiating the children of the working and middle classes.[89]

For many nuclear engineers, the quality of the school district was a paramount factor in their choice of where to live. Minkler told me that his coworkers made housing decisions in the same way as his father, who was also a Westinghouse engineer and who was transferred frequently. Minkler's father always chose their home based on the "reputation of the school system," which he determined through conversations with "colleagues and real estate agents."[90] Astronuclear engineer Carl Poplowski described how he and his wife were "serious about a school system, really serious." They were so serious that they interviewed school principals before they chose a house.[91]

Nuclear engineers in Pittsburgh's eastern suburbs gravitated to small school districts in residential suburbs, such as Edgewood and Churchill, that had long been home to Westinghouse's professional workforce. Thompson, an early employee of Westinghouse's Commercial Nuclear Division, purchased a home in Forest Hills, a "good middle-class community" with "a good school system." With the help of a fellow engineer's wife, who worked as a real estate agent, he sold this home several years later and purchased a house in Edgewood. He lovingly described Edgewood, calling it a "real enclave" and a "very nice area." Edgewood's minuscule school district stood out to Thompson; it was "like having a private school," he said.[92] Phil Thomas also moved to Edgewood, where he purchased a home sandwiched between the homes of

Bill Shoupp, the former technical director of Bettis and current director of the Astronuclear Laboratory, and Joe Rengel, the vice president of Westinghouse's Commercial Nuclear Division. He noted that "there were a number of others" in Edgewood, including the general manager of Bettis. He described the Edgewood School District as "golden in terms of education," "probably the best school district in the whole area."[93]

While the children of Thomas, Thompson, and other Westinghouse engineers thrived in the small Edgewood School District, students in the struggling nearby mill towns of Braddock and Rankin faced very different circumstances. Witnessing the socioeconomic and racial segregation of schools in Pittsburgh's eastern suburbs, in 1971 parents of children in the General Braddock School District filed a lawsuit arguing their school district was unconstitutionally segregated. In 1973 District Judge Gerald Weber agreed and issued a call for proposals to desegregate the district. Eight years of legal challenges, angry protests, and threatening mail followed. In June 1981, the U.S. Supreme Court denied a final appeal for delay and Weber consolidated the working-class districts of General Braddock, Swissvale, and Turtle Creek with the middle-class districts of Churchill and Edgewood, longstanding communities of choice for executives, engineers, and other white-collar professionals. At first known as "the New District," it was eventually named Woodland Hills.[94]

Anticipating the consolidation, officials in Churchill and Edgewood issued a $1.3 million tax refund to residents, an action that Weber halted and called a "pretty crummy thing" and "not in the form of an ordinance for the town of Skunk Hollow."[95] While parents with the organization Save Our Schools marched through downtown Pittsburgh vowing they would appeal to President Ronald Reagan to save them from Weber's "tyranny" and bearing a coffin with the names of the five school districts, students from Braddock traveled to Churchill to marvel that their new high school, located on the edge of the Westinghouse Research Center, had a swimming pool.[96]

As consolidation began to appear inevitable, parents rushed to enroll their children in private schools, with requests to bus children to St. Bartholomew in Penn Hills increasing from nine to twenty-five and to St. Coleman in Turtle Creek from fourteen to fifty-six. The Catholic Diocese tried to head off such "refugees." The principal at St. James in Wilkinsburg vetted prospective parents, noting, "They'll never say that to us [that they're seeking to avoid busing or other desegregation methods]. We have to talk for a while."[97]

Westinghouse employees Thompson and Thomas, who were then heading up Westinghouse operations in Belgium and Baltimore, respectively, were spared having to participate in the school consolidation battle. But both were strongly opposed, with Thomas noting it was "jammed down the throats of the people of Edgewood."[98] When Thompson prepared to return to Pittsburgh in 1979, he noted that "it was uncertain what was going to happen to Edgewood" and "we decided we wouldn't go back there because we still had kids in school." Instead he purchased a house in the wealthy suburb of Fox Chapel.[99] When Thomas returned, he purchased a mansion in the Pittsburgh neighborhood of Shadyside and had to "cheat and lie" to get his children enrolled at Taylor Allderdice, located in affluent Squirrel Hill. As the Woodland Hills consolidation withstood court challenge, many middle-class white parents either enrolled their children in private schools or moved further east to suburbs in Westmoreland County.

Two of the engineers I interviewed served on local school boards. Bill Jones, a Bettis engineer, was clearly as committed to his role in local schools as he was to nuclear engineering. He served on the board of a school district in Pittsburgh's eastern suburbs for more than twenty years, until he lost his reelection bid because he "took on the unions . . . one time too many." Jones told me that he brought an engineer's perspective to the management of schools. When he ran for the board in the 1960s, he did so because "I thought I had more smarts than some of the people sitting on the board." The district was in the midst of building a new school, and he felt his "engineering background" would allow him to contribute. As a member of the board, he promoted science fairs and "pushed very hard . . . to introduce some form of technology into the business aspects of running a school." His engineering and management background also prepared him to take on the teachers' union, which he considered the downfall of public education. After losing his reelection, he served for several years as a leader for school reform in Pennsylvania and based on his experience was appointed to a board of control that oversaw the operations of a school district in a mill town to the west of Pittsburgh. Replacing the locally elected school board, he and his fellow board members closed several schools, reformed hiring practices, and brought the school out of bankruptcy.[100]

Other Westinghouse engineers promoted science education in local schools. The Westinghouse Research Center had a long relationship with neighboring Churchill High School, and the Pittsburgh Chapter of the ANS had a number of programs, including supplying judges for science fairs, sponsoring a one-day Science-Teacher Symposium for local teachers, donating books to local high schools, and providing support to Boy Scouts trying to earn the Atomic Energy merit badge. The ANS even sponsored a Boy Scout Explorer Post of twenty local students "who plan to study nuclear science and engineering."[101]

As I argued in chapter 5, most engineers spent little time considering why they chose to move to particular suburbs. The social processes that caused certain neighborhoods to grow while others experienced decline were not of great interest to them. However, one Bettis engineer and Pleasant Hills resident spent a year investigating this question. In 1973 Westinghouse granted Larry Johnson a paid sabbatical to enroll at MIT's Sloan School, where the pioneer of systems theory Jay W. Forrester was based. Forrester, who developed the Whirlwind computer that formed the basis of the SAGE air defense system, had begun to apply systems theory to logistical, world, and urban systems. In the late 1960s, Forrester developed a highly complex model of the urban area as "a system of interacting industries, housing, and people." In Forrester's model, this urban system interacted with a surrounding "limitless environment." For all the math and time spent inputting data into computers, Forrester's conclusions were less than revelatory: (1) cities typically grow and then decline and (2) attempts to correct this decline often exacerbate it.[102]

At Bettis, Johnson was developing models to simulate reactors that were similar to those Forrester was using to "calculate how people move from cities to suburbs and how jobs change." He spent his sabbatical studying "how cities interact with suburbs." He tinkered with Forrester's model and eliminated the "limitless" potential for population growth. As he explained:

> I took that situation and I added a suburb to the city and I added a farming community and I punched some numbers in and I sort of proved that the problems in the city were because so many people were leaving the farms, and the city was more attractive and so it got overcrowded, but if you look at the numbers, the farm population had been so depleted by that time that the problem is going to go away all by itself.[103]

Forrester had reached "opposite conclusions," and Johnson's model "didn't sit too well with him."

What is remarkable about both Forrester's and Johnson's models is their tendency to disregard all previously existing research and public debate about cities and to instead believe that human behavior can be easily modeled using methods derived from engineering complex technical systems.[104] Both of these tendencies can be ascribed to the remarkable arrogance of engineering during this time period, the belief that all problems have technical solutions and only engineers are equipped to answer them. This was the way that many engineers approached the public who mindlessly opposed their reactors, the school systems that educated their children, the women who supported their daily lives, and the metropolitan regions where they lived. For Johnson, his time in Cambridge was "a nice diversion," but in 1974 he returned to Pleasant Hills and his work at Bettis simulating nuclear reactors.[105] The relationship between cities and suburbs remained as much of a mystery as when he left.

In the 1950s, sociologists such as C. Wright Mills and William H. Whyte subjected suburbanites *and* engineers to intense scrutiny in a number of widely read books. These studies, broad in their scope and sweeping in their conclusions, produced a clichéd portrayal of atomized and automatized American suburbanites and engineers. The "organization man" that Whyte and others described was not just a sociological invention. As this and the previous chapter have argued, science, engineering, and suburbanization came together to reshape American life during the early Cold War. An unprecedented federal investment in scientific research and military spending swelled the ranks of the country's engineers and scientists by hundreds of thousands. Not only was the employment of the young physicist or electrical engineer nearly guaranteed in the early 1950s, but the federal government or his employer often paid his way through graduate school. When he emerged from school, he was usually highly recruited and well paid and often had his choice of jobs across the country. Thus he relocated in droves from Iowa State University to Palo Alto, California, from Washington University to Holmdel, New Jersey, from MIT to Pleasant Hills, Pennsylvania. The young man of science was on the move, and when he arrived in his new home, he usually settled in a suburb and developed a way of looking at the world that often uncannily resembled those of his classmates who settled on the other side of the continent.

As the arms race and then the space race escalated, as polio was cured, as all manner of banal technologies captured America's attention, scientists and engineers offered themselves as the answers to the world's and America's problems. Their close coupling with private industry—one that had been developing for nearly a century—ensured that when these solutions were developed, they would be delivered not only by hallowed scientists and engineers but also by that most wholesome of American ideals—free enterprise. By the 1950s, with the most intransigent critics of industry silenced by red scares, science and engineering's love affair with industry was complete. Together engineers and scientists, corporate managers, and shareholders would deliver America and the world from the clutches of communism and into a world of unbridled freedom and prosperity.

When not perfecting their missiles and reactors and artificial hearts, scientists and engineers retreated to that most peaceful of refuge, the heavily subsidized suburban home. This too was the product of an even more unprecedented investment by the federal government. The trillions of dollars invested in roads and the subsidies granted to white homeowners and corporations alike ensured that by the close of the Cold War, the United States became a suburban nation in terms of employment and residence. Facilitated by massive federal investment, suburbanization and the ideology of technological rationality developed in tangent. The postwar suburbs developed as places intended to reproduce the class positions of the middle class. For scientists and engineers, this class position included their expertise—their ability to exercise control in their laboratories and the worlds outside them.

7

Warplace/Workplace

Technoscientific Jobs during the Cold War

On May 16, 1946, a week after seventy-six thousand Westinghouse workers ended a 115-day strike, the company hosted a three-day conference in Pittsburgh to commemorate the centennial of George Westinghouse's birth and probe the modest subject of "Science and Life in the World." Three thousand invitees from more than one hundred countries listened to prominent speakers, including Linus Pauling, Isaiah Bowman, and Charles Kettering, all of whom speculated on the future of the United States and the world in the wake of the political and scientific changes of World War II. On the first day, Robert Oppenheimer and Enrico Fermi told attendees about the possibility for the peaceful use of atomic energy and George Merck and Major General Aldan Watt discussed the benefits that biological and chemical weapons would yield in peacetime. Gwilym Price summed up the first day's proceedings by telling the audience how this "awesome power . . . for destruction" has provided "a new, and, I hope lasting realization of the impact of science on our affairs." This "newfound wealth," he continued, forces scientists and industry to "assume new and critical responsibilities."[1]

That evening, Vannevar Bush, whose recent report "Science: The Endless Frontier" undoubtedly inspired much of the day's proceedings, expanded on scientists' new responsibilities. In a speech titled "Planning in Science," Bush focused on the growing polarity between the United States and the Soviet Union. He described science as an important part of "planning," which "is basic to the proper functioning of the whole complex of industry, commerce, education, social action and government that goes to make the United States." It was up to scientists, by virtue of their "attitude toward factual data," to delineate a clear path for society. By taking a greater role in social and political life, scientists could "clear out extraneous side issues and focus attention and effort on the nub of the problem."[2] On the final day of the event, MIT president Karl Compton, following Bush's example, argued that scientists were the greatest tools in the U.S. military and economic arsenal. "For security against aggression and security against depression," he stated, "there is no element which is more important than to have the most adequate possible complement of able, well-trained scientific personnel in our country."[3]

Neatly contained within the proceedings of "Science and Life in the World" was a dichotomy between a scientific community committed to what Jessica Wang calls a "progressive left politics of science" and the leading figures of the military-industrial-academic complex, who had very different designs for science.[4] Scientists such as Oppenheimer and Pauling, as well as the recently formed Association of Pittsburgh Scientists, which only weeks earlier had hosted the first national meeting of the Federation of American Scientists, hoped to foster a scientific community committed to internationalism and peace.[5] Meanwhile, industry leaders, state officials, and the military increasingly opposed this progressive vision. To admirals and industrialists, scientific freedom was distinctly American, but military-industrial needs must dictate the path of research. To this end, while heady discussion about international cooperation, civilian control, and scientific freedom took place inside the conference, behind the scenes, Price took steps to secure Westinghouse a profitable place in the new era of Cold War science.

According to Westinghouse lore, the most important words spoken at "Science and Life in the World" were said not on the stage but in a short meeting between Price and naval captain Hyman Rickover, who stopped in Pittsburgh en route to a new assignment in Oak Ridge, Tennessee.[6] The hard-driving Rickover had already established a strong relationship with Westinghouse during World War II when he led the Electrical Bureau of the Division of Ships—one of the company's major customers during the war. He had developed a good working relationship with Westinghouse and found the company technically proficient and willing to submit to his often-demanding requests. During their short meeting in Pittsburgh, Price and Rickover discussed the prospects of nuclear-powered ships and Westinghouse's keen desire to participate and to commercialize nuclear power. This conversation between Price and Rickover marked the beginning of a half-century-long alliance between Westinghouse and the navy to develop and manufacture nuclear propulsion and power systems.

For the past seventy years, such sustained partnerships between the military and industry have radically transformed the work and everyday lives of engineers and scientists. During the Cold War, as Paul Forman describes, science "underwent a qualitative change in its purposes and character, an enlistment and integration of the bulk of its practitioners and its practices in the nation's pursuit of security through ever more advanced military technologies."[7] As many scientists and engineers spent a lifetime engaged in war work, they had to come to terms with their intimate relationship to the state, the military, and the Cold War. Their relationship to the Cold War and the military were visceral and violent in effect but heavily mediated by layers of bureaucracy and technoscience. The everyday lives of engineers and scientists encompassed a dichotomy between peace in their suburban homes and laboratories and the development of weapons of war that the United States frequently put to deadly use.

Such a dichotomy peaked during the Cold War, when, as Matthew Farish describes, Americans participated in "an uncertain, prolonged search for an impossible national security."[8] In this search, engineers and scientists had to master the seeming incongruity of living with war while finding their own lives at peace. At the same time, as previous chapters have argued, the "peace" that they experienced in racially and socioeconomically segregated suburbs was itself the product of structural violence. Nuclear scientists and engineers in Pittsburgh's suburbs created a dichotomy of war and peace in their everyday lives that allowed them to divide their own experiences from the violence that sustained them.[9] To nuclear scientists and engineers, war at best was an abstract and distant threat. War and structural violence became normalized in their lives while almost never becoming tangible. Their daily work developing reactors for submarines and ships that carried enough warheads to end the world became mundane.

This chapter traces Bettis's history as a place of war and a place of work. It begins by arguing that nationalism and war were intrinsic to many scientists' and engineers' work during the Cold War, but their experiences of war and nationalism were technologically and bureaucratically mediated. I then sketch a short history of the Bettis Atomic Power Laboratory and the Naval Nuclear Reactors Program, which is widely considered a model of the tight control that the military exercised over defense contractors' work. The next section explores how the tight strictures that the navy imposed on engineers and scientists at Bettis encouraged lab employees to see contributing to the Cold War as work. The final section explores how nuclear engineers and scientists saw the development of weapons not as part of a war with the Soviet Union but as a constant struggle to satisfy their "common enemy": the U.S. Navy.

Nationalism, War, and Technoscientific Work

As I argue in the introduction of this book, a key limitation of science and technology studies is that it usually fails to follow engineers and scientists outside their laboratories. It is as though scientists and engineers only inhabit labs and are constituted only through their "associations" with experiments and machines. STS also tends to neglect that science and engineering are work. In a critique of Bruno Latour's *Science in Action,* Steven Shapin notes that it contains "remarkably little on the work world of technoscience." According to Shapin, Latour falls victim to "a peculiar ophthalmological condition that appears preferentially to afflict the intellectual classes." Latour "can see the product of work, but the work itself seems to be invisible."[10] The reason for this is that Latour is highly averse to the suggestion that any "outside" force might decisively shape the work of scientists and engineers. Of course, he acknowledges that engineers and scientists are trained and managed, depend on wages, and occupy hierarchies like the rest of us, but this is merely the outcome of the settled alliances and networks that they help build. As a result, in *Science in Action* and other works, we get a strong sense that scientists and engineers are exercising an impressive level of autonomy and control over the labor process. This neatly parallels the perspective that industrial firms encouraged engineers and scientists to adopt: that their work was freeing, mental, and different from other work (see chapter 3).

Unsurprisingly, nuclear engineers and scientists considered Bettis as primarily a place of tightly regimented work. Sometimes their work was highly rewarding, and just as often it was very unpleasant. Even more than many others, their employer, an amorphous combination of Westinghouse and the navy, subjected them to impressively heavy levels of discipline. Indeed, the most consistent memory of the former Bettis employees I interviewed was the degree to which the navy, which they frequently named "the customer," exercised complete control over their work. Bettis employees could not attend a conference, publish a paper, pursue a project, or even travel abroad without the formal permission of the navy. This control did not end at the laboratory gates: the navy and the Federal Bureau of Investigation (FBI) also intensely scrutinized their personal lives.

Bettis engineers and scientists submitted to this difficult work regime because it was challenging, prestigious, and well paid. Just as important, they believed deeply in the importance of the naval nuclear program and that it contributed to human progress and national defense. By encouraging engineers and scientists to work hard at Bettis, the navy and Westinghouse enrolled them not only as allies in the development of nuclear reactors but also as national subjects who were contributing to the Cold War. Nationalism and militarism were key components of the technoscientific networks that the navy and Westinghouse employed engineers and scientists to create.

Bettis engineers and scientists genuinely saw their work as helping win the Cold War. It was through work—the harder and more disciplined the better—that they could develop the most reliable reactors and contribute to national defense. Scientists and engineers adopted a sense of themselves as national and military subjects through their work, but complex bureaucratic and technoscientific networks mediated their connection to the Cold War. This was representative of what Michael Mann describes as the shift from the "citizen warfare" of World War II to the "deterrence science militarism" of the Cold War. During World War II, there was intense emphasis on mass participation in national defense; during the Cold War, there was an increasing belief that the labor of select experts would guarantee national security.[11] Bettis engineers and scientists felt strongly that they contributed to national defense, not by making weapons that would kill, serving in the military, or conserving food as they would have during World War II but by refining an obscure component of a reactor, filling out forms in triplicate, and working hard to please the customer. As war increasingly became the business of technoscience, workers performed their national duties by complying carefully to the customer's needs.

This was the result of two important changes that began during World War II and became stronger still during the Cold War. First, the state adopted the negotiated contract between the military and businesses as the key means by which it distributed the work of defense research and manufacturing. As a result, war work increasingly adopted the form of a customer relationship. Second, a significant share of defense research and manufacturing was of the size and complexity of World War II–era big science projects, such as the Manhattan District and the Radiation Lab. Developing complex weapons systems required a maze of contracts and subcontracts spanning the military, universities, and industry.[12] It was often beyond the ability of any individual to understand his place within these complex networks. The emergence of a customer relationship with the state, the product of which were sophisticated technoscientific networks that supposedly guaranteed the defense of the nation and the free world, fundamentally reshaped the work of scientists and engineers and their sense of national belonging. Engineers and scientists felt a sense of national belonging through their work, but they also felt greatly removed from the military conflict to which they contributed.

The Cold War collapsed the relationship between technoscience, industry, and the state. Each became an overlapping component of an elaborate and comprehensive network that would guarantee national security. While this had origins in World War II, it differed in its lack of intensity, duration, and disconnect from the ferocity and immediacy of war. Thus if the fabrication of national identity and security go hand in hand, as Mark Neocleous has argued, and if during the Cold War such security was created through networks of state, industry, and technoscience, then engineers and scientists formed identities as scientific workers, engaged in the pursuit of rational and expert work, who in doing so offered the promise of national security.[13] In the remainder of this chapter, I follow engineers and scientists through the Bettis Laboratory to develop a sense of how this process played out.

Bettis: A Workplace of War

As early as 1939, the U.S. Navy was aware of the potential for nuclear-powered ships. Following the development of the atomic bomb, many naval officers considered nuclear propulsion vital to reducing the fleet's vulnerability. Nuclear propulsion allowed submarines to recharge their batteries underwater and freed surface ships from refueling at sea. The development of missile technology presented the opportunity for ship-based nuclear warheads. During the 1940s, Westinghouse executives and researchers tapped nuclear reactors for naval propulsion and civilian electricity generation as key future markets.[14] During and immediately after World War II, Westinghouse sought out contracts with the Manhattan Project and loaned employees to labs at Oak Ridge, Berkeley, and Los Alamos. The company's executives devoted these resources with the hope that they could obtain knowledge and cultivate connections that would allow them to be the first to commercialize nuclear power.

Immediately after his meeting with Price at "Science and Life in the World," Rickover traveled to Oak Ridge, where he joined a team of military officers, academics, and engineers working to develop a gas-cooled graphite-moderated reactor. Joining Rickover in Oak Ridge were seven engineers from Westinghouse, including John W. Simpson, who had worked with Rickover during the war. Simpson was soon living in a house with Rickover and three other engineers. During their time at Oak Ridge, Simpson and Rickover worked side by side, with Simpson helping with difficult calculations and Rickover explaining the political landscape of nuclear technology. Their relationship was formative for Westinghouse's entry into the nuclear industry.[15]

At Oak Ridge, Rickover became convinced that developing a reactor was a technical rather than a scientific challenge.[16] He believed that if the navy worked with a compliant firm, assembled a team of engineers rather than academic scientists, and followed the same management framework he used during World War II, it could quickly develop a nuclear submarine. As he put it, the development of naval reactors was "five percent theory and ninety-five percent engineering."[17] After the attempt to develop a gas-cooled reactor fell apart due to technical challenges and a leadership vacuum at the newly established Atomic Energy Commission (AEC), Rickover pushed the navy to take a greater lead in reactor development. Before the navy could begin developing a reactor, as Scott Frickel argues, Rickover first needed to forge an alliance with the AEC, which had congressionally mandated authority over nuclear technology.[18]

Early in 1948, the AEC moved responsibility for developing reactor designs from Oak Ridge to the Argonne Laboratory outside Chicago. Meanwhile, battles ensued in Washington over whether and where to develop the first nuclear reactors and the navy's role in this effort. While Rickover maneuvered for position within the navy and the AEC, he remained in close contact with Westinghouse executives, including Simpson, Price, and another wartime acquaintance, Charlie Weaver, a Churchill resident and former manager in the marine marketing department. Westinghouse sent several engineers to work at Argonne but otherwise focused on cultivating its relationship with Rickover and the navy. On June 2, 1948, the U.S. Navy's Bureau of Ships issued an $830,000 contract to Westinghouse, code-named Project Wizard, for "steam products." The contract made no mention of the source of the steam, which would have violated the Atomic Energy Act, but in fact authorized the company to create a study group on the development of a steam generator for a pressurized water reactor. The contract stressed that this work was confidential and as a result, "it is essential that the work be performed in an isolated facility." A separate contract outlined how such a facility "will be provided by the government, or by the contractor at government expense."[19]

Meanwhile, Rickover hammered out the details of a "dual organization" between the AEC and the navy to develop a naval reactor. As a result of this arrangement, Rickover assumed leadership positions in the reactor development offices of both the AEC and the navy.[20] In the final agreement, adopted in December 1948, Argonne would be responsible for developing the design of the reactor, and the navy's contractors—Westinghouse and GE—would engineer this design into prototypes and manufacture reactors. This division soon blurred as Rickover directed Westinghouse to take increasing responsibility for designing reactors as well.[21]

In October 1949, Westinghouse announced the formation of its Atomic Power Division, headed by Charlie Weaver. As a condition of its contract with the navy, Rickover required that Westinghouse devote its top engineers to the new division. Given carte blanche to recruit throughout the company, Weaver raided the staff of the Research Labs in order to form a team of the company's most talented scientists and engineers.[22] By the end of 1949, Weaver assumed the role of vice president of Westinghouse's nuclear activities and Rickover's old roommate Simpson became the general manager of the Bettis Laboratory. Building on the relationships developed during World War II, Rickover's Naval Reactors Division and Bettis operated seamlessly.

Written by a former employee of the Tennessee Valley Authority, the $6.1 million contract establishing Bettis was somewhat unusual for the time. Because it was not clear what the costs or timeframe of the project would be or even what design the reactor would take, the contract was a vague expression of good will between Westinghouse, the navy, and the AEC. Westinghouse was to pursue the project "in a spirit of partnership and cooperation with maximum effort and common sense in achieving their common objective." Otherwise the contract assumed the highly lucrative model of those administered during the Manhattan Project of "cost-plus-fixed-fee." Westinghouse earned a percentage of all funds spent, as well as a 5.1 percent overhead and administration fee.[23] As a result of the vague nature of the contract and Rickover's overbearing demeanor, Bettis immediately assumed the feel of a government-run research facility. Rickover and Naval Reactors exerted complete control over the lab, and as one engineer told me, "Westinghouse was simply the logo on our paycheck."[24]

After looking at several locations, Weaver settled on Bettis Field, an old airport to the southeast of Pittsburgh, because it was spacious and proximate to the company's Research Labs and East Pittsburgh Works, from which it would draw employees. Westinghouse purchased the airfield in January 1949, and the then tiny Atomic Power Division of around thirty people quickly moved into one existing office building and two hangars. Unlike the flagship research facilities of local industrial firms (see chapter 4), Bettis lacked any suggestion that an architect had set foot on the grounds. Built in Rickover's preferred spartan style, the laboratory was shabby and utilitarian. There was little attempt to landscape the grounds or to build structures that reflected the innovative work that was going on inside. The appearance of the lab mattered very little as it was accessible only to employees with a security clearance and was largely obscured by trees and a tall barbed wire fence.

Behind Bettis's fence, more than two thousand employees developed what Simpson called "a nuclear miracle": the world's first "fully engineered" nuclear reactor.[25] Bettis was responsible for "essentially all of the research, development, design, procurement, construction, and testing" for the Mark I and Mark II reactors.[26] The Mark I was built in a water-filled tank in the desert outside Idaho Falls, Idaho. There, in what Westinghouse called the "Kitty Hawk of the Atomic Age," Rickover pushed engineers to take the Mark I reactor to the breaking point, running it for one hundred consecutive hours to simulate a submerged Atlantic crossing.[27] Based on the design of the Mark I, the Mark II was installed in the U.S.S. *Nautilus*.

In total, Bettis-designed reactors powered 11 aircraft carriers and 110 submarines, 42 of which were armed with Polaris missiles.[28] By 1965 Bettis's operating budget was $62.6 million, making it the fifth-largest AEC laboratory in terms of funding, behind Lawrence-Livermore ($151.6 million), Los Alamos ($97.5 million), Oak Ridge ($78.7 million), and Argonne ($77.9 million).[29] While Bettis never earned the notoriety or the budget of the major "multi-use labs" that primarily produced nuclear warheads, it nonetheless was the leading center for reactor research and development and had a significant role in strengthening the U.S. military power during the Cold War. It was one site among many where scientists and engineers did the mundane work of maintaining the United States' military arsenal.

The Zirconium Curtain

Retired Bettis employees persistently told me what they called "Rickover stories." One engineer told me that I "must" read Rickover's biography and that he "would flunk [me] if [I] didn't."[30] I did not set out to speak about Rickover, but it became clear that this larger-than-life character deeply shaped how Bettis engineers and scientists saw their work. Through these Rickover stories, they impressed on me that "the Admiral" had left a lasting and exceptional impact on their work. What was shockingly routine about the practice of telling Rickover stories was that after telling several, many that I heard before, when I asked interviewees if they had ever met Rickover, most admitted that they had rarely encountered him. Rickover's impact on their work was deeply personal, but few had spoken to him. He personified and embodied their relationship with the state and the Cold War—representing in human terms the bureaucracy that they struggled with daily. This was, as Richard G. Hewlett and Francis Duncan note, Rickover's strategy: "he did not see himself as the casual agent of a faceless bureaucracy but as a personification of the government itself."[31]

Rickover stories and the mythology they create provide a window into the relationship that developed between Bettis employees and the military. Bettis engineers were more likely to identify as hard-working employees trying to satisfy an exacting bureaucracy than as patriotic Cold Warriors. However, the entrenchment of the military-industrial complex in their everyday lives blurred the distinction between war and bureaucracy. Bettis employees believed they were contributing to the Cold War, but they did so by developing obscure technologies and answering the uncompromising daily requests of their customer. Their sense that they contributed to national security was defined by their struggle with Rickover and the Naval Reactors Division.

One of the defining traits of the Naval Reactors Division, according to its apostles and Bettis employees, was its strong focus on discipline, consistency, and centralized power.[32] Even for the many engineers and scientists who were skeptical of the state and its intrusion into research and development, Naval Reactors was the program that broke the mold. As one former Bettis employee described it, Naval Reactors "was one of the best-run government programs we ever had in this country."[33] The reason it was exceptional, many offered, was the character of Rickover and the practices he established. They explained that Rickover's tight control of Bettis created a culture of hard work and accountability that resulted in success.

Rickover's oversight of Bettis was notoriously demanding and comprehensive. All paperwork at the lab included a pink carbon copy that was sent to his office in Washington. He had a direct line installed between Washington and the general manager's office at Bettis. The red phone had only two functions: to provide a direct connection between Rickover and the general manger and to allow the general manger to contact any division head at the laboratory to immediately answer whatever question the Admiral asked.[34] Each week, every divisional manager at Bettis was required to submit a report of his current top challenge to Rickover, a management technique that, according to one engineer, Rickover adopted from Napoleon.[35] From his scrappy office in Washington, Rickover exercised greater control over Westinghouse than was typical of most contractors.[36] Working from a model he developed during World War II, he cultivated a talented staff, ninety-seven of whom were permanently based at Bettis, that provided intensive oversight over its contractors.[37] To staff his offices in Washington and West Mifflin, the Admiral gleaned the top graduates of the naval Reserve Officer Training Course (ROTC) program and sent them to the Naval Reactor Engineering School at Bettis, where they studied an intensive course on reactor engineering.[38] Within his carefully selected "cadre" of "very, very bright" people, Rickover maintained an "incredible esprit de corps."[39] This "cadre" kept a watchful eye over all the navy's contractors and laboratories, including Bettis.

Rickover also kept a close watch over Bettis, making frequent "nocturnal visits" and often staying at an apartment Westinghouse maintained for him in Pleasant Hills. Among Rickover's "unorthodox tactics" were surprise visits to the lab on evenings, holidays, and weekends.[40] Zalman Shapiro, who began work with Bettis in 1949 and led the development of a process for manufacturing large quantities of zirconium alloy, explained that Rickover's favorite time to come to the lab was in the late evening, when he would "spur me on in his own inimitable way."[41] Rickover was not, according to most employees, interested in details and had a deep aversion to scientific research, which he considered impractical. Based on his experience at Oak Ridge, he favored engineering and considered the development of a naval nuclear reactor a technical rather than a scientific challenge.[42] "He had a very short attention span," Bill Jones explained. "He really didn't want to know how you got there; he wanted to know what the answer was."[43] He also was particularly withering to those in authority, and several employees happily noted that both Bettis's upper management and Ivy League professors cowered in his presence. One of his favorite techniques was to ask a question, silence a manager, and then ask a subordinate to respond instead.

Most Bettis employees expressed an odd mixture of animosity and reverence for Rickover—he was both "a great visionary" and "not a nice man."[44] Larry Johnson told me "people feared him" but also that "he insisted on super high quality" and "was a very effective leader."[45] Simpson described his "blend of admiration and ambivalence" toward Rickover and called the Admiral "masterfully Machiavellian."[46] Jake Hubert, who eventually left Bettis to assume an executive position with Westinghouse, was influenced by Rickover's "management discipline" and had "tremendous respect" for him but "didn't like him as an individual." Rickover, he said, had no "people skills" and "would use people and then destroy them."[47]

All the employees I spoke with believed that Bettis and Rickover outperformed other divisions of the military and their contractors and that this was a direct result of the Admiral's tight discipline. According to David Lebowitz, who eventually left Bettis for a career as a consultant, what he learned at the lab was an emphasis on quality. "At Bettis," he said, "things were done right the first time." Like many employees, he contrasted Bettis's record to the aerospace industry, which he considered unreliable and overfunded. He believed that if Rickover had taken over the space program at its beginning, "you wouldn't have had any of that trial and error, the stuff would have been done right, and that would have been launched." "The Naval Reactors program reflected Rickover's personality of get it done right," he said, "and it was fantastic for our country."[48] While many employees struggled under Rickover's despotic style of management, they also believed that it was necessary for the good of the United States. Rickover personified the level of discipline that they believed was needed in order to develop the complex technological systems that were vital for the United States to win the Cold War.

Bettis employees nicknamed the navy's absolute authority over their work the "Zirconium Curtain." The Zirconium Curtain referred to Rickover prohibiting employees from finding employment in other divisions of Westinghouse or transferring information out of the lab. Rickover enforced these restrictions to reduce the advantage Westinghouse received from its role as a defense contractor and also to retain talent at Bettis, where employees were often paid less than peers in Westinghouse's commercial divisions. As Peter Copeland explained, because of the Zirconium Curtain, "you could leave, but you weren't going to get a job with Westinghouse."[49] Jones remembered several instances where an engineer left Bettis for "better pay or some other reason," only to find that their new job "didn't exist anymore because once the Admiral found out . . . he contacted this thing and [*slams table*]."[50] Similarly, Lebowitz relayed the story of a coworker whose going-away party he attended, only to find him back at Bettis the following week: "I asked him, 'Sam, what are you doing here; I thought you were at Astronuclear?' 'Well, the Admiral made a phone call and my job disappeared. . . .' So that gives you some idea of the power Admiral Rickover had over us." Phil Thomas, a former Bettis employee who eventually worked in management at Westinghouse's Commercial Nuclear Division, told me "it was well known" that you did not hire anyone from Bettis "without approval from the Admiral himself."[51]

When Bettis was formed, Westinghouse gave its general manager, Charlie Weaver, permission to "cherry pick" scientists and engineers from Westinghouse Research Laboratories and its manufacturing divisions.[52] Westinghouse always intended to use Bettis as a stepping-stone to commercializing nuclear power. As a compromise with the Admiral, a small percentage of management was permitted to leave Bettis each year for the company's commercial divisions. In addition to this percentage, occasionally "windows" opened in the Zirconium Curtain in order to allow employees and information to leave Bettis. These windows usually corresponded to downturns at Bettis, a technical problem with commercial reactor technology that could have disastrous results for the nuclear industry, or Westinghouse ignoring the Admiral.[53] Bettis served as a state-funded apprenticeship and research and development program for Westinghouse's Commercial Nuclear Power Division.

Bettis, like all government nuclear laboratories, used a complex system of security classification. This made it difficult for employees to publish their research. For example, Tim Smith, who worked on reactor methods, became "frustrated" early in his career when he submitted five papers, all of which the navy's censors rejected.[54] Employees were also prohibited from attending conferences unless censors cleared their papers well in advance. In the mid-1950s, Bettis developed a journal, the *Bettis Technical Review* (*BTR*), that was intended to accelerate the publication of the work of scientists and engineers at the labs. As one former employee explained, the lab's censors funneled publications into the *Review*. If a lab employee tried to submit a piece "to *Mathematica* or something . . . the reviewers would say, don't you think this ought to be in the [*BTR*]?"[55] Many employees managed to have significant scholarly careers, but petty and cumbersome barriers to research were daily reminders that at Bettis, engineers' and scientists' ultimate purpose was to serve the customer.[56]

Considering the annoyances of working at Bettis, it is remarkable that all the former employees I interviewed had a positive account of both the laboratory and Rickover. Hubert, who celebrated the Admiral's "management discipline," told me that Bettis employees "had a tremendous amount of pressure put on us by the navy nuclear organization," and he considered it "one of the most disciplined and stressful organizations I have ever seen."[57] Dan Stein, who eventually was a manager at the lab, added that "in the Rickover tradition," it was "a very strict meritocracy." He continued:

> I had been there thirty years, I was quite successful, and nobody ever gave me a compliment. Rickover didn't believe in that. If you're doing a good job, that should be satisfaction enough, and so it was not the kind of place where everyone went around telling everyone how great they are and what a great job they were doing. The satisfaction came in the work.[58]

Due to the "high-stress situation," one employee told me how he collapsed at the laboratory from an ulcer and had a significant portion of his stomach removed.[59] The central message of Rickover stories was employees' strong faith that their adherence to excessive discipline allowed them to develop complex technological systems that in turn preserved national security. Rickover personified their belief in three components of the engineering politics I discussed in the previous chapter: that hard work was morally virtuous in its own right; that the state, Westinghouse, and society would always meritocratically reward hard work; and that the hard work carried out at that lab was technical, not political.

"Common Enemy"

I began interviewing retired nuclear engineers and scientists with the hope that they would hold strong opinions about communism and capitalism, the United States and the Soviet Union—that they would identify as patriots and important actors in the Cold War.[60] One of my earliest interviews in the basement of the Pleasant Hills Library with Tim Smith, a nuclear engineer who had worked for both the U.S. Army and Bettis, complicated my perspective. I asked Smith what it was like working at Bettis and he responded, "There was a great sense of camaraderie and working together; sometimes in order to make a team you have to have some common enemy and we had a common enemy." Assuming that the common enemy was the Soviet Union, I was surprised when he told me that "the Pittsburgh Naval Reactors office" was "a more focused . . . present enemy" than the Soviet Union. I asked why a seeming ally was an enemy and he explained:

> Naval Reactors to some degree was our common enemy because Naval Reactors in the style of Rickover was not accustomed to praising; they were always accustomed to finding fault and criticizing and tearing you down and beating you up and so it was sort of a depressing place that you would always get bad reviews from the customer, they always criticized you for this, and wanted it to be better. So there was a lot of camaraderie there as we tried to fight against our common enemy and there was a lot of cooperation.[61]

For Smith and other Bettis employees, their experience of the Cold War was defined by their relationship to the customer: Admiral Rickover, the Naval Reactors program, and the state. They experienced the Cold War more as a daily struggle with the customer than as an international conflict between the Soviet Union and the United States. They needed to please the customer and in doing so contributed to national defense.

Bettis employees tended to invoke bureaucratic and technical challenges, rather than war, as their primary motivation. Their goal was never to wage open war with the Soviets, a possibility they considered highly unlikely and irrational, but to ensure that the U.S. naval nuclear fleet operated without the possibility of error. Maintaining the fleet required that they not consider political questions, including how the United States used the weapons they developed. Hugh Gusterson observed similar tendencies among weapons scientists at Lawrence-Livermore National Laboratory. After interviewing engineers and scientists with a range of political beliefs, he was forced to discard traditional political labels and "think of science itself—the ideology that claims not to be one—as a source of binding energy capable of holding the scientists together despite their apparent political differences." This ideology was marked by weapons scientists' tendencies toward "privatization of moral thinking," "consequentialism," and the belief that "nuclear weapons offer the best hope of preventing war and saving lives." The "internalization" of such beliefs is an essential part of the work of the lab. "As the laboratory reproduces its scientists," Gusterson argues, "it not only works on their beliefs and their vocabularies; it also molds their fears, their joys, and their excitements, turning them to the service of nuclear deterrence."[62]

Every Bettis engineer and scientist I spoke with believed that nuclear reactors—for war and peace—had provided an important benefit to the United States and the world. Many identified very strongly with and even dedicated their lives to nuclear technology. They rarely, if ever, saw building nuclear submarines and aircraft carriers as an irresolvable moral quandary or even as a quandary at all. They tended to see the Cold War as a remote "political" conflict that they needed to isolate from their "technical" work at the labs. They assiduously maintained an impenetrable division between their reactors and the politics of the Cold War. Such beliefs were not simply the product of an "ideology of science" but resulted from the technoscientific and bureaucratic networks through which scientists and engineers worked for the nation. Severed from the politics of the Cold War by the customer relationship, engineers and scientists understandably came to see war as work.

Tom Boreland, a physicist and longtime employee of Westinghouse Research Labs who joined the company in the late 1930s and worked on defense research throughout his career, drew a distinction between times of hot and cold war. He contrasted his experience during World War II, "where everybody was really busting their neck to try to get things done," to the Cold War, which "didn't have that same intensity to it." During the Cold War, he told me, scientists and engineers "were contributing to technology and science, in general for whatever use," rather than concerning themselves with the Soviet Union.[63] This contrast between hot and cold war was also shared by John Peters, a metallurgical engineer who joined Westinghouse during World War II and continued in various positions with the company's jet engine and nuclear activities during the Cold War. His memories of working at explosive and turbine plants during World War II were so vivid that, "even today, I'm emotionally upset over it."[64] He told me that during the war, "you were proud of your fellow officers, civilians, everyone putting their shoulder to the wheel" and that Americans were brought together by a "terrible vindictive feeling about those bastards." Of German ancestry, Peters admitted that he harbored a deep and continued hatred toward Japan. Like many Americans, he remembered the war in the Pacific as a race war between the civilized world and Japanese barbarism.[65] World War II was a time like no other, Peters told me, and he has "never seen a country or an organization pull together as a team with a goal, and the goal was to get back at the Japanese."[66]

In his nineties, Peters found his memory at times understandably cloudy and contradictory, yet he could recall the exact moment when he learned of the attack on Pearl Harbor as well as his visit years later to the Pearl Harbor Memorial. His memories of key moments that occurred much later in his life were often much less clear. He did not harbor the same hatred toward the Soviets that he did the Japanese. "I never liked communism," he told me. "In that respect, I guess I disliked Russia, but not really enough to really be upset. Not the way I was at Pearl Harbor. That hit hard." When I asked whether he feared the Soviet Union or nuclear attack, he told me:

> I felt we would be able to deter one another because [*paused*]. Yeah, I recognized the Cold War, obviously everybody did, and I knew that Russia had nuclear bombs, I knew that we did, I knew that Russia didn't want any dropped on them and we didn't want any dropped on us. So it was sort of a standoff and it looked like a feasible arrangement. You're not going to put the genie back in the box—it's out, it's there. I guess that was my only feeling about it.[67]

Peters drew a direct contrast between the deep feeling of immediacy and participation he felt during World War II and his dispassionate and rational feelings about the Cold War. He acknowledged that his hatred of Japan was problematic but also appropriately irrational. The Cold War, in contrast, was "a feasible arrangement" premised on the mutual threat of apocalypse.

Most of the Bettis employees I interviewed shared this dispassionate feeling about the Cold War, "the overwhelming rationality of this irrational enterprise," as Marcuse termed it at the time.[68] I spoke at length about this with Herman Schwartz, an affable physicist and the only Bettis employee to express even fleeting doubts about working for a defense contractor. After receiving their PhDs, many of his former graduate school classmates went to Los Alamos and Livermore, where "they'd be able to have their own bomb." Echoing several Bettis employees, he told me, "I disliked that," but he admitted that he never addressed the contradiction that "here I came along and helped build nuclear submarines. No matter how far out it is, it's like a bomb, you know what I mean? I didn't—I passed it off, I passed it off. And I rationalized, I said, 'You know, it's okay.'" Schwartz came to terms with his work at Bettis. He accepted, like most Bettis employees, that the Cold War was an inevitable but limited conflict and that the platforms that carried nuclear weapons were necessary for national security. When I asked if he ever had doubts about working at Bettis, he told me:

> SCHWARTZ: Yes, over my lifetime I have given thought to what I was doing, of course; I was working in the defense industry. I did not give very much thought to that, but it did cross my mind. But I had already been in it, I had been involved in it—it was not a bad thing to do, I felt. It was a necessary thing to do.
>
> VITALE: Necessary for you or necessary for the . . . ?
>
> SCHWARTZ: Necessary for the government to maintain its military power, I felt it important. Yes, I still do. So would I go out and join a defense industry? I see nothing wrong with that. I think that's necessary. Unfortunately.

Schwartz believed that most of his coworkers shared this perspective—they did not approach their work with "political overtones." As an example, he told me of his former boss, who would sit eagerly by the phone waiting for a problem to develop at the shipyards so he could assemble a team to fix it. This boss "loved the excitement of getting things done—repairing the ships." It was the technical challenge that motivated him, the desire to "get things done for Bettis, for Bettis's sake." Scientists and engineers were more inspired by their interest in technical challenges than any explicitly political or military motive. People at Bettis were "gung ho," Schwartz said. "I don't think it was for the glory of America political winning against the Soviets but to keep the ships afloat."[69]

Larry Johnson, Schwartz's neighbor and an electrical engineer who worked on the development of the first nuclear-powered aircraft carrier, the U.S.S. *Enterprise,* agreed with Schwartz that it was the "smaller challenge[s]" that motivated his work at Bettis. Like Tim Smith, he also invoked a customer relationship, likening Bettis's relationship to the navy to that between a mechanic and a car owner. Bettis employees, like auto mechanics, were concerned only with the navy's technical requirements, not the uses to which they put their ships. "The navy ran their ships and we were the maintenance guys," he said. "The guy who changes your brakes doesn't care where you drive your car—it's a different category, it's a different department of the navy." Johnson remembered other engineers occasionally expressing misgivings about doing military work, but he never felt this way because he was working on the "safety aspects" of naval nuclear reactors—"taking care of the problems that might make it unsafe."[70] Johnson considered his work as technical, not political.

Engineer Dan Stein began his university studies in 1957, only a few months before the Soviets launched Sputnik 1. "At that time" he recalled, "everybody was very concerned that this race we were on with the Soviets was very serious business."[71] He attended graduate school on an AEC fellowship—the first major federal program to fund doctoral degrees. Stein chose nuclear engineering because he felt nuclear power would become a "great energy source for the world." He remembered his time in graduate school as one of uncertainty, in which he was concerned about "how we are going to come out vis-à-vis the Soviets." Yet Stein, who was an "environmentalist" and "had no interest in bombs," believed that the battle with the Soviets would be won through "our brainpower . . . and continuing to develop our society and electrical energy." A direct product of Atoms for Peace, Stein believed that nuclear power "would be too cheap to meter." Later, when he arrived at Bettis, he first worked on the Shippingport Atomic Power Station and then joined management. He and fellow managers tried to impart "a bigger view of what was going on" to employees and encouraged them to attend the commissioning of ships and even to go to sea with the navy. But on the whole, the work was "highly focused and demanding so you're focused on what you're doing," not the context of the work.[72]

Not everyone I interviewed was reluctant to contribute to the military-industrial complex. Physicist Jake Hubert was not reluctant to claim that he contributed to the Cold War and believed "everybody I dealt with felt the same way." He told me that he remembered being "quite concerned with the friction between the United States and the Soviet Union. I could see the value of what we were doing and really felt a strong sense of pride that if we weren't successful here, we could end up jeopardizing the future of the United States." Hubert believed that he contributed to a technical battle between "rational" enemies and that without reliable deterrents, "we would have had war with the Soviet Union." His coworkers "knew the strategic importance of these [submarines and aircraft carriers] to the navy and to the overall defense of the country and I would say unanimously everybody . . . expressed an opinion . . .

[that] we were doing something that made our country stronger." Even in the case of a "controversial war" like Vietnam, his "thought process" was that "if our country entered what we felt was a just war, then we should be able to utilize the weapons that we developed."[73]

Yet even Hubert, who of the Bettis employees I interviewed felt most strongly about the positive impact of his work on national security, nonetheless described the work at Bettis as apolitical. If asked, he certainly believed the work was patriotic, but this did not foreground his experience working at the labs. Rather, he separated building the technical "backbone" of national defense from the politics of the Cold War. Engineers, scientists, and other Bettis employees, he claimed, simply created technologies. It was not their business what "our country" did with them.

This sense that work at Bettis was apolitical—or technical—was reinforced by many employees' emphasis that they were only doing a job. A few engineers described their decision to work at Bettis as primarily dictated by their need for stable employment and income. "I was not a Cold Warrior," Frank Sampson said, after explaining to me that he rarely considered the politics of his work. He was motivated to support his family, and when working six days a week, he did not have time to mull over the effects of his work. He was certain that many of his coworkers felt the same way. If you asked them, most would say, "We should defeat Communism or something," he told me, but "most people lived their lives. They got enough going on that they don't worry about things like that."[74] When I asked Peter Copeland, another longtime engineer at Bettis, whether he was motivated by a desire to defeat the Soviet Union, he told me he was not very "imaginative in that type of interest." Like Sampson, his primary motive was that he "had a family to support and deal with the education of six kids and all the other associated distresses that you're aware of. There wasn't much of any sophisticated or philosophical factors that I really claimed."[75] This was also the perspective of Johnson, an electrical engineer, who said that his coworkers' "first priority is get a job and then worry about the secondary issues."[76]

When I asked Copeland, a veteran of World War II who joined Bettis after attending university on the GI Bill and working at Oak Ridge National Laboratory, about his feelings about the Vietnam War, he again told me that he "wasn't very imaginative about those kinds of things." He then convolutedly explained how his work addressed technical rather than political concerns.

> Throughout my Olympic career with Westinghouse, there was enough distraction—the job itself and the responsibilities of making sure that you didn't make a mistake—the fact that I [later] worked . . . in the oversight of the defense department in Washington suggests that it's not enough to entertain, you might say, the good output or the accomplishments that your product that you're working with would have. What's the downside, what can go wrong?

Copeland continued by offering the example of the Challenger explosion, which he argued resulted from engineers being forced by "the big boys" to not cancel the launch due to oxidized O-rings. He used the "horrible experience" of the Challenger as an example of the "downside." Such "downsides" rarely occurred in the naval nuclear program because "the lifestyle of Rickover's people" resulted in Bettis engineers putting "in a good amount of conservatism to make sure things don't break as smoothly and as nice as you like—you don't end up in trouble."[77]

It is hard to know what to make of an answer to a simple question about the Vietnam War that spans from his career at Bettis, to his later position as a government regulator, to the Challenger explosion. What I take it to mean is that engineers and scientists do not do politics. In fact, in order to work effectively, they must keep politics and science and engineering separate. This is what Copeland meant when he twice claimed that he was "not imaginative" about the fuller "accomplishments" of his work. By not doing politics—by being concerned only with "the job itself"—engineers and scientists help their employer avoid the "downside." Somewhat contradictorily, the downside is the failure of a technology, not the "good output" that results—that is, that the aircraft carrier Sampson helped develop was the launching point for countless bombing runs on Vietnam. According to Sampson, by keeping politics and engineering separate, engineers can most effectively do their work. This sentiment was widely shared by Bettis engineers and scientists and no doubt millions of other workers employed by the military-industrial complex during the Cold War.

Johnson devoted his entire career to developing nuclear reactors for the navy and commercial utilities. Much of his work remains classified, and he could not talk about it three decades later. Yet despite his lengthy and intimate involvement in an important defense industry, he could remember only a few moments when the Cold War felt "real." He recalled attending a graduate course at Carnegie Tech where his professor allowed the students to listen to President John F. Kennedy's speech during the Cuban Missile Crisis. "That was a really tense time, you really didn't know where that was going to go," he said, "but that really was the only time where the nuclear thing really became kind of real."[78] After thirty years of building "nuclear things," during which time his employer and the navy often explained and celebrated the immediate impact of his work on the United States and the world, the Cold War nonetheless felt unreal to Johnson. It is this sense of detachment that defines the Cold War for many who participated directly in it. Bettis engineers and scientists participated in technoscientific and bureaucratic networks that framed their experience of war as rational, peaceful, and apolitical technical work.

For seventy years, the Bettis Atomic Power Laboratory has sat quietly alongside Pittsburgh McKeesport Boulevard, one small piece of a mind-boggling array of laboratories and factories that maintain, produce, and develop technologies that allow the United States to exert its influence across and even beyond the globe. For the engineers and scientists who worked at Bettis in the 1950s and 1960s, there was little that was glorious about their work. A few were motivated by patriotism, but most thought of their work at Bettis as just a job. They worked long hours, the navy was incredibly demanding, and the small technical details they often spent months addressing seemed far removed from the exercise of American hegemony. Yet these small details and hard work did contribute to American hegemony. Engineers and scientists contributed very small components to vast weapons systems, and these systems integrated the mundane aspects of their work lives into a larger technoscientific network designed to protect and extend the power of the United States.

The Bettis Laboratory was unusual for Pittsburgh. With the exception of the "arsenals of democracy" along the rivers that produced steel and aluminum for weapons and the Westinghouse Research Center and the universities that pursued military research contracts, the military-industrial complex had a limited physical presence in Pittsburgh during the Cold War. In comparison to Boston, Los Angeles, or the Bay Area, there were far fewer engineers and scientists employed in defense industries.[79] Yet this limited presence did not lessen the military-industrial complex's effect. Throughout the Cold War, civic leaders constantly advocated for more defense contracts, even developing state agencies to solicit them. What little defense spending there was they proudly advertised as proof that the region was moving beyond steel and in doing so was contributing to national security. In the 1950s and 1960s, Bettis as well as Westinghouse Astronuclear Laboratory, which developed reactors for rockets and space travel, became key evidence on which to hang this claim. The Pittsburgh region, or at least those who spoke for it, was proud to contribute to the Cold War, however remote and alien it seemed.

Epilogue

Did Science Save Pittsburgh?

Today the story of Pittsburgh's rebirth through science and engineering that this book traces has come to its full fruition. It is now commonplace to argue that a partnership of state and business leaders has successfully remade Pittsburgh into a vibrant center of high-tech research, higher education, and medicine. Travel magazines cite Pittsburgh's "extreme metropolitan makeover" as a must-see destination alongside London, Congo's Virunga volcanoes, and Mongolia.[1] Policy makers, politicians, academics, media commentators, and corporate executives consider Pittsburgh a model not only for other Rust Belt cities—the envy of Cleveland and Detroit, as they often describe it—but also for urban areas in need of renewal around the world. They often highlight science and technology and scientists and engineers as key to Pittsburgh's successful remaking.[2] Pittsburgh's promoters argue that its renewal is the product of both a bold civic partnership and the work of its scientists and engineers. A sundry assortment of robot designers, software developers, medical researchers, and engineers populate reports of the region's rebirth. According to these accounts, these brilliant minds both brought about Pittsburgh's renewal and are the people in whose interests a civic partnership initiated this renewal in the first place.

There are some broad lessons that we can draw from the place of technoscience and scientists and engineers within the ceaseless renewal and suburbanization of postwar and twenty-first-century Pittsburgh. In the first section, I summarize the key ways that the social, economic, and political context of Cold War suburban Pittsburgh shaped the work of scientists and engineers. As I have argued repeatedly, this context is a vital but usually invisible part of technoscientific networks. In the second section, I move to the present and explore one key instance, Barack Obama's visit to the city for the Group of 20 (G20) Summit in 2009, where local and global elite once again used Pittsburgh, as they had sixty years earlier at Shippingport's unveiling, as a setting to reinforce the myth that science and technology can resolve the crisis tendencies of capitalism.

The Sociospatial Context of Science and Engineering Matters

Science and engineering often operate on the premise that scientists and engineers need to eliminate the impact of the local context on their work. Their goal is to ensure replicability so that other scientists and engineers can produce the same knowledge or machine anywhere. Many geographers and other scholars have challenged this placeless perspective and traced how space shapes science and engineering.[3] This book has added to this scholarship by arguing that not just the explicit spaces of technoscience matter but also the spaces that help socially reproduce scientists and engineers; their gender, race, and class positions; and their shared dispositions toward the world.

For scientists in seventeenth-century England, these spaces were parlors; for mathematicians in the Soviet Union, they were dachas; for contemporary tech workers in Cambridge and San Francisco, they were gentrified neighborhoods; and for Cold War scientists and engineers in the United States, they were the suburbs.[4] Nuclear engineers and scientists in Pittsburgh give us one example of how the production of facts and machines and the social reproduction of scientists and engineers were embedded in suburban spaces during the Cold War. The same conclusions that I draw about nuclear scientists and engineers in Pittsburgh could easily be extended to those who worked on rockets in Huntsville or radar in Baltimore's southern suburbs or aerospace in Southern California. There are a series of conclusions that we can draw about the specific suburban character of Cold War science and the more general role that cloistered spaces play in reproducing the lives and work of scientists and engineers from the example of nuclear engineers and scientists in Pittsburgh's suburbs.

While, like all workers, scientists and engineers during the Cold War undoubtedly faced serious constraints to their work and everyday lives, there is also no doubt that, by any measure, they had a life of privilege in relation to the vast majority of Americans. On average, they earned significantly higher incomes; benefited from extraordinary levels of state subsidy for education, housing, and research; lived healthier and longer lives; had greater control over their work; and secured status that allowed them to shape social and political life. In addition to these class, gender, and racial benefits of being a scientist or engineer, built into these professions is the idea that technoscientific workers are more free than other workers. Employers, educational institutions, and the state repeatedly reassured scientists and engineers that their role within the workplace was to think freely, and this freedom was contrasted with the situation of workers whose labor was more tightly controlled. As I explore in part II of this book, this class formation of supposedly free scientific workers was created in part through the production of exclusive suburban spaces for scientists and engineers.

Scientists and engineers in Cold War Pittsburgh lived very different lives from steelworkers and coal miners who resided only a few miles away; they saw the world differently, and this was the product of not only their work but also the communities where they lived. Integral to the growth of science and engineering in Cold War Pittsburgh was the ability to attract scientists and engineers to the region. Westinghouse and other companies did this by touting the appeal of middle-class suburbs where scientists and engineers could live alongside fellow white-collar professionals who looked like them and supposedly shared similar values. The racially and socially segregated and gendered spaces of Cold War Pittsburgh were essential ingredients of the technoscientific networks that allowed for the development of nuclear technology. It is not coincidental that if you traveled to other regions across the United States where technoscientific work was being done, you would have found nearly identical neighborhoods of scientists and engineers clustered alongside other supposedly like-minded members of the middle class. In federal laboratories—communities that were planned from scratch as sites of technoscience—designers, managers, and state officials often developed neighborhoods that explicitly segregated employees by race, gender, and class.[5]

The segregated spaces of the suburbs and the race, class, and gender positions they produced were essential to Cold War technoscience, but their existence and function were usually invisible to scientists and engineers. From the very beginnings of their education, scientists and engineers embraced meritocratic ideas about work, success, and expertise that they learned were essential to their professions. They deeply believed that their education, unlike that of the broader public, prepared them to make objective decisions that would ultimately accrue benefits to the rest of society. They contrasted their expertise and social worth both to the irrationality of a less-educated public and the dependency of those who supposedly could not freely support themselves. Nuclear scientists and engineers in Pittsburgh embraced the idea that they were uniquely independent and free thinking. The vast constellation of state institutions and programs that were embedded in the suburbs and that supported scientists and engineers needed to be invisible in order to maintain the aura that scientists and engineers were free and independent. Scientists' and engineers' tendency to live alongside and socialize with each other helped reinforce their sensibility that they had a special position in society.

The social position of scientists and engineers as irreplaceable professionals who were independent, could freely choose where to live, and would bring progress and economic growth made them the perfect subjects around which Pittsburgh elites and businesses could center their remaking of the region. At the close of World War II, Pittsburgh was plagued by strikes and dominated by heavy industry; the air was dark with smoke and the cityscape bleak and gray. It was against this backdrop that Pittsburgh's leaders set out to renew the region, and fittingly it was scientists and engineers whom they enrolled in their efforts. Pittsburgh-based corporations invested heavily in facilities for scientists and engineers during the Cold War and hoped that these investments would pay off by improving corporate images, developing new products, luring government contracts, and providing places that helped attract scientists and engineers. Meanwhile, the ACCD, a regional alliance of business and political elite, described many of its renewal efforts as taking place for the benefit of scientists and engineers. While strategies to make cities appealing to the "creative class" are now commonplace, it was in Pittsburgh and other declining industrial cities where these practices were first put into place. By claiming that they were carrying out Pittsburgh's renewal to meet the needs of scientists and engineers, the region's leaders boosted the legitimacy of their efforts to remake the region in the interests of business.

Rather than lessen inequalities and injustices, science and engineering often built on and exacerbated them. The incomes of many white Americans increased greatly during the Cold War, but even despite the gains won by unions, the incomes of workers in Westinghouse and in U.S. Steel's mills fell well behind those of engineers and scientists in their labs and white-collar professionals in downtown skyscrapers. Meanwhile, African Americans, who were often excluded from many industrial and nonindustrial jobs, faced ongoing poverty and segregation. Predominantly white male scientists and engineers emerged from the Cold War not only with higher incomes and greater access to education, housing, health care, and leisure but also with a sense that the state, employers, and society saw them as valuable. None of these divisions was new, but the effort to create a new Pittsburgh focused on science and engineering and other postindustrial activities did not alleviate—and likely worsened—the inequalities and injustices that have long defined the region.

Pittsburgh Reborn Again

At the top of the agenda for the White House press conference on May 28, 2009, was the location of the G20 Summit. The G20 had met a month earlier in London, but dire economic news called for another meeting. Press secretary Robert Gibbs opened the press conference by announcing that the United States would host the G20 in Pittsburgh. Microphones captured the laughter and calls of "why?" Gibbs glanced at his notes and haltingly responded that President Barack Obama had chosen Pittsburgh because it is "an area that has seen its share of economic woes in the past but because of foresight and investment is now renewed—giving birth to renewed industries that are creating the jobs of the future.... The President believes it would be a good place to highlight some of that."[6]

Over the next months, the White House and local leaders in Pittsburgh repeatedly invoked a well-trod narrative that Pittsburgh, a reborn industrial region, was the perfect site for the G20 at a moment of economic crisis. In Pittsburgh, the ACCD partnered with local governments and Visit Pittsburgh to form the Pittsburgh G20 Partnership, the host committee for the summit. The partnership led neighborhood cleanup days, prepared businesses for disruption, and ensured that Pittsburgh's renaissance story was not eclipsed by the G20. Local leaders highlighted how Pittsburgh could provide valuable lessons to world leaders at a time when the global economy itself required renewal. In Washington, Obama did his part to support this narrative. In a statement before the summit, he called Pittsburgh "a bold example of how to create new jobs and industries while transitioning to a 21st century economy." Pittsburgh, he explained, "has transformed itself from the city of steel to a center for high-tech innovation." As a result of this remaking, "Pittsburgh will provide both a beautiful backdrop and a powerful example for our work."[7]

During the G20, leaders met inside the heavily fortified and "green" David Lawrence Convention Center. From inside, Obama again highlighted Pittsburgh as "a perfect venue." He observed that world leaders "were so impressed with the revitalization" and "pointed to lessons they could take away in revitalizing manufacturing towns in their own home countries." Pittsburgh, he explained, was once a symbol of industry, but today the city represented capitalism's capacity to reinvent itself. After "hard times," Obama said, "Pittsburgh picked itself up, and dusted itself off, and is making the transition to job-creating industries of the future. . . . It serves as a model for turning the page to a 21st century economy."[8] He then turned to the G20's response to the economic crisis, calling for stimulus and global financial coordination, while laying out a path for austerity in the years ahead.

The G20 was not Obama's first trip to Pittsburgh, nor would it be his last. For a president in the midst of terms dominated by economic malaise, a visit to Pittsburgh served a valuable purpose. Obama is one very visible character in a cast of hundreds of state leaders, business executives, and urban boosters who have transformed Pittsburgh into a stage on which they can endlessly replay capitalism's salvation: a region devastated by industrial decline can be reborn as a center of the high-tech economy. Invisible in this performance, of course, is any sense of the unevenness of Pittsburgh's rebirth: that poverty and injustice pervade a region that is constantly being reborn for precisely the people—the surgeons, engineers, financiers, and corporate executives—for whom it never died in the first place. In the hands of the powerful, from Richard King Mellon to Barack Obama, this narrative represents the creative promise of capitalist renewal at every scale from the neighborhood to the region to the globe.

Science and technology often play a major role in this story of crisis and redemption. Before the summit, the Pittsburgh G20 Partnership's president, Bill Flanagan, presented media with a list of locations that he called "transformational visuals." Included were the site of the 1892 Homestead strike, redeveloped into a U.S. Steel research center and strip mall; the Westinghouse Air Brake factory, renovated to house the Pittsburgh Opera; and the Hot Metal Bridge that once transported molten iron now repurposed to carry cyclists from the Pittsburgh Technology Center to a mixed-use commercial and office center. But the "'money shot,' that tells the whole story," is the view from Mount Washington. There, on what used to be called Coal Hill, onlookers could see "one of the most inspiring views anywhere": smoke-free skies, skyscrapers, the Technology Center, and universities all encapsulating the seventy-year effort to remake the region.[9]

During the G20 Summit, journalists from far and wide visited these "transformational visuals" and sent home stories about Pittsburgh's rebirth.[10] The *Toronto Star* hailed a visit to the city as "promising a glimpse of a clean, green post-industrial future." The BBC declared Pittsburgh "a text-book example of how a globalized economy works." When manufacturing leaves, "your population educates itself; then moves into cleaner, more sophisticated service sectors." Seeking an exception to this dream world, the BBC traveled an hour and a half to Youngstown, Ohio, to find even a hint of dissatisfaction. Former Pittsburgher Caitlan Smith, writing in *The Atlantic,* told world leaders that they could find "inspiration on how to revive their economies" on a "walk through Pittsburgh's neighborhoods, which brim with reminders that just about everything old can be new again."[11]

Those brave enough to walk through Pittsburgh during the G20 found a city that looked more like a military encampment than a "clean, green example of regeneration."[12] The usual presummit raids detained activists. Soldiers roamed downtown in armored vehicles. A maze of impenetrable fences surrounded the David Lawrence Convention Center. The Pittsburgh police department debuted its ear-splitting long-range acoustical device, the sound cannon, on the streets of Lawrenceville. On the final day of the summit, a police riot broke out in Oakland, during which police gassed, beat, and jailed more than one hundred students and demonstrators on the University of Pittsburgh's campus. For the students, joggers, journalists, and protestors who faced the full-scale police repression usually reserved for those who are Black or poor, the violence that sustains the city's remaking was, for a fleeting moment, very evident. From Pittsburgh's streets, it seemed less like a city that symbolized capitalism's renewal and more like one in danger of being overwhelmed by its contradictions.

Inside the well-barricaded Convention Center, this contrast was apparent to local television correspondent John Delano, who asked Obama for his response to the thousands of demonstrators who saw the G20 as "something devilish and destructive of the world economy, and particularly the economy of the poor." Obama cast the protestors as unreasonable and unrealistic.

"You know," he replied, "I think many of these protestors are just directed generically at capitalism. And they object to the existing free market system." If "they're actually interested in knowing what was taking place," which he suspected they were not, then they could read the summit's communiqué and discover that leaders were developing an economy that ensures that "growth is bottom up."[13]

It is not surprising that the president of the United States would make such a statement. But even so, we should consider the work that it does. In 2009 the world economy teetered on the precipice of a global depression brought on by callous speculation. Even despite the financial crisis, the Pittsburgh region is a place where the devastation of capitalism is abundantly apparent. In spite of the significance of this moment and this place, Obama foreclosed the possibility of alternatives to capitalism. In the face of much evidence to the contrary, he argued that it was protestors who were unreasonable. Using Pittsburgh as an example, just as the ACCD's leaders had done seventy years earlier and have done so repeatedly ever since, Obama did the heavy discursive labor of proclaiming capitalism's inevitability.

Creating this sense of inevitability was an important part of Pittsburgh's remaking during the Cold War. Pittsburgh was not exceptional in this role, but there is little doubt that it has made a formable contribution to a globally comprehensible narrative about capitalism's potential for creative renewal through science and technology. This book has explored how during the Cold War, the region's elite—its corporate executives, university administrators, political leaders, and regional boosters—transformed Pittsburgh into an internationally recognizable allegory for urban renaissance. Beginning in the 1940s, this coalition led a campaign of urban renewal, environmental reform, and economic diversification. While large corporations always dominated Pittsburgh (as they still do), the regional elite cast scientists and engineers in the starring role of the Renaissance. As local leaders often explained, if they succeeded in attracting these ideal metropolitan citizens, they would develop the new technologies that would ensure the region's, as well as the nation's and the world's, renewal. To attract these citizens, Pittsburgh's elite built the cultural and educational facilities, parks, laboratories, highways, office complexes, and suburbs that would transform the city from a place for making things into a postindustrial economy. Through this remaking, they renewed Pittsburgh into not only a center of technoscience but also a technology itself, a globally deployable symbol of capitalism's renewal.

The Cold War invigorated a long-standing class alliance between scientists and engineers, industrialists, financiers, and the federal government. For more than a century, this alliance has offered science and technology, and scientists and engineers, as the solutions to both the region's and the world's problems. If Pittsburgh is to prosper, it must create laboratories, suburbs, and, increasingly, dynamic urban neighborhoods where scientists and engineers are cloistered from the messy problems they hope to solve. These spaces protect and reproduce the position and privileges of scientists and engineers and in doing so grant them the power to carry out their work. These bubbles are intrinsic to technoscience and its networks.

Far from being isolated from the region and the world's problems, these bubbles are founded in violence and exclusion. Now, as in the past, they are maintained by violence against poor, working-class, and Black Pittsburghers; against women whose work is invisible but essential to their reproduction; against people from Vietnam to Yemen who find themselves on the wrong side of U.S. military interventions; and against those who fight to create a different world. Fittingly, it is the same daily violence that sustains Pittsburgh's status as a symbol of capitalist rebirth.

Acknowledgments

Like a lot of academics, I find that my social and intellectual worlds are blurred. Some of the people mentioned here engaged with this book and have shaped it for the better in numerous ways. Others have no idea what this book is about but have nonetheless made meaningful contributions to my life.

My thanks to the staff at the University of Minnesota Press for their care producing this book, especially Pieter Martin and Anne Carter, as well as Sheila McMahon.

I am grateful to the many librarians and archivists who made this work possible, including David Grinnell and Mark Scott at the University of Pittsburgh; Mary Jones and former employees Arthur Louderback, Cassie Nespor, and Lauren Zabelsky at the Detre Library & Archives of the Senator John Heinz History Center; and Willis Shirk Jr. at the Pennsylvania State Archives.

My interviewees, former and current employees of Westinghouse, were uniformly kind, generous with their time, and open about their lives. I regret that it took me so long to finish this book and that some of them will never have a chance to read it.

I greatly appreciate urban historians who have welcomed a geographer into their field, including Peter Baldwin, Andrew Busch, Stephanie Frank, Mark Healey, Joseph Heathcott, John McCarthy, Alyssa Riberio, Andrew Simpson, and Allen-Dietrich Ward. I have been learning from Ted Muller since 1999, and I am thankful for his unstinting enthusiasm for my work. I met Tracy Neumann in the Pennsylvania State Archives in Harrisburg. My research during that trip was a bust, but her friendship has been far more valuable than any archival find.

Thank you to Josh Akers (University of Michigan, Dearborn), Max Andrucki (Temple University), Ken Foote and Scott Stephenson (University of Connecticut), Asher Ghertner (Rutgers University), and Sabina Dietrich (University of Pittsburgh) for inviting me to their campuses to share portions of this book.

At New York University, I am deeply indebted to my postdoctoral colleagues in the Draper Program, Lori Cole, Emma Heaney, and Justin Jackson, for being fun and collegial folks to share a workplace with. Thank you as well to Robert Dimit, Joanna Epstein, Robin Nagle, and Nicole Pandolfo for all their support. I also appreciate those outside Draper who took time to open up their communities to me, especially Kafui Attoh, Sophie Gonick, Sam Markwell, Hudson McFann, Karen Miller, Andrew Needham, Rich Nisa, Emma Shaw Crane, and Andrew Urban. Marilyn Young kindly welcomed me to New York, twice, as both a doctoral fellow and a postdoctoral fellow, and is dearly missed. My life in New York would have been much less fun without Toronto transplants Brett Story and Martine August.

In Connecticut, I am appreciative that I work alongside wonderful colleagues in the Department of Political Science, Philosophy, and Geography at Eastern Connecticut State University, including Courtney Broscious, Ana Funes Maderey, Kevin Generous, Nicole Krassas, Katie Mazer, Martín Mendoza-Botehlo, Akihiko Michimi, Matt Rukgaber, Brenda Schiavetti, and Karl Stocker. Thanks as well to colleagues outside the department for creating a collegial place to work, including Nancy Brennan, Denis Canterbury, Caitlin Carenen, Carmen Cid, Jessica Cook, Maeve Doyle, Kristen Epp, Amy Groth, Ania Jaroszyńska-Kirchmann, Stefan Kamola, Mary Kenny, Joan Meznar, Jamel Ostwald, Niti Pandey, Ricardo Pérez, Kim Silcox, and David Stoloff. Many Eastern students are great, but a few have made Eastern an especially rewarding place to teach, including Aschly Abarzua, Rachel Bobadilla, Tess Candler, Abby Demarkey, Shawn Dousis, Phillip Hoeps, Sheran Smith, and Sara Terry. Beyond the university, my thanks go to Sarah Harrigan, Maggie Harrigan-Thorp, Jed Thorp, Mia Karpov, Emily Mitchell-Eaton, Sung Choe, and Kieran Choe for making southern New England a livelier place to live.

This book began in Toronto, and a lot of folks there created a fantastic environment for learning and living. I am thankful to Robert Lewis, Matt Farish, Emily Gilbert, and Jason Hackworth for their generosity, patience, and long engagement with an earlier version of this book. My thanks to Elspeth Brown and Scott Prudham for reading this earlier version and for much encouragement during my time in Toronto. I am also thankful to a slew of other current and formerly Toronto-based people for fostering a wonderful time of my life, most especially Emily Eaton, Lisa Freeman, Paul Jackson, Vanessa Mathews, Kate Parizeau, Roger Picton, Jen Ridgley, Amy Siciliano, Josh Akers, Martine August, Alana Boland, JP Catungal, Dan Cohen, Deb Cowen, Martin Danyluk, Heather Dorries, Jamey Essex, Kanishka Goonwardena, Prasad Khanolkar, Nick Lombardo, Nick McGee, Annie McKenzie, Jaby Mathews, Katie Mazer, Jacob Nerenberg, James Nugent, Shiri Pasternak, Laura Pitkanen, Dustin Raab, Brett Story, and Simon Vickers. My special thanks to Caitlin Henry, who has been a steadfast friend for many years and who now lives too far away.

Thanks to others scattered in places other than New York, Toronto, and Connecticut, including Trevor Barnes, Matt Himley, Paul Kershaw, Jenna Loyd, Aman Luthra, Don Mitchell, Reecia Orzeck, Clayton Rosati, Monique Rosati, Bob Ross, Owen Toews, Joaquín Villanueva, and Katie Wells.

My family in Toronto, Avery Leah, Jack Leah, Jess Leah, Allison McLennan, Alex Mazer, Elliot Mazer, and Attiya Khan, have all contributed a lot to this book, mostly by giving me lots of opportunities to be a kid again. In Prince Edward Island, Anne, Don, and Isaac Mazer have provided a wonderful place to relax, great company, and a seemingly bottomless deep freezer of cookies.

My family has been unconditionally supportive of my academic work for a little less than four decades. My parents, Linda and Steve Vitale, have shared news of this book with anyone who will listen. They have given me the greatest gift that parents can give to their child: I have never once doubted that they are proud of me. My sister, Elaina Vitale, has always been a great friend, and I am excited to enter a new phase of life with her, Matt DiClemente, and Ramona DiClemente.

Frances Mazer-Vitale was born in the last months of this project. Besides being the most effective deadline I have ever had, she has contributed little to this book. I am sure it will be many decades (if ever) before she finds this book interesting. By the time she reads it, I hope that she will be hard at work making a world that is more just than the one this book describes and that we currently live in.

Katie Mazer has been living with me and this project for more than ten years. She has read, commented on, and improved most of this book. She has always remained confident—when I have not been—that this book was worth writing. She has the remarkable ability to spark curiosity and insight at even the most difficult times. The world is an unjust place, but I am very fortunate to live in and struggle to make it better with her.

Notes

Archives and Manuscript Collections

Archives Service Center (UPASC), University of Pittsburgh, Pittsburgh
  Allegheny Conference on Community Development Collection (ACCD)
  Edward Litchfield Papers (ELP)

Avery Library (ALCU), Columbia University, New York
  Max Abramovitz Papers

Carnegie Library of Pittsburgh (CLPGH)

Churchill Borough Municipal Records (CBMR), Churchill, Pennsylvania

Detre Library & Archives (DL&A), Senator John Heinz History Center, Pittsburgh
  Allegheny Conference on Community Development Papers (ACCD)
  George Westinghouse Museum Collection
  Westinghouse Electric Corporation Archives (WECA)

Introduction

1. Robert D. Lewis, ed., *The Manufacturing Suburb: Building Work and Home on the Metropolitan Fringe* (Philadelphia: Temple University Press, 2004); Richard Harris, *Unplanned Suburbs: Toronto's American Tragedy, 1900 to 1950* (Baltimore: Johns Hopkins University Press, 1996); Becky Nicolaides, *My Blue Heaven: Life and Politics in the Working-Class Suburbs of Los Angeles* (Chicago: University of Chicago Press, 2002).

2. Andrew Wiese, *Places of Their Own: African American Suburbanization in the Twentieth Century* (Chicago: University of Chicago Press, 2004); Wendy Cheng, *The Changs Next Door to the Díazes: Remapping Race in Suburban California* (Minneapolis: University of Minnesota Press, 2013); Andrew Friedman, *Covert Capital: Landscapes of Denial and the Making of U.S. Empire in the Suburbs of Northern Virginia* (Berkeley: University of California Press, 2013).

3. John Archer, Paul J. P. Sandul, and Katherine Solomonson, eds., *Making Suburbia: New Histories of Everyday America* (Minneapolis: University of Minnesota Press, 2015).

4. Lily Geismer, *Don't Blame Us: Suburban Liberals and the Transformation of the Democratic Party* (Princeton, N.J.: Princeton University Press, 2014); Layne Karafantis and Stuart W. Leslie, "'Suburban Warriors': The Blue-Collar and Blue-Sky Communities of Southern California's Aerospace Industry," *Journal of Planning History* 18, no. 1 (2019): 3–26.

5. According to Donna Haraway and Bruno Latour, technoscience refers to the broad networks of industries, states, universities, scientists and engineers, nonhuman actants, and many others that converge around the production of scientific knowledge and technology. As Latour broadly defines it, technoscience includes "all the elements tied to the scientific contents no matter how dirty, unexpected, or foreign they seem." Bruno Latour, *Science in Action* (Cambridge, Mass.: Harvard University Press, 1987), 174–75. See also Bruno Latour, *Pandora's Hope: Essays on the Reality of Science Studies* (Cambridge, Mass.: Harvard University Press, 1999), 203–4; and Donna Haraway, *Modest_Witness@Second_Millenium.FemaleMan_Meets_OncoMouse: Feminism and Technoscience* (London: Routledge, 1997), 50, 279.

6. For examples of suburbanites' search for order and control, see Robert Fishman, *Bourgeois Utopias: The Rise and Fall of Suburbia* (New York: Basic Books, 1987); Robert Fogelson, *Bourgeois Nightmares: Suburbia, 1870–1930* (New Haven, Conn.: Yale University Press, 2005); David Freund, *Colored Property: State Policy and White Racial Politics in Suburban America* (Chicago: University of Chicago Press, 2007); Kevin Kruse, *White Flight: Atlanta and the Making of Modern Conservativism* (Princeton, N.J.: Princeton University Press, 2005); Kenneth T. Jackson, *Crabgrass Frontier: The Suburbanization of the United States* (New York: Oxford University Press, 1985); Robert Self, *American Babylon: Race and the Struggle for Postwar Oakland* (Princeton, N.J.: Princeton University Press, 2005); Thomas Sugrue, *The Origins of the Urban Crisis: Race and Inequality in Postwar Detroit* (Princeton, N.J.: Princeton University Press, 1998).

7. For accounts of similar suburban bubbles, see Laura R. Barraclough, *Making the San Fernando Valley: Rural Landscapes, Urban Development, and White Privilege* (Athens: University of Georgia Press, 2011); Jim Duncan and Nancy Duncan, "Deep Suburban Irony: The Perils of Democracy in Westchester County," in *Visions of Suburbia*, ed. Roger Silverstone (New York: Routledge, 1997), 161–79; and Jim Duncan and Nancy Duncan, *Landscapes of Privilege: The Politics of the Aesthetic in an American Suburb* (New York: Routledge, 2004). On displacement, see Rob Nixon, *Slow Violence and the Environmentalism of the Poor* (Cambridge, Mass.: Harvard University Press, 2013).

8. Richard Walker, "The Suburban Solution: Urban Geography and Urban Reform in the Capitalist Development of the United States" (PhD diss., Johns Hopkins University, 1977); Richard Walker, "A Theory of Suburbanization: Capitalism and the Construction of Urban Space in the United States," in *Urbanization and Urban Planning*

in Capitalist Society, ed. Michael Dear and Allen Scott (New York: Methuen, 1981), 383–430; Barry Checkoway, "Large Builders, Federal Housing Programs, and Postwar Suburbanization," *International Journal of Urban and Regional Research* 4, no. 1 (1980): 21–45; David Gordon, "Capitalist Development and the History of American Cities," in *Marxism and the Metropolis,* ed. William K. Tabb and Larry Sawers (Oxford: Oxford University Press, 1984), 21–53; David Harvey, *The Urban Experience* (Baltimore: Johns Hopkins University Press, 1989).

9. Mark Neocleous, "Against Security," *Radical Philosophy* 100 (March/April 2000): 7–15; Elaine Tyler May, "Security Against Democracy: The Legacy of the Cold War at Home," *Journal of American History* 97, no. 4 (2011): 939–57.

10. David Harvey, *The Limits to Capital,* 2nd ed. (London: Verso, 2006).

11. Vannevar Bush's 1945 report "Science: The Endless Frontier" is a landmark example of the faith that scientific innovation would lead to endless progress during the postwar period. Bush wrote: "Advances in science when put to practical use mean more jobs, higher wages, shorter hours, more abundant crops, more leisure for recreation, for study, for learning how to live without the deadening drudgery, which has been the burden for common man for ages past. Advances in science will also bring higher standards of living, will lead to the prevention or cure of disease, and will assure means of defense against aggression." Vannevar Bush, "Science: The Endless Frontier," *Transactions of the Kansas Academy of Science* 48, no. 3 (1945): 232. For an even greater level of faith in postwar science, see William H. Whyte, *The Organization Man* (New York: Simon & Schuster, 1956), 7, 22–33.

12. Robert A. Beauregard, *When America Became Suburban* (Minneapolis: University of Minnesota Press, 2006); Nancy Kwak, *A World of Homeowners: American Power and the Politics of Housing Aid* (Chicago: University of Chicago Press, 2015).

13. Paul Ceruzzi, *Internet Alley: High Technology in Tysons Corner* (Cambridge, Mass.: MIT Press, 2008); Alex Sayf Cummings, *Brain Magnet: Research Triangle Park and the Idea of the Idea Economy* (New York: Columbia University Press, 2020); Joseph Heathcott and Maire Agnes Murphy, "Corridors of Flight, Zones of Renewal: Industry, Planning, and Policy in the Making of Metropolitan St. Louis, 1940–1980," *Journal of Urban History* 31, no. 2 (2005): 151–89; David Kaiser, "The Postwar Suburbanization of American Physics," *American Quarterly* 56, no. 4 (2004): 851–88; Karafantis and Leslie, "'Suburban Warriors'"; Scott G. Knowles and Stuart W. Leslie, "'Industrial Versailles': Eero Saarinen's Corporate Campuses for GM, IBM, and AT&T," *Isis* 92, no. 1 (March 2001): 1–33; Stuart W. Leslie, *The Cold War and American Science: The Military-Industrial-Academic Complex at MIT and Stanford* (New York: Columbia University Press, 1993); Reinhold Martin, *The Organizational Complex: Architecture, Media, and Corporate Space* (Cambridge, Mass.: MIT Press, 2003); Louise Mozingo, *Pastoral Capitalism: A History of Suburban Corporate Landscapes* (Cambridge, Mass.: MIT Press, 2011); Margaret Pugh O'Mara, *Cities of Knowledge: Cold War Science and the Search for the Next Silicon Valley* (Princeton, N.J.: Princeton University Press, 2005); William J. Rankin, "The Epistemology of the Suburbs: Knowledge, Production, and Corporate Laboratory Design," *Critical Inquiry* 36, no. 4 (2010): 771–806.

14. Elaine Tyler May, *Homeward Bound: American Families in the Cold War Era* (New York: Basic Books, 1989).

15. Feminist geographers have broadly challenged notions that the home is a space of refuge. See Katherine Brickell, "'Mapping' and 'Doing' Critical Geographies of Home," *Progress in Human Geography* 36, no. 2 (2012): 225–44; Alison Blunt and Robyn Dowling, *Home* (Abingdon: Routledge, 2006); and Linda McDowell, *Gender, Identity, and Place: Understanding Feminist Geographies* (Minneapolis: University of Minnesota Press, 1999), 71–95.

16. Ruth Wilson Gilmore, "Globalization and US Prison Growth: From Military Keynesianism to Post-Keynesian Militarism," *Race and Class* 40, nos. 2/3 (September 1998): 171–88; Ruth Wilson Gilmore, "Fatal Couplings of Power and Difference: Notes on Racism and Geography," *Professional Geographer* 54, no. 1 (2002): 15–24; Ruth Wilson Gilmore, *Golden Gulag: Prisons, Surplus, Crisis, and Opposition in Globalizing California* (Berkeley: University of California Press, 2007); Ira Katznelson, *When Affirmative Action Was White* (New York: W. W. Norton, 2005); Jenna M. Loyd, *Health Rights Are Civil Rights: Peace and Justice Activism in Los Angeles, 1963–1978* (Minneapolis: University of Minnesota Press, 2014); Laura Pulido, "Flint, Environmental Racism, and Racial Capitalism," *Capitalism Nature Socialism* 27, no. 3 (July 2, 2016): 1–16.

17. Catherine Lutz, "Making War at Home in the United States: Militarization and the Current Crisis," *American Anthropologist* 104, no. 3 (2002): 725.

18. Seymour Melman, *Pentagon Capitalism: The Political Economy of War* (New York: McGraw-Hill, 1970); Seymour Melman, *The Permanent War Economy: American Capitalism in Decline* (New York: Simon & Schuster, 1974).

19. Deborah Cowen, *Military Workfare: The Soldier and Social Citizenship in Canada* (Toronto: University of Toronto Press, 2008); Deborah Cowen and Emily Gilbert, "Citizenship in the 'Homeland,'" in *War, Citizenship, Territory*, ed. Deborah Cowen and Emily Gilbert (Toronto: University of Toronto Press, 2008), 261–79; Mary L. Dudziak, *War Time: An Idea, Its History, Its Consequences* (New York: Oxford University Press, 2012); Michel Foucault, *"Society Must Be Defended": Lectures at the College de France, 1975–1976*, trans. D Macey (New York: Picador, 2003); Stephen Graham, *Cities under Siege: The New Military Urbanism* (London: Verso, 2010); Derek Gregory, "War and Peace," *Transactions of the Institute of British Geographers* 35, no. 2 (2010): 154–86; Scott Kirsch and Colin Flint, "Introduction: Reconstruction and the Worlds That War Makes," in *Reconstructing Conflict: Integrating War and Post-War Geographies*, ed. Scott Kirsch and Colin Flint (Surrey, England: Ashgate, 2011), 3–28; Jenna M. Loyd, "'Peace Is Our Only Shelter': Questioning Domesticities of Militarism and White Privilege," *Antipode* 43, no. 3 (2011): 845–73; Lutz, "Making War at Home in the United States"; Erica Schoenberger, "The Origins of the Market Economy: State Power, Territorial Control, and Modes of War Fighting," *Comparative Studies in Society and History* 50, no. 3 (2008): 663–91; Charles Tilly, "War Making and State Making as Organized Crime," in *Bringing the State Back In*, ed. Peter B. Evans, Dietrich Rueschemeyer, and Theda Skocpol (Cambridge: Cambridge University Press, 1985); Marilyn Blatt Young, "'I Was Thinking, as I Often Do These Days, of War': The United States

in the Twenty-First Century," *Diplomatic History* 36, no. 1 (2012): 1–15; Rachel Woodward, "From Military Geographies to Militarism's Geographies: Disciplinary Engagements with the Geographies of Militarism and Military Activities," *Progress in Human Geography* 29, no. 6 (2005): 719–40.

20. Mark Neocleous, "War as Peace, Peace as Pacification," *Radical Philosophy* 159 (January/February 2010): 8–17.

21. There is a vast literature on alliances of local elites, which political scientists, geographers, and sociologists have variously named urban growth machines, urban regimes, growth coalitions, and regional alliances. This research shares an understanding that locally based actors form cooperative coalitions in order to advance the prosperity of a region. While much of this work emphasizes the importance of locally fixed property investments as the genesis of these coalitions, the members of Pittsburgh's elite alliance, the ACCD, were not property developers but corporate executives, financiers, and leaders of the region's universities and foundations (see part I for more details about the ACCD and its membership). Their primary motivation was not rent seeking but to renew Pittsburgh as a business center. Scientists and engineers were not included in the ACCD unless they led local corporations or universities, but the ACCD nonetheless enrolled scientists and engineers as allies in its remaking of the region (see chapter 2). For more on regional alliances, see Kevin Cox and Andrew Mair, "Urban Growth Machines and the Politics of Local Economic Development," *International Journal of Urban and Regional Research* 13, no. 1 (1989): 137–46; David Harvey, "The Geopolitics of Capitalism," in *Social Relations and Spatial Structures,* ed. Derek Gregory and John Urry (London: Macmillan, 1985), 128–63; David Harvey, *The Urbanization of Capital: Studies in the History and Theory of Capitalist Urbanization* (Baltimore: Johns Hopkins University Press, 1985); Andrew E. G. Jonas and David Wilson, eds., *The Urban Growth Machine: Critical Perspectives, Two Decades Later* (Albany: State University of New York Press, 1999); Harvey Molotch, "The City as a Growth Machine: Toward a Political Economy of Place," *American Journal of Sociology* 82, no. 2 (September 1976): 309–32; John Mollenkopf, "The Post-War Politics of Urban Development," *Politics & Society* 5, no. 3 (January 1, 1975): 247–95.

22. The Pittsburgh Renaissance refers to the efforts of a regional alliance of local business, nonprofit, and political leaders to remake the region from a center of industry to one of finance, education, medicine, and corporate administration. Typically historians associate the Renaissance with urban renewal and flood and smoke control. This book adds making spaces for science and technology, and scientists and engineers as central components of Pittsburgh's first and subsequent Renaissances. On the Renaissance, see David Houston, "A Brief History of the Process of Capital Accumulation in Pittsburgh: A Marxist Interpretation," in *Pittsburgh-Sheffield Sister Cities,* Praxis/Poetics 3, ed. Joel Tarr (Pittsburgh: Carnegie Mellon University, 1986), 29–70; Roy Lubove, *Twentieth-Century Pittsburgh,* vol. 1, *Government, Business, and Environmental Change* (Pittsburgh: University of Pittsburgh Press, 1969); Sherie Mershon, "Corporate Social Responsibility and Urban Revitalization: The Allegheny Conference on Community Development, 1943–1968" (PhD diss., Carnegie Mellon University, 2000);

Shelby Stewman and Joel A. Tarr, "Public-Private Partnerships in Pittsburgh: An Approach to Governance," in *Pittsburgh-Sheffield Sister Cities,* Praxis/Poetics 3, ed. Joel A. Tarr (Pittsburgh: Carnegie Mellon University, 1986), 141–82; Andrew Simpson, *The Medical Metropolis: Health Care and Economic Transformation in Pittsburgh and Houston* (Philadelphia: University of Pennsylvania Press, 2019); Joel A. Tarr, ed., *Devastation and Renewal: An Environmental History of Pittsburgh and Its Region* (Pittsburgh: University of Pittsburgh Press, 2003); John Teaford, *The Rough Road to Renaissance: Urban Revitalization in America, 1940–1985* (Baltimore: Johns Hopkins University Press, 1990); Michael P. Webber, *Don't Call Me Boss: David L. Lawrence, Pittsburgh's Renaissance Mayor* (Pittsburgh: University of Pittsburgh Press, 1988). Journalists who visited Pittsburgh at the time best captured the ethos of the Renaissance. Two fine examples are Alfred Steinberg, "Pittsburgh, a New City," *National Municipal Review* 44, no. 3 (1955): 126–31; and "Pittsburgh's New Powers," *Fortune* 35 (February 1947): 69–77, 182–87.

23. Latour, *Science in Action,* 90.

24. Latour, 29; Sergio Sismondo, *An Introduction to Science and Technology Studies,* 2nd ed. (Malden, Mass.: Wiley-Blackwell, 2010), 11.

25. Latour, *Pandora's Hope,* 58.

26. Latour, *Science in Action,* 252.

27. Haraway, *Modest_Witness,* 23–29. See also Nina E. Lerman, "Categories of Difference, Categories of Power," *Technology and Culture* 51, no. 4 (2010): 893–918; Erika Lorraine Milam and Robert A. Nye, "An Introduction to Scientific Masculinities," *Osiris* 30, no. 1 (2015): 1–14; and Kara W. Swanson, "Rubbing Elbows and Blowing Smoke: Gender, Class, and Science in the Nineteenth-Century Patent Office," *Isis* 108, no. 1 (2017): 40–61.

28. Haraway, *Modest_Witness,* 35–37.

29. Donna Haraway, *Simians, Cyborgs, and Women: The Reinvention of Nature* (New York: Routledge, 1991), 188.

30. Silvia Federici, *Caliban and the Witch: Women, the Body and Primitive Accumulation* (Brooklyn, N.Y.: Autonomedia, 2004); Silvia Federici, *Revolution at Point Zero: Housework, Reproduction, and Feminist Struggle* (Oakland, Calif.: PM Press, 2012); Katharyne Mitchell, Sallie A. Marston, and Cindi Katz, eds., *Life's Work: Geographies of Social Reproduction* (Malden, Mass.: Wiley-Blackwell, 2004); Katie Meehan and Kendra Strauss, eds., *Precarious Worlds: Contested Geographies of Social Reproduction* (Athens: University of Georgia Press, 2015); Jamie Winders and Barbara Ellen Smith, "Social Reproduction and Capitalist Production: A Genealogy of Dominant Imaginaries," *Progress in Human Geography* 43, no. 5 (2019): 871–89.

31. Trevor J. Pinch, "The Social Construction of Facts and Artifacts: Or How the Sociology of Science and the Sociology of Technology Might Benefit Each Other," in *The Social Construction of Technological Systems: New Directions in the Sociology and History of Technology,* ed. Wiebe E. Bjiker, Thomas P. Hughes, and Trevor J. Pinch (Cambridge, Mass.: MIT Press, 1987), 17–50; Michel Callon, "Society in the Making: The Study of Technology as a Tool for Sociological Analysis," in *The Social Construction*

of Technological Systems: New Directions in the Sociology and History of Technology, ed. Wiebe E. Bjiker, Thomas P. Hughes, and Trevor J. Pinch (Cambridge, Mass.: MIT Press, 1987), 83–103.

32. In 1960 *Nuclear News,* the magazine of the American Nuclear Society, surveyed its members on what profession they identified with; of the 90 percent of ANS members who responded, 20 percent identified as nuclear scientists, 38 percent as nuclear engineers, and 42 percent as a specific type of scientist or engineer, such as a physicist or mechanical engineer. "ANS Member Analysis," *Nuclear News,* February 1960.

33. Scott Kirsch, "Peaceful Nuclear Explosions and the Geography of Scientific Authority," *Professional Geographer* 52, no. 2 (2000): 179–92; David Livingstone, "The Spaces of Knowledge: Contributions towards a Historical Geography of Science," *Environment and Planning D: Society and Space* 13, no. 1 (1995): 5–34; David Livingstone, *Putting Science in Its Place: Geographies of Scientific Knowledge* (Chicago: University of Chicago Press, 2003); Simon Naylor, "Introduction: Historical Geographies of Science—Places, Contexts, Cartographies," *British Journal for the History of Science* 38, no. 1 (2005): 1–12; Richard C. Powell, "Geographies of Science: Histories, Localities, Practices, Futures," *Progress in Human Geography* 31, no. 3 (2007): 309–29; Steven Shapin, "Placing the View from Nowhere: Historical and Sociological Problems in the Location of Science," *Transactions of the Institute of British Geographers* 23, no. 1 (1998): 5–12.

34. Lubove, *Twentieth-Century Pittsburgh,* 106.

1. Going Critical

1. Fred Remington, "Atom-Lit City Was Thrilling in National Telecast," *Pittsburgh Press,* February 11, 1958, 41.

2. See, for example, Stephen M. Spencer, "Atomic Power for American Homes," *Saturday Evening Post,* February 8, 1958; "Atoms for Peace," *New York Times,* December 20, 1957, 26; "Power Flows from First Big U.S. Atomic Plant in Shippingport, Pa.," *Wall Street Journal,* December 19, 1957, 24.

3. John Krige, "The Peaceful Atom as Political Weapon: Euratom and American Foreign Policy in the Late 1950s," *Historical Studies in the Natural Sciences* 38, no. 1 (2008): 5–44; John Krige, *American Hegemony and the Postwar Reconstruction of Science in Europe* (Cambridge, Mass.: MIT Press, 2006).

4. Isadore Shrensky, "Atom Power Plant Becoming 'University,'" *Pittsburgh Press,* January 18, 1959.

5. "Shippingport Atomic Power Dedication Issue," *Westinghouse News,* May 1958.

6. Albert W. Bloom, "Ceremonies Dedicate Shippingport A-Plant," *Pittsburgh Post-Gazette,* May 27, 1958, 1, 5.

7. Spencer, "Atomic Power for American Homes."

8. Philip Fleger, "The Shippingport Atomic Power Plant," *Electrical Engineering* 74, no. 10 (October 1955): 892–94.

9. Matthew Farish, *The Contours of America's Cold War* (Minneapolis: University of Minnesota Press, 2010), xvii, xii.

10. Krige, "The Peaceful Atom as Political Weapon."

11. Westinghouse, "Nuclear Market Acceptance and Comparative Experience," January 1, 1984, WECA, DL&A.

12. On the development of submarine-based ballistic missiles, see Donald MacKenzie, *Inventing Accuracy: A Historical Sociology of Nuclear Missile Guidance* (Cambridge, Mass.: MIT Press, 1993). On the strategic value of naval nuclear propulsion, see Richard G. Hewlett and Francis Duncan, *Nuclear Navy: 1946–1962* (Chicago: University of Chicago Press, 1974). For an account of Westinghouse's role in the development of the nuclear navy, see John Simpson, *Nuclear Power from Underseas to Outer Space* (LaGrange Park, Ill.: American Nuclear Society, 1995).

13. "The Enterprise Begins Rest Tour," *New York Times*, January 16, 1966, 4.

14. David Vine, *Island of Shame: The Secret History of the U.S. Military Base on Diego Garcia* (Princeton, N.J.: Princeton University Press, 2009).

15. John DiMoia, "Atoms for Sale? Cold War Institution-Building and the South Korean Atomic Energy Project, 1945–1965," *Technology and Culture* 51, no. 3 (2010): 589–618; Gabrielle Hecht, "Negotiation Global Nuclearities: Apartheid, Decolonization, and the Cold War in the Making of the IAEA," *Osiris* 21, no. 1 (2006): 25–48; John Krige, "Atoms for Peace, Scientific Internationalism, and Scientific Intelligence," *Osiris* 21, no. 1 (2006): 161–81; John Krige, "The Politics of Phosphorus-32: A Fable Based on Fact," *Studies in the Physical and Biological Sciences* 36, no. 1 (2005): 71–91.

16. Krige, "The Peaceful Atom as Political Weapon," 8; Krige, *American Hegemony.*

17. Kanishka Goonewardena and Stefan Kipfer, "Postcolonial Urbicide: New Imperialism, Global Cities and the Damned of the Earth," *New Formations* 59 (Autumn 2006): 25.

18. Edward Said, *Culture and Imperialism* (New York: Vintage Books, 1994), 10.

19. Christina Klein, *Cold War Orientalism: Asia in the Middlebrow Imagination, 1945–1961* (Berkeley: University of California Press, 2003), 7.

20. Inez Robb, "Pioneer Venture," *Pittsburgh Press,* May 10, 1954, 10.

21. "144 Communities Use Atom Power," *Pittsburgh Post-Gazette,* May 27, 1958; "City Starts Getting Power from Atom," *Pittsburgh Post-Gazette,* December 19, 1957, 1, 6.

22. William J. Gill, "Pittsburgh, Pattern for Progress," photographs by Clyde Hare, *National Geographic* 127, no. 3 (March 1965): 364.

23. Rose Demorest, "Pittsburgh a Bicentennial Tribute," Carnegie Library of Pittsburgh, 1958, ACCD, UPASC.

24. "Age of Atom . . . Westinghouse to Shippingport," *Pittsburgh Press,* January 18, 1959.

25. Al Knight, "Surge in Research," July 1959, 1–5, ACCD, UPASC. It is not clear what publication this article appeared in.

26. Ketchum Incorporated, "The New Pittsburgh, the Most Talked about City in America," Pittsburgh Chamber of Commerce, 1954, ACCD, UPASC.

27. Albert W. Bloom, "Shippingport: Key to Knowledge, 'Flameless Fire' May Rival Man's Discovery of Fire," *Pittsburgh Post-Gazette,* May 27, 1958, 15; "A-Plant Effect: Neither Fears Nor Hopes Realized in Tiny Pa. Town," *Washington Post,* August 24, 1972; Leo Marx, *The Machine in the Garden: Technology and the Pastoral Ideal in America* (New York: Oxford University Press, 1964).

28. Spencer, "Atomic Power for American Homes."

29. Fleger, "The Shippingport Atomic Power Plant."

30. Gabrielle Hecht, "Nuclear Ontologies," *Constellations* 13, no. 3 (2006): 322. See also Gabrielle Hecht, "The Power of Nuclear Things," *Technology and Culture* 51, no. 1 (2010): 1–30.

31. Mel Seidenberg, "Open Vast Avenues of Progress: Research Makes Area Dynamic Center on Industry," *Pittsburgh Post-Gazette*, May 17, 1958, 8.

32. "City A-Power 'Capital,'" *Pittsburgh Sun-Telegraph*, February 9, 1956, 2.

33. "City A-Power 'Capital'"; "City Called Free World 'A' Capital," *Pittsburgh Post-Gazette*, February 9, 1956; "City Proclaimed World A-Center," *Pittsburgh Press*, February 9, 1956, 2.

34. Westinghouse Bettis Atomic Power Division, "Bettis Plant Tenth Anniversary, 1948–1958," 1958, 25, DL&A.

35. Seidenberg, "Open Vast Avenues of Progress," 8. This estimate, made during the height of Pittsburgh's research mania, is exaggerated. A more accurate estimate is the forty-one major research laboratories that Ira Lowry counted in 1963. Ira S. Lowry, *Portrait of a Region*, vol. 2 of *The Economic Study of the Pittsburgh Region* (Pittsburgh: University of Pittsburgh Press, 1963), 96.

36. Seidenberg, "Open Vast Avenues of Progress," 8.

37. Gabrielle Hecht, *Being Nuclear: Africans and the Global Uranium Trade* (Cambridge, Mass.: MIT Press, 2012).

38. There is a long history of illustrious people looking down on Pittsburgh from Mount Washington. In its early years, the view of the smoky city was celebrated for the prosperity it represented. Later it was recognized as a vantage of industrial capitalism run amuck. By 1958 the view represented how local leaders had banded together in order to reform industrial capitalism. While earlier views showed steel mills that maimed and polluted, in 1958 nuclear power lit a city supposedly freed from the smoke, chaos, and crises of industrial capitalism. On earlier vantages from Mount Washington, see Barbara L. Jones, *Born of Fire: The Valley of Work; Industrial Scenes of Southwestern Pennsylvania* (Greensburg, Pa.: Westmoreland Museum of Art, 2006); David E. Nye, *American Technological Sublime* (Cambridge, Mass.: MIT Press, 1994); Edward Steven Slavishak, *Bodies of Work: Civic Display and Labor in Industrial Pittsburgh* (Durham, N.C.: Duke University Press, 2008); and Cecelia Tichi, "Pittsburgh at Yellowstone: Old Faithful and the Pulse of Industrial America," *American Literary History* 9, no. 3 (1997): 522–41.

39. "Pittsburgh's New Powers," *Fortune* 35 (February 1947): 69, 71, 73; "San Diego: A Big Market (550,000) Near 4,000,000 Others," *Fortune* 35 (February 1947): 187.

40. "Pittsburgh's New Powers," 77, 182.

41. "Pittsburgh's New Powers," 76.

42. Between 1946 and 1959, the executive committee of the ACCD included five representatives of universities, foundations, or scientific institutions and thirty-two representatives of the private sector. Of those private sector executives, fifteen came from industrial firms, three from the resource sector, three from department stores,

three from the utility or transport sector, and one each from real estate development and law. Six members of the committee were from banks or insurance companies, but four of these represented Mellon Bank, which had a controlling interest in many of Pittsburgh's industrial firms. In 1965 Arnold Auerbach cataloged the social characteristics of the ACCD's executive committee. Reflecting the dominance of the Scotch-Irish in Pittsburgh, thirteen of twenty-five members were Presbyterian, four Episcopalian, two Catholic, one Methodist, and one Jewish. Eight had degrees from Princeton, six from Yale, five from Harvard, and two each from the University of Pittsburgh, Penn, and MIT. Twenty-four of the twenty-five were members of the exclusive Duquesne Club; Edgar Kaufman, the only Jew on the executive committee, was not. Arnold J. Auerbach, "Power and Progress in Pittsburgh," *Society* 2, no. 6 (1965): 15–20; Sherie Mershon, "Corporate Social Responsibility and Urban Revitalization: The Allegheny Conference on Community Development, 1943–1968" (PhD diss., Carnegie Mellon University, 2000). On regional alliances, see John Mollenkopf, "The Post-War Politics of Urban Development," *Politics & Society* 5, no. 3 (January 1, 1975): 247–95; Harvey Molotch, "The City as a Growth Machine: Toward a Political Economy of Place," *American Journal of Sociology* 82, no. 2 (September 1976): 309–32; David Harvey, "The Geopolitics of Capitalism," in *Social Relations and Spatial Structures,* ed. Derek Gregory and John Urry (London: Macmillan, 1985), 128–63; and John R. Logan and Harvey Molotch, *Urban Fortunes: The Political Economy of Place,* 2nd ed. (Berkeley: University of California Press, 2007).

43. Mershon, "Corporate Social Responsibility and Urban Revitalization," 3.

44. Joel A. Tarr, ed., *Devastation and Renewal: An Environmental History of Pittsburgh and Its Region* (Pittsburgh: University of Pittsburgh Press, 2003).

45. Roy Lubove, *Twentieth-Century Pittsburgh,* vol. 1, *Government, Business, and Environmental Change* (Pittsburgh: University of Pittsburgh Press, 1969); John Teaford, *The Rough Road to Renaissance: Urban Revitalization in America, 1940–1985* (Baltimore: Johns Hopkins University Press, 1990); Mershon, "Corporate Social Responsibility and Urban Revitalization."

46. "Pittsburgh's New Powers," 187.

47. Leaders from around the world did not just observe Pittsburgh's remaking from afar. By 1955 delegations from thirty-nine American cities, as well as European and South American cities, had visited Pittsburgh to "find inspiration and practical means to reclaim their own dying cities." Alfred Steinberg, "Pittsburgh, a New City," *National Municipal Review* 44, no. 3 (1955): 126; Tracy Neumann, *Remaking the Rust Belt: The Postindustrial Transformation of North America* (Philadelphia: University of Pennsylvania Press, 2016).

48. Arthur B. Van Buskirk, "What Business Has Learned about Rebuilding a City," in *The Little Economies: Problems of U.S. Area Development* (New York: Committee for Economic Development, 1958), 30.

49. Arthur B. Van Buskirk, "Opening Remarks," September 18, 1951, ACCD, DL&A.

50. P. I. Prentice, "An Outsider Looks at Pittsburgh," September 18, 1951, 18, ACCD, DL&A.

51. Austin Pardue, "An Insider Looks at Pittsburgh," September 18, 1951, 18, ACCD, DL&A.

52. Pardue, "An Insider Looks at Pittsburgh," 25–28.

53. Shelby Stewman and Joel A. Tarr, "Public-Private Partnerships in Pittsburgh: An Approach to Governance," in *Pittsburgh-Sheffield Sister Cities*, Praxis/Poetics 3, ed. Joel A. Tarr (Pittsburgh: Carnegie Mellon University, 1986), 146.

54. Van Buskirk, "What Business Has Learned about Rebuilding a City," 25–26.

55. Van Buskirk, 27–29.

56. Van Buskirk, 29.

57. Mindy Thomson Fullilove, *Root Shock: How Tearing Up City Neighborhoods Hurts America, and What We Can Do about It* (New York: One World Books, 2005), 29.

58. Steinberg, "Pittsburgh, a New City," 131.

59. Lubove, *Twentieth-Century Pittsburgh*, 1:131.

60. Van Buskirk, "What Business Has Learned about Rebuilding a City," 29.

61. Samuel Zipp, *Manhattan Projects: The Rise and Fall of Urban Renewal in Cold War New York* (Oxford: Oxford University Press, 2010), 5, 161.

62. Van Buskirk, "What Business Has Learned about Rebuilding a City," 29.

63. Van Buskirk, 30.

64. Lowry, *Portrait of a Region*, 95–100.

65. Louise Mozingo, *Pastoral Capitalism: A History of Suburban Corporate Landscapes* (Cambridge, Mass.: MIT Press, 2011); William J. Rankin, "The Epistemology of the Suburbs: Knowledge, Production, and Corporate Laboratory Design," *Critical Inquiry* 36, no. 4 (2010): 771–806.

66. For the period between 1940 and 1970, I categorized professional, managerial, sales, and clerical workers as white-collar workers and craftsmen, operatives, and laborers as blue collar. For the period between 1980 and 1990, I categorized managerial and technical as white collar and precision and operators as blue collar. In both time periods, I classified all other occupations besides service as other.

67. Figures 1 and 2 are derived from the U.S. Censuses, 1940–90, as noted in Tables 1 and 2.

68. These figures do not include professors at local universities or medical researchers. Between 1950 and 1970, the number of college teachers grew by 266.3 percent.

69. This is an admittedly flawed way of accounting for the growth of suburbanization, as many of the communities outside the city were aging industrial centers that were not suburban in character. For a much more detailed evaluation, see Kent James, "Public Policy and the Postwar Suburbanization of Pittsburgh, 1945–1990" (PhD diss., Carnegie Mellon University, 2005).

70. James, "Public Policy," 179.

2. Research and Renaissance

1. PBPE, *Pittsburgh Is a Good Place to Live* (Pittsburgh: PBPE, 1955), 17, 41, 59.

2. Josie Carey and Marty Wolfson, *This Is Pittsburgh and Southwestern Pennsylvania: We Live Here . . . We Like It!* (Pittsburgh: RIDC, 1963), 2, 3, ACCD, DL&A.

3. I am borrowing the term *enrollment* from STS, which uses it to describe how scientists and engineers create alliances with human and nonhuman entities in order to produce facts and machines. However, unlike STS, I am interested in exploring how the figure of the scientist is created not only through scientific work but also through the wider networks that valorize scientists as figures uniquely suited to the needs of progress and growth at the urban, national, and global scales. Bruno Latour, *Science in Action* (Cambridge, Mass.: Harvard University Press, 1987); Bruno Latour, *Pandora's Hope: Essays on the Reality of Science Studies* (Cambridge, Mass.: Harvard University Press, 1999).

4. Frank Giarratani and David Houston, "Structural Change and Economic Policy in a Declining Metropolitan Region: Implications of the Pittsburgh Experience," *Urban Studies* 26, no. 6 (1989): 549–58; Mariel P. Isaacson, "Pittsburgh's Response to Deindustrialization: Renaissance, Renewal, and Recovery" (PhD diss., City University of New York, 2014).

5. Econometric Institute, "The Long-Range Outlook for the Pittsburgh Industrial Area," 1946, ACCD, DL&A.

6. Patrick Vitale, "Anti-Communism, the Growth Machine and the Remaking of Cold-War-Era Pittsburgh," *International Journal of Urban and Regional Research* 39, no. 4 (2015): 772–87.

7. ACCD, "Challenge and Response," 1947, DL&A.

8. Joy Bilharz, *The Allegany Senecas and Kinzua Dam: Forced Relocation through Two Generations* (Lincoln: University of Nebraska Press, 1998).

9. Mindy Thomson Fullilove, *Root Shock: How Tearing up City Neighborhoods Hurts America, and What We Can Do about It* (New York: One World Books, 2005); Joe William Trotter and Jared N. Day, *Race and Renaissance: African Americans in Pittsburgh since World War II* (Pittsburgh: University of Pittsburgh Press, 2010).

10. Laura Grantmyre, "'They Lived Their Life and They Didn't Bother Anybody': African American Female Impersonators and Pittsburgh's Hill District, 1920–1960," *American Quarterly* 63, no. 4 (2011): 983–1011.

11. Roy Lubove, *Twentieth-Century Pittsburgh,* vol. 1, *Government, Business, and Environmental Change* (Pittsburgh: University of Pittsburgh Press, 1969), 136, 115.

12. Pennsylvania Economy League Inc., "A More Effective Industrial Development Program for the Pittsburgh Region," 1954, 46, ACCD, UPASC.

13. Pittsburgh Regional Planning Association (PRPA), *Region in Transition,* vol. 1 of *The Economic Study of the Pittsburgh Region* (Pittsburgh: University of Pittsburgh Press, 1963), 415–16.

14. PRPA, 416.

15. Fullilove, *Root Shock,* 29.

16. Pittsburgh Urban Redevelopment Authority (PURA), "An All Purpose Civic Auditorium for the New Pittsburgh and Allegheny County," n.d., ACCD, DL&A.

17. ACCD, "The Lower Hill Center . . . a Perspective," n.d., ACCD, DL&A.

18. PURA, "Lower Hill Redevelopment Project: Residential and Commercial Sites Available for Redevelopment," n.d., ACCD, DL&A.

19. PURA, "An All Purpose Civic Auditorium."

20. Leland Hazard, "Presentation of the Study on the Lower Hill Cultural Center and Housing Development," February 26, 1953, ACCD, DL&A.

21. Robert Pease, "The Problem of Relocation," *Real Estate,* July 1963.

22. Fullilove, *Root Shock.*

23. Between 1950 and 1960, there was a 40 percent increase in white-collar jobs in the Pittsburgh region. In 1960 13 percent of African Americans and 37 percent of white people were employed in such positions. In 1960 0.2 percent of the region's engineers and 0.7 percent of its natural scientists were African American. Between 1950 and 1960, the number of African American engineers in the region shrunk from 42 to 31, while the total number of engineers increased from 11,695 to 14,574. Residential segregation also increased. In the 1940s, the dissimilarity index for African Americans was 64.3, and in the late 1960s, it reached 74.5. In 1950 the mean income of an African American in the Pittsburgh region was 68 percent of the mean income for white residents. In 1980 African American median household income in the region was 57 percent of white households. *1950 United States Census of Population* (Washington, D.C.: Bureau of the Census, 1950); *1960 Census of Population and Housing, Pittsburgh, Pa., Standard Metropolitan Statistical Area,* PHC(1)-118 (Washington, D.C.: Bureau of the Census, 1960); *1980 Census of Population and Housing: Pittsburgh, Pa., Standard Metropolitan Statistical Area,* PHC80-2-286 (Washington, D.C.: Bureau of the Census, 1980); Trotter and Day, *Race and Renaissance,* 53, 213, 214, 68.

24. Jonathan Peyton, "Corporate Ecology: BC Hydro's Stikine-Iskut Project and the Unbuilt Environment," *Journal of Historical Geography* 37, no. 3 (2011): 358–69; Jamie Peck, "Struggling with the Creative Class," *International Journal of Urban and Regional Research* 29, no. 4 (2005): 740–70; Patrick Vitale, "Cradle of the Creative Class: Reinventing the Figure of the Scientist in Cold War Pittsburgh," *Annals of the American Association of Geographers* 106, no. 6 (2016): 1378–96.

25. The wives of scientists, engineers, and corporate executives were important characters in the narrative of Pittsburgh's Renaissance. Corporate leaders often told national media that they were renewing downtown at the request of their wives, who considered it dirty and lacking the cultural and shopping opportunities of other major cities. As Richard King Mellon told the *National Municipal Review,* his concern about Pittsburgh developed when his wife, Constance, told him, "You've got to do something about Pittsburgh or we'll move away." He explained that he "couldn't afford to lose such a wonderful wife . . . so I decided to do something." Alfred Steinberg, "Pittsburgh, a New City," *National Municipal Review* 44 (1955): 128.

26. WEC, "Materials Engineering Departments," 1958, 23, WECA, DL&A.

27. WEC, 18.

28. WEC, 22.

29. WEC, 23.

30. WEC, "Your Future with Westinghouse Research," 1962, 3–4, WECA, DL&A.

31. WEC, 8, 14, 26

32. WEC, 16–26.

33. For examples, see David Kaiser, "Cold War Requisitions, Scientific Manpower, and the Production of American Physicists after World War II," *Historical Studies in the Physical Sciences* 33, no. 1 (2002): 131–59; David Kaiser, "The Postwar Suburbanization of American Physics," *American Quarterly* 56, no. 4 (2004): 851–88; and Layne Karafantis and Stuart W. Leslie, "'Suburban Warriors': The Blue-Collar and Blue-Sky Communities of Southern California's Aerospace Industry," *Journal of Planning History* 18, no. 1 (2019): 3–26.

34. Kaiser, "Postwar Suburbanization," 867.

35. Chemical engineering (American Institute of Chemical Engineers, AIChE) joined the United Engineering Trust in 1958.

36. Mary Ann Hoffman, "The United Engineering Building: A Vision of Andrew Carnegie," *Proceedings of the IEEE* 94, no. 10 (October 2006): 1896–1901.

37. United Engineering Trust, "History and Plans for the Engineering Center Project," September 1957, ACCD, DL&A; Max Page, *The Creative Destruction of Manhattan, 1900–1940* (Chicago: University of Chicago Press, 1999).

38. Pittsburgh Engineering Trust, "Agreement of Trust," 1953, ACCD, DL&A.

39. Price and Monteith to Trustees of Pittsburgh Engineering Trust, February 8, 1954; Price and Monteith to Trustees of Pittsburgh Engineering Trust, August 20, 1954, ACCD, DL&A.

40. Memorandum of Special Meeting called by President Snyder of the ACCD, November 23, 1953, ACCD, DL&A.

41. PURA, "Let's Bring the 'Engineering Center' Building to Pittsburgh," 1953, ACCD, DL&A.

42. ACCD, "The Pittsburgh Story as Presented to the United Engineering Trustees," September 1953, ACCD, DL&A.

43. ACCD, "The Pittsburgh Story."

44. ACCD, "Pittsburgh's Offer for the New Engineering Center Building," 1954, ACCD, DL&A.

45. *Pittsburgh Post-Gazette,* September 7, 1953; "Engineering Center," *Pittsburgh Press,* September 11, 1953; "Pittsburgh Is Logical Center for Engineering Research Center," *Pittsburgh Sun-Telegraph,* September 12, 1953; "Best Place," *Pittsburgh Sun-Telegraph,* September 4, 1953.

46. ACCD, "Pittsburgh's Offer," 12.

47. ACCD, 15, 18; ACCD, "The Logical Location for the New Engineering Center Building Is Pittsburgh," 1954, 11, ACCD, DL&A.

48. ACCD, "Pittsburgh's Offer," 15, 18.

49. Monteith to Trustees of Pittsburgh Engineering Trust, February 10, 1955, ACCD, DL&A.

50. Arthur Van Buskirk to Elgin Robertson, February 15, 1955, ACCD, DL&A.

51. A. C. Monteith to Trustees, February 10, 1955, ACCD, DL&A.

52. R. K. Mellon to A. C. Monteith, March 31, 1955, ACCD, DL&A.

53. Gwilym Price to UET Site Selection Committee, April 6, 1955, and August 5, 1955, ACCD, DL&A.

54. UET, "History and Plans of the Engineering Center Project," September 1957, n.p., ACCD, DL&A; Samuel Zipp, *Manhattan Projects: The Rise and Fall of Urban Renewal in Cold War New York* (Oxford: Oxford University Press, 2010).

55. ACCD, "The Allegheny Conference on Community Development Presents . . . Pittsburgh and Allegheny County, an Era of Progress and Accomplishment," 1956, 33–35, ACCD, UPASC.

56. Francis G. Couvares, *The Remaking of Pittsburgh: Class and Culture in an Industrializing City, 1877–1919* (Albany: State University of New York Press, 1984); Edward K. Muller and John F. Bauman, "The Olmsteds in Pittsburgh: Part II, Shaping the Progressive City," *Pittsburgh History* 76, no. 4 (1994): 191–205; Robert H. Kargon and Scott G. Knowles, "Knowledge for Use: Science, Higher Learning, and America's New Industrial Heartland, 1880–1915," *Annals of Science* 59, no. 1 (2002): 1–20.

57. D. S. Greenberg, "Pittsburgh the Rocky Road to Excellence, Part II," *Science* 151, no. 3711 (February 1966): 658.

58. D. S. Greenberg, "Pittsburgh the Rocky Road to Excellence, Part I," *Science* 151, no. 3710 (February 1966): 552.

59. Greenberg, 549–50.

60. Paul A. Weinstein, "University and Community Activities to Attract Industry: Supplementary Special Report to the Chancellor, University of Pittsburgh," October 1961, ELP, UPASC.

61. Paul A. Weinstein, "Research and Development in the Pittsburgh Region: Special Report to the Chancellor, University of Pittsburgh," October 1961, 3, 9, ELP, UPASC.

62. "Educational-Cultural Center in Pittsburgh," 1961, ELP, UPASC.

63. The population numbers presented here are approximate and are based on the crude map produced by the University of Pittsburgh. *U.S. Censuses of Population and Housing: 1960, Pittsburgh, Pa., Standard Metropolitan Statistical Area,* PHC(1)-118 (Washington, D.C.: Bureau of the Census, 1960).

64. University leaders in Cleveland also likened its University Circle neighborhood to an "island." However, by 1962, as relations soured with the city's African American community, the University Circle Community Foundation began to recommend against the use of word *island* to describe the neighborhood. See J. Mark Souther, "Acropolis of the Middle-West: Decay, Renewal, and Boosterism in Cleveland's University Circle," *Journal of Planning History* 10, no. 1 (2011): 30–58.

65. "Educational-Cultural Center in Pittsburgh."

66. Minutes of meeting with Prudential Insurance Company, January 22, 1962, ELP, UPASC.

67. George E. Barbour, "We Must Have Hill: 'Will Help Relocate Families,' Litchfield Says in Interview," *Pittsburgh Courier,* April 21, 1962.

68. "Upper Hill Will Remain Residential," *Pittsburgh Courier,* April 28, 1962.

69. Edward Litchfield, "Research: The Key to Pittsburgh's Economic Growth," speech to Pennsylvania Economy League, May 14, 1962, ELP, UPASC.

70. Litchfield; Pittsburgh Regional Planning Association, "A Plan for Pittsburgh's Cultural District Oakland," Pittsburgh, 1961.

71. This valley was named Junction Hollow, but Pitt's Public Relations Department determined that the name of Panther Hollow was "more colorful, distinctive, and memorable." University of Pittsburgh Public Relations Department letter, n.d., ELP, UPASC.

72. "Engineers Popping Eyes with Wonders; Panther Hollow Research Park Is One," *Pittsburgh Press,* January 5, 1964.

73. John Harwood and Janet Parks, *The Troubled Search: The Work of Max Abramovitz* (New York: Miriam and Ira D. Wallach Art Gallery, Columbia University, 2004).

74. OakCorp, "This Is an Urban Area," 1963, 25, ELP, UPASC.

75. OakCorp, 9.

76. OakCorp, 16.

77. Burtson-Marsteller Associates, "Pittsburgh Plans Massive Research Center," press release, June 5, 1963, ELP, UPASC.

78. William J. Gill and Clyde Hare, "Pittsburgh, Pattern for Progress," *National Geographic* 127, no. 3 (March 1965): 343–71; "In the Picture," *The Observer,* April 19, 1964, 29; David R. Francis, "Panther Hollow: Pittsburgh Project Clicks," *Christian Science Monitor,* June 11, 1963, 10.

79. "Panther Hollow," 1963, Max Abramovitz Papers, Avery Library, Columbia University.

80. OakCorp, "This Is an Urban Area," 8.

81. Burtson-Marsteller Associates, "Pittsburgh Plans Massive Research Center," June 5, 1963, ELP, UPASC.

82. OakCorp, "This Is an Urban Area," 9, 13.

83. OakCorp, 22.

84. OakCorp, 9.

85. Burtson-Marsteller Associates, "Pittsburgh Plans."

86. OakCorp, "This Is an Urban Area."

87. Max Abramovitz, "The City of Tomorrow," *Pitt,* October 1963, 11, 13.

88. Abramovitz, 13, 14.

89. "Years of Change," *Pittsburgh Press,* January 15, 1963.

90. "City Boomed for Research Center," *Pittsburgh Post-Gazette,* May 14, 1963.

91. David Bollinger, "Industrialist Hails 'People' in Renaissance," *Pittsburgh Press,* November 21, 1963.

92. M. Kyle Tudor, "Lawrence Litchfield Jr. of Alcoa," *Mines Magazine,* April 1970.

93. Frederick Terman, "The Newly Emerging Community of Technical Scholars," in *Colorado and the New Technological Revolution: Proceedings of the University-Industry Liaison Conference,* ed. William Miernyk (Boulder: Bureau of Economic Research, Institute of Behavioral Science, University of Colorado, 1963), 43–53; Stuart W. Leslie and Robert H. Kargon, "Selling Silicon Valley: Frederick Terman's Model for Regional Advantage," *Business History Review* 70, no. 4 (1996): 435–72.

94. Sabina Deitrick and Tracy Soska, "The University of Pittsburgh and the Oakland Neighborhood: From Conflict to Cooperation, or How the 800-Pound Gorilla Learned to Sit with—and Not on—Its Neighbors," in *The University as Urban Developer: Case*

Studies and Analysis, ed. David C. Perry and Wim Wiewal (New York: M. E. Sharpe and Lincoln Land Institute, 2005), 25–44.

95. Andrew Simpson, *The Medical Metropolis: Health Care and Economic Transformation in Pittsburgh and Houston* (Philadelphia: University of Pennsylvania Press, 2019).

96. Peyton, "Corporate Ecology."

97. Joseph Heathcott and Maire Agnes Murphy, "Corridors of Flight, Zones of Renewal: Industry, Planning, and Policy in the Making of Metropolitan St. Louis," *Journal of Urban History* 31, no. 2 (2005): 151–89.

98. J. Mark Souther, *Believing in Cleveland: Managing Decline in "the Best Location in the Nation"* (Philadelphia: Temple University Press, 2017); Margaret Pugh O'Mara, *Cities of Knowledge: Cold War Science and the Search for the Next Silicon Valley* (Princeton, N.J.: Princeton University Press, 2005).

99. Richard L. Florida, *The Rise of the Creative Class: And How It's Transforming Work, Leisure, Community and Everyday Life* (New York: Basic Books, 2002).

3. The Invention of Research Man

1. Louise Mozingo, "To Rethink Sprawl, Start with Offices," *New York Times,* November 26, 2011; Louise Mozingo, *Pastoral Capitalism: A History of Suburban Corporate Landscapes* (Cambridge, Mass.: MIT Press, 2011), 51–53.

2. Doreen B. Massey, *Spatial Divisions of Labour: Social Structures and the Geography of Production* (London: Macmillan, 1984).

3. Massey.

4. Melissa Wright, *Disposable Women and Other Myths of Global Capitalism* (New York: Routledge, 2006).

5. Harry Braverman, *Labor and Monopoly Capital* (New York: Monthly Review Press, 1974), 242; David Noble, *Forces of Production: A Social History of Industrial Automation* (New York: Knopf, 1984). The sociospatial division between mental and physical labor is always incomplete. Even in the most mechanized workplaces manual work involves thinking (and vice versa). This chapter explores: (1) how firms produced a division between mental and physical labor and a corresponding class relationship between different types of workers and (2) how this division and class relationship were essential to industry's ability to extract surplus value.

6. William J. Rankin, "The Epistemology of the Suburbs: Knowledge, Production, and Corporate Laboratory Design," *Critical Inquiry* 36, no. 4 (2010): 775.

7. Jason W. Moore, "Remaking Work, Remaking Space: Spaces of Production and Accumulation in the Reconstruction of American Capitalism, 1865–1920," *Antipode* 34, no. 2 (2002): 176–209; Richard Walker, "Class, Division of Labour and Employment in Space," in *Social Relations and Spatial Structures,* ed. Derek Gregory and John Urry (London: Macmillan, 1985), 164–89.

8. Karl Marx and Friedrich Engels, *The German Ideology,* ed. C. J. Arthur (New York: International Publishers, 1947), 53. See also David Montgomery, *Workers' Control in America* (Cambridge: Cambridge University Press, 1979).

9. Karl Marx, *Capital: A Critique of Political Economy,* vol. 1, *The Process of Capitalist Production* (London: Penguin Books, 1976), 481–82.

10. Karl Marx, *Grundrisse,* trans. Martin Nicolaus (London: Penguin Books, 1973), 695.

11. Braverman, *Labor and Monopoly Capital,* 155; Marx, *Capital,* 1:509, 550.

12. Marx and Engels, *The German Ideology,* 78.

13. Steven Shapin, "Who Is the Industrial Scientist?," in *The Science-Industry Nexus: History, Policy, Implications,* ed. Karl Grandin, Nina Wormbs, and Sven Widmalm (Sagamore Beach, Mass.: Science History Publications, 2004), 337–64.

14. William Walker, "Education for Research," *Journal of Industrial and Engineering Chemistry* 7, no. 1 (January 1915): 2–4; R. A. Millikan, "Research in America after the War," *Transactions of the American Institute of Electrical Engineers* 37, no. 2 (1919): 1723–46; Robert E. Rose, "The Education of the Research Chemist," *Journal of Industrial and Engineering Chemistry* 12, no. 10 (1920): 947–51; Willis R. Whitney, "Research as a National Duty," *Science* 43, no. 1114 (1916): 629–37.

15. F. B. Jewett, "Industrial Research with Some Notes Concerning Its Scope in the Bell Telephone System," *Transactions of the American Institute of Electrical Engineers* 36 (January–December 1917): 842.

16. W. D. Richardson, "The Analyst, the Chemist and the Chemical Engineer," *Science* 28, no. 717 (1908): 396–402; Julius Stieglitz, "Chemical Research in American Universities," *Science* 26, no. 673 (1907): 699–703; M. C. Whitaker, "The Training of Chemical Engineers," *Journal of Industrial and Engineering Chemistry* 3, no. 1 (1911): 36–39.

17. Perley G. Nutting, "The Application of Organized Knowledge to National Welfare," *Scientific Monthly* 6, no. 5 (1918): 411.

18. Perley G. Nutting, "Research and Industries," *Scientific Monthly* 7, no. 2 (1918): 149.

19. Stieglitz, "Chemical Research in American Universities," 702.

20. Nutting, "The Application of Organized Knowledge to National Welfare," 412.

21. Donna Haraway, *Modest_Witness@ Second_Millenium.FemaleMan_Meets_OncoMouse: Feminism and Technoscience* (London: Routledge, 1997); Jennifer S. Light, "When Computers Were Women," *Technology and Culture* 40, no. 3 (1999): 455–83; Kara W. Swanson, "Rubbing Elbows and Blowing Smoke: Gender, Class, and Science in the Nineteenth-Century Patent Office," *Isis* 108, no. 1 (2017): 40–61.

22. David Noble, *America by Design: Science, Technology, and the Rise of Corporate Capitalism* (Oxford: Oxford University Press, 1977), 152.

23. Nutting, "The Application of Organized Knowledge to National Welfare," 412.

24. Millikan, "Research in America after the War," 137, 135.

25. Millikan, 135.

26. Whitney, "Research as a National Duty," 630; C. Alfred Jacobson, "Some Aspects of Scientific Research," *Science* 42, no. 1087 (1915): 599.

27. Richardson, "The Analyst, the Chemist and the Chemical Engineer," 398.

28. Nutting, "The Application of Organized Knowledge to National Welfare," 415.

29. Richardson, "The Analyst, the Chemist and the Chemical Engineer," 398.

30. G. A. Pearson, "Some Conditions for Effective Research," *Science* 60, no. 1543 (1924): 11. For similar statements, see James Rowland Angell, "The Organization of Research," *Scientific Monthly* 11, no. 1 (1920): 30, 35; and Walker, "Education for Research," 4.

31. Millikan, "Research in America after the War," 132.

32. Jewett, "Industrial Research," 850; Willis R. Whitney, "American Engineering Research," *Proceedings of the American Institute of Electrical Engineers* 38, no. 2 (1919): 9.

33. Millikan, "Research in America after the War," 138.

34. C. E. Skinner, "Industrial Research and Its Relation to University and Governmental Research," *Transactions of the American Institute of Electrical Engineers* 36 (January–December 1917): 871.

35. Charles P. Steinmetz, "Scientific Research in Relation to the Industries," *Journal of the Franklin Institute* 182, no. 6 (1916): 711–18.

36. Angell, "The Organization of Research," 35.

37. Noble, *America by Design,* 29, 175.

38. Whitaker, "The Training of Chemical Engineers," 38.

39. Noble, *America by Design,* 33–34.

40. Noble, 263.

41. S. M. Kinter, "Making Research Profitable," *Manufacturing Industries* 14, no. 6 (December 1927): 416; Nutting, "Research and Industries." Noble estimates that between 1904 and 1929, upward of two-thirds of engineers became managers within fifteen years of graduating from postsecondary institutions. Noble, *America by Design,* 304.

42. Edward R. Weidlein, "The Administration of Industrial Research," *Journal of Industrial and Engineering Chemistry* 18, no. 1 (January 1926): 99–100.

43. Jacobson, "Some Aspects of Scientific Research," 600, 602.

44. L. A. Hawkins, "Research Man or Engineer? A Discussion of the Selection of Men for Research," *Ohio State Engineer* 11, no. 2 (1927): 8.

45. Noble, *America by Design,* 183.

46. Herman Schneider, *Education for Industrial Workers: A Constructive Study Applied to New York City* (Yonkers-on-Hudson, N.Y.: World Book Company, 1915), 12.

47. Shapin, "Who Is the Industrial Scientist?"

48. C. E. Skinner, "Commercial Research," *Electric Journal* 5 (April 1908): 203.

49. C. E. Kenneth Mees, *The Organization of Industrial Scientific Research* (New York: McGraw-Hill, 1920), 94–95.

50. Edward R. Weidlein, "Selecting Research Man," *Science News-Letter* 14, no. 383 (August 11, 1928): 84.

51. Robert H. Wiebe, *The Search for Order, 1877–1920* (New York: Hill and Wang, 1967).

52. Richardson, "The Analyst, the Chemist and the Chemical Engineer"; Steinmetz, "Scientific Research in Relation to the Industries."

53. Nutting, "The Application of Organized Knowledge to National Welfare," 409.

54. Weidlein, "The Administration of Industrial Research," 101.

55. Stanley Aronowitz, "Marxism, Technology, and Labor," *New Political Science* 1, nos. 2–3 (1979): 105–17; Barbara Ehrenreich and John Ehrenreich, "The Professional-Managerial Class," in *Between Labor and Capital,* ed. Pat Walker (Boston: South End, 1979), 5–45; André Gorz, "Technical Intelligence and the Capitalist Division of Labor," *Telos* 1972, no. 12 (1972): 27–41; David Noble, "The PMC: A Critique," in *Between Labor and Capital,* ed. Pat Walker (Boston: South End, 1979), 121–42.

56. Erik Olin Wright, *Classes* (London: Verso, 1985).

57. E. P. Thompson, *The Making of the English Working Class* (New York: Vintage Books, 1963); Wright, *Classes.*

58. Alfred Chandler, *The Visible Hand: The Managerial Revolution in American Business* (Cambridge, Mass.: Belknap Press of Harvard University Press, 1977); Daniel Nelson, *Managers and Workers: Origins of the Twentieth-Century Factory System in the United States, 1880–1920* (Madison: University of Wisconsin Press, 1995).

59. *Adventures in Power: A Fact History of Westinghouse* (East Pittsburgh: Westinghouse Electric and Manufacturing, 1936).

60. Skinner, "Industrial Research," 877–78.

61. Lillian Hoddeson, "The Emergence of Basic Research in the Bell Telephone System, 1875–1915," *Technology and Culture* 22, no. 3 (July 1981): 512; Noble, *America by Design,* 111.

62. Steven W. Usselman, "From Novelty to Utility: George Westinghouse and the Business of Innovation during the Age of Edison," *Business History Review* 66, no. 2 (Summer 1992): 251–304.

63. The off-site laboratory was established by William Stanley Jr., a key researcher at Westinghouse who was sickened by the air in Pittsburgh and moved to the Berkshires. Stanley operated it on contract and somewhat independently from Westinghouse. See Ronald R. Kline and Thomas Lassman, "Competing Research Traditions in American Industry: Uncertain Alliances Between Engineering and Science at Westinghouse Electric, 1886–1935," *Enterprise & Society* 6, no. 4 (2005): 608. For more on the struggle between Westinghouse and Edison, see Jill Jonnes, *Empires of Light* (New York: Random House, 2004).

64. Roy Lubove, *Twentieth-Century Pittsburgh,* vol. 1, *Government, Business, and Environmental Change* (Pittsburgh: University of Pittsburgh Press, 1969), 5.

65. Edward K. Muller, "Industrial Suburbs and the Growth of Metropolitan Pittsburgh, 1870–1920," *Journal of Historical Geography* 27, no. 1 (2001): 66.

66. Andrew Needham and Allen Dieterich-Ward, "Beyond the Metropolis: Metropolitan Growth and Regional Transformation in Postwar America," *Journal of Urban History* 35, no. 7 (2009): 943–69.

67. Robert D. Lewis, ed., *The Manufacturing Suburb: Building Work and Home on the Metropolitan Fringe* (Philadelphia: Temple University Press, 2004); Robert D. Lewis, *Manufacturing Montreal: The Making of an Industrial Landscape, 1850–1930* (Baltimore: Johns Hopkins University Press, 2000).

68. Thomas J. Misa, *A Nation of Steel: The Making of Modern America, 1865–1925* (Baltimore: Johns Hopkins University Press, 1995), 25–28; Chandler, *The Visible Hand,* 258–69.

69. Andrew Carnegie, *The Autobiography of Andrew Carnegie and His Essay: The Gospel of Wealth* (Mineola, N.Y.: Dover, 2014), 132, 133, 136.

70. Francis G. Couvares, *The Remaking of Pittsburgh: Class and Culture in an Industrializing City, 1877–1919* (Albany: State University of New York Press, 1984), 84.

71. David Gordon, "Capitalist Development and the History of American Cities," in *Marxism and the Metropolis,* ed. W. Tabb and L. Sawers (Oxford: Oxford University Press, 1984), 21–53; Anne E. Mosher, *Capital's Utopia: Vandergrift, Pennsylvania, 1855–1916* (Baltimore: Johns Hopkins University Press, 2004).

72. Marx, *Grundrisse,* 639.

73. Robert H. Kargon and Scott G. Knowles, "Knowledge for Use: Science, Higher Learning, and America's New Industrial Heartland, 1880–1915," *Annals of Science* 59, no. 1 (2002): 1–20.

74. For most Pittsburgh-based firms and Westinghouse in particular, their relationship was not limited just to local universities and colleges. Westinghouse and GE in fact provided the first equipment for MIT's electrical engineering department. Westinghouse maintained a close relationship with and supported research at MIT, the University of Pennsylvania, the Stevens Institute of Technology, Cornell, Purdue, and many other universities. Noble, *America by Design,* 136.

75. Local firms also joined with the Pittsburgh School Board and the very active local chapter of the National Association of Corporate Training to develop the "Pittsburgh Idea," one of the first vocational training programs for skilled workers in the country. Noble, 196.

76. John Servos describes the Mellon Institute as "dedicated not to the enlargement of human understanding but to the creation and improvement of industrial technologies." John Servos, "Changing Partners: The Mellon Institute, Private Industry, and the Federal Patron," *Technology and Culture* 35, no. 2 (1994): 234.

77. Braverman, *Labor and Monopoly Capital,* 164.

78. Noble, *America by Design,* 304.

79. William Allen Hamor, "Pittsburgh as a Chemical Research Center," *Journal of Industrial and Engineering Chemistry* 14, no. 9 (1922): 764–71.

80. Noble, *America by Design,* xxv.

81. Chandler, *The Visible Hand;* David Hounshell, "The Evolution of Industrial Research in the United States," in *Engines of Innovation: U.S. Industrial Research at the End of an Era,* ed. Richard Rosenbloom and William J. Spencer (Boston: Harvard Business School Press, 1996), 13–85; David C. Mowery and Nathan Rosenberg, *Technology and the Pursuit of Economic Growth* (Cambridge: Cambridge University Press, 1989); Leonard S. Reich, *The Making of American Industrial Research: Science and Business at GE and Bell, 1876–1926* (Cambridge: Cambridge University Press, 1985); John Kenly Smith Jr., "The Scientific Tradition in American Industrial Research," *Technology and Culture* 31, no. 1 (1990): 121–31.

82. Paul Ceruzzi, *Internet Alley: High Technology in Tysons Corner* (Cambridge, Mass.: MIT Press, 2008); Alex Sayf Cummings, "'Brain Magnet': Research Triangle Park and the Origins of the Creative City, 1953–1965," *Journal of Urban History* 43, no. 3 (2017): 470–92; Scott G. Knowles and Stuart W. Leslie, "'Industrial Versailles': Eero Saarinen's Corporate Campuses for GM, IBM, and AT&T," *Isis* 92, no. 1 (March 2001): 1–33; Mozingo, *Pastoral Capitalism*; Margaret Pugh O'Mara, *Cities of Knowledge: Cold War Science and the Search for the Next Silicon Valley* (Princeton, N.J.: Princeton University Press, 2005); Rankin, "The Epistemology of the Suburbs."

83. Mees, *The Organization of Industrial Scientific Research,* 68, 109, 111.

84. David Hounshell and John Kenly Smith Jr., *Science and Corporate Strategy: Du Pont R&D, 1902–1980* (Cambridge: Cambridge University Press, 1988).

85. George Wise, "A New Role for Professional Scientists in Industry: Industrial Research at General Electric, 1900–1916," *Technology and Culture* 21, no. 3 (July 1980): 408.

86. Hounshell, "The Evolution of Industrial Research in the United States," 53. See also Noble, *America by Design.*

87. David C. Mowery, "The Development of Industrial Research in U.S. Manufacturing," *American Economic Review* 80, no. 2 (1990): 345–49; Noble, *America by Design,* 108.

88. Hounshell and Smith, *Science and Corporate Strategy;* Thomas P. Hughes, *American Genesis* (Chicago: University of Chicago Press, 1989); David C. Mowery and Nathan Rosenberg, *Paths of Innovation: Technological Change in 20th-Century America* (Cambridge: Cambridge University Press, 1999); Tom Nicholas, "The Role of Independent Invention in U.S. Technological Development, 1880–1930," *Journal of Economic History* 70, no. 1 (2010): 57–82.

89. Hounshell, "The Evolution of Industrial Research in the United States," 53.

90. Hounshell and Smith, *Science and Corporate Strategy,* 5; Chandler, *The Visible Hand*; Alfred D. Chandler, *Scale and Scope the Dynamics of Industrial Capitalism* (Cambridge, Mass.: Belknap Press of Harvard University Press, 1990).

91. Mowery and Rosenberg, *Paths of Innovation*; National Research Council, *Research Laboratories in Industrial Establishments of the United States of America,* Bulletin of the National Research Council 2 (Washington, D.C.: National Research Council, 1920); National Research Council, *Industrial Research Laboratories of the United States Including Consulting Research Laboratories,* Bulletin of the National Research Council 104 (Washington, D.C.: National Research Council, 1940).

92. Kline and Lassman, "Competing Research Traditions," 610.

93. T. K. Phares, *History of the Westinghouse Research Laboratories* (East Pittsburgh: Westinghouse, 1941) 4, WECA, DL&A.

94. Kinter, "Making Research Profitable," 415.

95. Kline and Lassman, "Competing Research Traditions," 603.

96. Skinner, "Commercial Research," 185–86.

97. Mees, *The Organization of Industrial Scientific Research,* 114.

98. Mees, 63, 67.

99. Mees, 63, 67.

100. Kinter, "Making Research Profitable," 418.

101. Mozingo, *Pastoral Capitalism*, 54.

102. C. E. Skinner and R. W. E. Moore, "The New Westinghouse Research Building," *Electrical World*, June 1, 1918, 1132–33.

103. C. E. K. Mees, "Planning a Research Laboratory for an Industry," *Scientific Monthly* 7, no. 1 (1918): 59.

104. Arthur Percy Morris Fleming, "Planning a Works Research Organization," *Journal of the Institution of Electrical Engineers* 57, no. 279 (1919): 157.

105. Skinner and Moore, "The New Westinghouse Research Building," 1132.

106. Kinter, "Making Research Profitable," 415.

107. Mees, *The Organization of Industrial Scientific Research*, 94.

108. Mees, 112; Skinner and Moore, "The New Westinghouse Research Building," 1132.

109. Steven Shapin, "The Invisible Technician," *American Scientist* 77, no. 6 (1989): 554–63; Park Doing, "'Lab Hands' and the 'Scarlet O': Epistemic Politics and (Scientific) Labor," *Social Studies of Science* 34, no. 3 (2004): 299–323.

110. Stephen R. Barley and Beth A. Bechky, "In the Backrooms of Science: The Work of Technicians in Science Labs," *Work and Occupations* 21, no. 1 (1994): 88.

111. Kinter, "Making Research Profitable," 416.

112. R. E. Peterson, "Recollections of the Research Laboratories on Ardmore Boulevard," June 19, 1980, WECA, DL&A.

113. Kinter, "Making Research Profitable," 416.

114. Nutting, "Research and Industries," 156.

115. Peterson, "Recollections."

116. Address and telephone list, research laboratories, April 1948, WECA, DL&A.

117. J. A. Hutcheson to H. W. Reding, June 29, 1951, WECA, DL&A; J. A. Hutcheson to L. D. Rigdon, April 2, 1951, WECA, DL&A.

118. C. E. Kenneth Mees and John A. Leermakers, *The Organization of Industrial Scientific Research*, 2nd ed. (New York: McGraw-Hill, 1950), 112, 130–31.

119. Mees and Leermakers, 144–45.

120. Aluminum Company of America, *Aluminum Research Laboratories* (Pittsburgh: Aluminum Company of America, 1935).

4. The Monroeville Doctrine

1. Carol Pickens, "Diversified Development Will Benefit the Borough for Many Years to Come," *Times Express*, September 25, 1969, 1; Monroeville Chamber of Commerce, "Residential Research Center of the Nation . . . Monroeville, Pennsylvania, Gateway to Pittsburgh," March 1964, Monroeville clippings file, CLPGH.

2. Pickens, "Diversified Development Will Benefit the Borough," 1; Allen Dieterich-Ward, "From Mill Towns to 'Burbs of the Burgh': Suburban Strategies in the Postindustrial Metropolis," *Research in Urban Sociology* 10 (2010): 83.

3. Advertisement, *Times Express*, September 25, 1969.

4. Ira S. Lowry, *Portrait of a Region,* vol. 2 of *Economic Study of the Pittsburgh Region* (Pittsburgh: University of Pittsburgh Press, 1963), 98.

5. For a similar example of how aerospace firms helped create exclusive communities around their research labs, see Layne Karafantis and Stuart W. Leslie, "'Suburban Warriors': The Blue-Collar and Blue-Sky Communities of Southern California's Aerospace Industry," *Journal of Planning History* 18, no. 1 (2019): 3–26.

6. Tracy Neumann, "Reforging the Steel City: Symbolism and Space in Postindustrial Pittsburgh," *Journal of Urban History* 44, no. 4 (2018): 582–602.

7. Unsurprisingly, Westinghouse president Gwilym Price had a hand in the formation of the economic study. At the time, he was the chairman of the RIDC and sent a letter of support to the Ford Foundation. Kent James and Sherie Mershon, "Academic Initiative, Economic Analysis, and Regional Planning during the 1960s: The Hoover Study of Pittsburgh," n.d., unpublished paper in author's possession.

8. Lowry, *Portrait of a Region,* v.

9. Pittsburgh Regional Planning Association (PRPA), *Region in Transition,* vol. 1 of *The Economic Study of the Pittsburgh Region* (Pittsburgh: University of Pittsburgh Press, 1963), 382.

10. PRPA, 386–88.

11. PRPA, *Region with a Future,* vol. 3 of *The Economic Study of the Pittsburgh Region* (Pittsburgh: University of Pittsburgh Press, 1963), 183.

12. PRPA, *Region in Transition,* 382.

13. PRPA, *Region with a Future,* 117.

14. PRPA, *Region in Transition,* 412.

15. PRPA, 390.

16. Lowry, *Portrait of a Region,* 98.

17. Lowry, 98.

18. Lowry, 98–99.

19. Lowry, 99.

20. Pittsburgh Airways Inc., "Application to the Pennsylvania Public Utility Commission," Docket No. A. 83743, folder 3, September 21, 1962, folder "Westinghouse Research Laboratories Heliport," CBMR.

21. Margaret Pugh O'Mara, *Cities of Knowledge: Cold War Science and the Search for the Next Silicon Valley.* (Princeton, N.J.: Princeton University Press, 2005), 28–36.

22. Thomas W. Hanchett, "U.S. Tax Policy and the Shopping-Center Boom of the 1950s and 1960s," *American Historical Review* 101, no. 4 (1996): 1082–1110; O'Mara, *Cities of Knowledge,* 30.

23. David Freund, *Colored Property: State Policy and White Racial Politics in Suburban America* (Chicago: University of Chicago Press, 2007).

24. From 1916 to 1956, Westinghouse's research facilities in Forest Hills were known as the Westinghouse Research Lab; in 1956, when they moved to Churchill, they became the plural Westinghouse Research Laboratories; and in 1962 they became known as the Westinghouse Research and Development Center.

25. John Harlon, "Analysis of Shift in Research Professions at Westinghouse R&D Center," 1973, WECA, DL&A; R. D. Haun, "Westinghouse Central Corporate Research and Development," October 7, 1971, WECA, DL&A.

26. J. A. Hutcheson to L. D. Rigdon, April 19, 1951, WECA, DL&A.

27. J. A. Hutcheson, letter and draft memorandum to A. C. Monteith, November 11, 1951, WECA, DL&A.

28. J. A. Hutcheson to L. D. Rigdon, April 19, 1951.

29. J. A. Hutcheson to H. W. Reding, June 29, 1951, WECA, DL&A.

30. J. A. Hutcheson to L. D. Rigdon, April 19, 1951.

31. J. A. Hutcheson to H. W. Reding, June 29, 1951.

32. Kenneth McArdle, "'Civil War' Faced by Wilkins Township as Big Property Owners Try to Secede," *Pittsburgh Press,* February 4, 1934, 2.

33. "Council Keeps Close Eye on 'Ideal' Borough," *Pittsburgh Press,* June 10, 1934.

34. Edwin H. Beachler, "Jack-and-Beanstalk Town Built around Parkway," *Pittsburgh Press,* May 9, 1951.

35. *Research Newsletter,* October–November 1955, 10–11, WECA, DL&A; *Research Newsletter,* August 31, 1948, 11, WECA, DL&A.

36. Churchill Borough Minute Books, September 11, 1950, CBMR.

37. Petition of Westinghouse Electric Corporation, January 7, 1952, folder "Westinghouse Zoning Ordinance," CBMR.

38. The first zoning ordinance limited to research facilities was for the Bell Laboratories built in Summit, New Jersey, in the early 1940s. A similar zoning ordinance was also put in place in Palos Verdes, California. Louise Mozingo, *Pastoral Capitalism: A History of Suburban Corporate Landscapes* (Cambridge, Mass.: MIT Press, 2011), 63; Karafantis and Leslie, "'Suburban Warriors,'" 14.

39. Ordinance No. 120, February 11, 1952, folder "Westinghouse Zoning Ordinance," CBMR.

40. E. M. Elkin to Churchill Borough Council, January 28, 1952, folder "Westinghouse Zoning Ordinance," CBMR.

41. Charles A. Williams to Churchill Borough Council, January 21, 1952, folder "Westinghouse Zoning Ordinance," CBMR.

42. Public hearing RE proposed Ordinance No. 120, February 11, 1952, 55–58, Churchill Borough Council Minutes, 1951–1953, CBMR.

43. Public hearing RE proposed Ordinance No. 120, 7–8. Tellingly, in the early 1940s, Bell Laboratories also met little resistance when it moved to the exclusive suburb of Summit, New Jersey. As with the Westinghouse Labs, the presence of Bell employees as residents of Summit paved the way for its relocation. Frank Jewett, director of Bell Labs, made a nearly identical defense to the one Hutcheson made for Westinghouse. At a council meeting, he assured residents that the lab's employees were "mostly of the scientific and engineering type who will want to live with their families somewhere in the territory between Short Hills and New Providence." He added that the lab "is not a manufacturing concern: it is a laboratory." Finally, it would be landscaped by Olmsted Brothers and "will in no way harm the growth of this entire section as a

residential community but rather will be of great assistance in keeping this territory on a high plain of a suburban residential community." Mozingo, *Pastoral Capitalism,* 56.

44. Public hearing RE proposed Ordinance No. 120, 23–30.

45. J. A. Hutcheson to Earl Gulbransen, May 19, 1952, WECA, DL&A; J. A. Hutcheson to A. C. Monteith, September 8, 1952, WECA, DL&A.

46. J. A. Hutcheson to R. M. Wilson, July 18, 1952, WECA, DL&A.

47. J. A. Hutcheson to A. C. Monteith, September 8, 1952; Glen Ross Asner, "The Cold War and American Industrial Research" (PhD diss., Carnegie Mellon University, 2006), 391–93.

48. J. A. Hutcheson to Charles R. Miller, November 28, 1952, WECA, DL&A.

49. J. A. Hutcheson to A. C. Monteith, March 19, 1953, WECA, DL&A.

50. J. A. Hutcheson, Memorandum Necessity Certificate—TA-21260, September 16, 1954, WECA, DL&A.

51. Asner, "The Cold War," 393.

52. J. A. Hutcheson to Hugh Nielson and Henry Schwartz, April 25, 1952, WECA, DL&A.

53. J. A. Hutcheson to L. S. Houk, September 2, 1952, WECA, DL&A.

54. Mozingo, *Pastoral Capitalism,* 63, 53.

55. William J. Rankin, "The Epistemology of the Suburbs: Knowledge, Production, and Corporate Laboratory Design," *Critical Inquiry* 36, no. 4 (2010): 776.

56. "Westinghouse Research Labs Looks beyond Tomorrow," *Plant Engineering,* November 1956, 114–15.

57. Vorhees, Walker, Foley, & Smith Architects and Engineers, "Westinghouse Research Laboratories Fundamental Design Report," November 11, 1952, CBMR.

58. Public hearing RE proposed Ordinance No. 120, 12.

59. *Research Newsletter,* April 25, 1950, WECA, DL&A.

60. Gardening was a frequent topic in the *Research Newsletter* after World War II, when many researchers were buying new homes. In a lengthy article, a researcher noted that "the field of horticulture is peculiarly suited to raise questions which embrace the whole realm of the scientist." *Research Newsletter,* April 30, 1952, 7–8, WECA, DL&A.

61. *Research Newsletter,* April 1955, 2–5, WECA, DL&A.

62. Clarence Zener, "To Our Neighbors in Churchill Borough," May 20, 1957, folder "Westinghouse Permit #789," CBMR; Westinghouse R&D Center, "Landscaping Guide," 1968, WECA, DL&A.

63. Borough of Churchill to Neil D. Cole, December 16, 1958, folder "Westinghouse Permit #789," CBMR.

64. W. E. Richards to William E. Shoupp, November 17, 1966, folder "Westinghouse Fence," CBMR.

65. Larry F. Cervi, "That Unneighborly Fence," November 9, 1966, folder "Westinghouse Fence," CBMR.

66. WEC, "Westinghouse Breaks Ground for Most Modern Research Center," press release, June 12, 1953, WECA, DL&A.

67. J. Hutcheson to C. Zener, August 6, 1956, WECA, DL&A.

68. A. Nelkin, dedication newsletter, September 5, 1956, WECA, DL&A.

69. "Westinghouse Research Laboratories Dedication," 1956, WECA, DL&A.

70. A. Nelkin, dedication newsletter, September 11, 1956, WECA, DL&A.

71. *Research Newsletter,* June 1955, 14, WECA, DL&A.

72. Coverage appeared in the Associated Press, the *New York Times, Popular Science,* the *Wall Street Journal, Reader's Digest,* and many other newspapers. "Dedication Press List," WECA, DL&A.

73. Among other publications, the advertisement ran in *Time, Newsweek,* the *Wall Street Journal, Business Week,* and *U.S. News & World Report.*

74. "Westinghouse Research Laboratories Dedication."

75. A. Nelkin, dedication newsletter, September 17, 1956, WECA, DL&A.

76. A. Nelkin, dedication newsletter, September 4, 1956, WECA, DL&A.

77. A. Nelkin, dedication newsletter, September 21, 1956, WECA, DL&A.

78. Gwilym Price, "The Role of Research in Our Society," September 20, 1956, 2, WECA, DL&A.

79. Price, 4.

80. Price, 3–6.

81. Price, 11.

82. Price, 12.

83. Vannevar Bush, "Science: The Endless Frontier," *Transactions of the Kansas Academy of Science* 48, no. 3 (1945): 232–33.

84. Daniel J. Kevles, "The National Science Foundation and the Debate over Postwar Research Policy, 1942–1945: A Political Interpretation of Science—The Endless Frontier," *Isis* 68, no. 1 (1977): 5–26.

85. Gregory Hooks, "The Rise of the Pentagon and U.S. State Building: The Defense Program as Industrial Policy," *American Journal of Sociology* 96, no. 2 (1990): 370; Michael S. Sherry, *In the Shadow of War: The United States since the 1930s* (New Haven, Conn.: Yale University Press, 1995), 138.

86. "Research . . . an Investment in Tomorrow," *Industrial Laboratories,* November 1956, 38–43.

87. "Westinghouse Research and Development in Churchill Borough," 1959, 1, WECA, DL&A.

88. WEC, "Westinghouse Proposes Expansion of Research Laboratories in Churchill," press release, June 1959, folder "Westinghouse—Ord. #236," CBMR; "Westinghouse Research and Development in Churchill Borough," 2.

89. "Westinghouse Research and Development in Churchill Borough," 4.

90. S. W. Herald, "To Our Friends in Churchill Borough," July 8, 1959, folder "Westinghouse—Ord. #236," CBMR.

91. "Partial Report of Proceedings before Council of the Borough of Churchill," August 18, 1959, folder "Westinghouse—Ord. #236," CBMR.

92. "Presentation to the Capital Expenditures Committee: Office Building for R&D Center," February 3, 1969, 2–5, WECA, DL&A.

93. "People Ideas Capabilities at the Westinghouse Research Laboratories," 1974, WECA, DL&A.

94. Public hearing transcript, Westinghouse R&D Rezoning, September 15, 1964, 7, 10, folder "Westinghouse Expansion," CBMR.

95. Public hearing transcript, 17–18.

96. Minutes of recessed meeting of Council, November 11, 1978, CBMR.

97. Minutes of exploratory meeting, August 31, 1964, folder "Westinghouse Expansion R.C.H.," CBMR.

98. Asner, "The Cold War," 401.

99. Ann R. Markusen et al., *The Rise of the Gunbelt: The Military Remapping of Industrial America* (Oxford: Oxford University Press, 1991).

100. Scott G. Knowles and Stuart W. Leslie, "'Industrial Versailles': Eero Saarinen's Corporate Campuses for GM, IBM, and AT&T," *Isis* 92, no. 1 (2001): 1–33.

5. Finding a Home in the Nuclear Suburbs

1. The Mark I was the first successful reactor intended to operate as a means of propulsion and differed greatly from previous reactors in terms of its careful engineering and tight space requirements. Scott Frickel, "Engineering Heterogeneous Accounts: The Case of Submarine Thermal Reactor Mark-I," *Science, Technology, and Human Values* 21, no. 1 (1996): 28–53.

2. See, for example, Stephen Graham, *Cities under Siege: The New Military Urbanism* (London: Verso, 2010); Mark L. Gillem, *America Town: Building the Outposts of Empire* (Minneapolis: University of Minnesota Press, 2007); and Catherine Lutz, *Homefront: A Military City and the American 20th Century* (Boston: Beacon, 2001).

3. Elaine Tyler May, *Homeward Bound: American Families in the Cold War Era* (New York: Basic Books, 1988).

4. Robert A. Beauregard, *When America Became Suburban* (Minneapolis: University of Minnesota Press, 2006).

5. David Harvey, *The Urban Experience* (Baltimore: Johns Hopkins University Press, 1989), 39; Marshall Feldman and Richard Florida, "Housing in US Fordism: The Class Accord and Postwar Spatial Organization," *International Journal of Urban and Regional Research* 12, no. 2 (1988): 187–210.

6. Nancy Kwak, *A World of Homeowners: American Power and the Politics of Housing Aid* (Chicago: University of Chicago Press, 2015).

7. Greg Castillo, *Cold War on the Home Front: The Soft Power of Midcentury Design* (Minneapolis: University of Minnesota Press, 2010), 122–24.

8. Daniel Bell, *The End of Ideology: On the Exhaustion of Political Ideas in the Fifties* (Glencoe, Ill.: Free Press, 1960); Herbert Marcuse, *One-Dimensional Man: Studies in the Ideologies of Advanced Industrial Societies* (Boston: Beacon, 1964).

9. David Freund, *Colored Property: State Policy and White Racial Politics in Suburban America* (Chicago: University of Chicago Press, 2007); Kevin Kruse, *White Flight: Atlanta and the Making of Modern Conservativism* (Princeton, N.J.: Princeton University Press, 2005); Lisa McGirr, *Suburban Warriors: The Origins of the American*

Right (Princeton, N.J.: Princeton University Press, 2001); Thomas Sugrue, *The Origins of the Urban Crisis: Race and Inequality in Postwar Detroit* (Princeton, N.J.: Princeton University Press, 1998).

10. Lily D. Geismer, *Don't Blame Us: Suburban Liberals and the Transformation of the Democratic Party* (Princeton, N.J.: Princeton University Press, 2014).

11. Beauregard, *When America Became Suburban;* Lizabeth Cohen, *A Consumer's Republic: The Politics of Mass Consumption in Postwar America* (New York: Knopf, 2003); May, *Homeward Bound;* Patrick Vitale, "Learning to Be Suburban: The Production of Community in Westwood Hills, Pennsylvania, 1952–1958," *Journal of Historical Geography* 35, no. 4 (2009): 743–68.

12. Stuart W. Leslie, *The Cold War and American Science: The Military-Industrial-Academic Complex at MIT and Stanford* (New York: Columbia University Press, 1993); David Noble, *America by Design: Science, Technology, and the Rise of Corporate Capitalism* (Oxford: Oxford University Press, 1977); David Noble, *Forces of Production: A Social History of Industrial Automation* (New York: Knopf, 1984).

13. James R. Newman and Byron S. Miller, "The Socialist Island," *Bulletin of the Atomic Scientists* 5, no. 1 (1949): 13–15; Kim Phillips-Fein, *Invisible Hands: The Businessmen's Crusade Against the New Deal* (New York: W. W. Norton, 2009); Gwilym Price, "The Role of Research in Our Society," September 20, 1956, 11, 12, WECA, DL&A.

14. Quoted in Peter J. Westwick, *The National Labs: Science in an American System, 1947–1974* (Cambridge, Mass.: Harvard University Press, 2003), 21.

15. Katharyne Mitchell, Sallie Marston, and Cindi Katz, eds., *Life's Work: Geographies of Social Reproduction* (Malden, Mass.: Wiley-Blackwell, 2004); Katie Meehan and Kendra Strauss, *Precarious Worlds: Contested Geographies of Social Reproduction* (Athens: University of Georgia Press, 2015).

16. James Burnham, *The Managerial Revolution: What Is Happening in the World* (New York: John Day, 1941); John Kenneth Galbraith, *The New Industrial State* (Boston: Houghton Mifflin, 1967); Marcuse, *One-Dimensional Man*; C. Wright Mills, *White Collar: The American Middle Classes* (New York: Oxford University Press, 1951); William H. Whyte, *The Organization Man* (New York: Simon & Schuster, 1956).

17. Marcuse, *One-Dimensional Man,* ix–x, 16, 11, 32.

18. Noble, *America by Design,* xxv.

19. Whyte, *The Organization Man,* 10.

20. Pierre Bourdieu, "Social Space and Symbolic Power," *Sociological Theory* 7, no. 1 (1989): 18; Pierre Bourdieu, *Distinction: A Social Critique of the Judgement of Taste,* trans. Richard Nice (Cambridge, Mass.: Harvard University Press, 1984), 6, 170; Joe Painter, "Pierre Bourdieu," in *Thinking Space,* ed. Mike Crang and Nigel Thrift (New York: Routledge, 2000), 242–43.

21. Bourdieu, *Distinction,* 170.

22. E. P. Thompson, *The Making of the English Working Class* (New York: Vintage Books, 1963); E. P. Thompson, *The Poverty of Theory and Other Essays* (New York: Monthly Review Press, 1978).

23. Richard Walker, "Class, Division of Labour and Employment in Space," in *Social Relations and Spatial Structures*, ed. Derek Gregory and John Urry (London: Macmillan, 1985), 164–89; Andrew Herod, *Labor Geographies: Workers and Landscapes of Capitalism* (New York: Guilford, 2001).

24. On three occasions, the interviewee's spouse participated in the interview.

25. Tim Smith, interview by author, August 11, 2008. I have changed all the interviewees' names to protect their anonymity.

26. Dan Stein, interview by author, August 15, 2008.

27. Stein interview; Peter Copeland, interview by author, July 14, 2008; Frank Sampson, interview by author, October 7, 2008.

28. Edwin Beachler, "Growing Pains in the Suburbs—No. 6: West Mifflin Borough," *Pittsburgh Press*, May 11, 1951.

29. *1940 United States Census of Population: Pittsburgh, Pa., and Adjacent Area* (Washington, D.C.: Bureau of the Census, 1940); *1970 Census of Population and Housing: Pittsburgh, PA. Standard Metropolitan Statistical Area.* PHC(1)-162 (Washington, D.C.: Bureau of the Census, 1970).

30. Between 1950 and 1970, Clairton lost 23.4 percent of its population, Duquesne 35.2 percent, Homestead 39.9 percent, and McKeesport 26.3 percent. Population loss did not end in 1970, and all four of these communities have continued to lose population.

31. Sugrue, *The Origins of the Urban Crisis*; Patrick Vitale, "Learning to Be Suburban: Working Class Formation and Suburbanization in Post-World War II McKeesport, Pennsylvania" (MA thesis, Syracuse University, 2005).

32. Bill Jones, interview by author, July 7, 2008.

33. Noble, *America by Design*, 34.

34. Doris MacArthur, interview by author, July 18, 2008.

35. Whyte, *The Organization Man*, 267–80; May, *Homeward Bound*, 19.

36. General Dynamics, "In San Diego: A Climate for Creativity at General Atomic Division," *Program for the Annual American Nuclear Society Meeting*, 1967.

37. Westinghouse, "Secure Your Future Today with Westinghouse Nuclear Energy Systems," *Preliminary Program for the Annual American Nuclear Society Meeting*, 1969.

38. WEC, "Tomorrow's Opportunity Today at Westinghouse's Bettis Plant," 1956, WECA, DL&A.

39. WEC, "Bettis Atomic Power Laboratory: Employe Handbook," 196[?], WECA, DL&A.

40. Robert Self, *American Babylon: Race and the Struggle for Postwar Oakland* (Princeton, N.J.: Princeton University Press, 2005), 16.

41. Whyte, *The Organization Man*, 267–80; May, *Homeward Bound*, 19.

42. Herman Schwartz, interview by author, August 15, 2008.

43. Schwartz interview.

44. Stein interview

45. Schwartz interview.

46. Larry Johnson, interview by author, October 6, 2008.

47. Jake Hubert, interview by author, November 11, 2008.

48. Smith interview.

49. David Lebowitz, interview by author, October 29, 2008.

50. Copeland interview.

51. Sampson interview.

52. Sampson interview.

53. For a discussion of such communities, see Andrew Wiese, *Places of Their Own: African American Suburbanization in the Twentieth Century* (Chicago: University of Chicago Press, 2004).

54. See Freund, *Colored Property*; and Kenneth T. Jackson, *Crabgrass Frontier: The Suburbanization of the United States* (New York: Oxford University Press, 1985).

55. Joe William Trotter and Jared N. Day, *Race and Renaissance: African Americans in Pittsburgh since World War II* (Pittsburgh: University of Pittsburgh Press, 2010).

56. The percentage of engineers in the Pittsburgh metropolitan area who were African American ranged from 0.4 percent in 1950 to 0.8 percent in 1970 (see Table 2 in ch. 1). In Pittsburgh and nationally, African Americans remain highly underrepresented in science and engineering. "Women, Minorities, and Persons with Disabilities in Science and Engineering" (special report, National Science Foundation, Division of Science Resources Statistics, Arlington, Va., 2011), http://www.nsf.gov/statistics/wmpd/.

57. Steven Hoffman, "A Plan of Quality: The Development of Mount Lebanon, a 1920s Automobile Suburb," *Journal of Urban History* 18, no. 2 (1992): 168.

58. Laura Pace, "Mount Lebanon's Past of Not Selling Homes to Minorities Is Highlighted by Muhammad Ali's Efforts to Buy in Virginia Manor," *Pittsburgh Post-Gazette*, February 21, 2001.

59. Sugrue, *The Origins of the Urban Crisis*, 245.

60. Freund, *Colored Property*, 9, 13.

61. Stein interview.

62. Vitale, "Learning to be Suburban."

63. Large Site History Committee, "Westinghouse at Large Scrapbook," 1987, in possession of author.

64. Kent James, "Public Policy and the Postwar Suburbanization of Pittsburgh, 1945–1990" (PhD diss., Carnegie Mellon University, 2005).

65. Layne Karafantis and Stuart W. Leslie, "'Suburban Warriors': The Blue-Collar and Blue-Sky Communities of Southern California's Aerospace Industry," *Journal of Planning History* 18, no. 1 (2019): 3–26; Geismer, *Don't Blame Us*.

6. Invisibilities of Nuclear Engineering

1. In this chapter, I use *nuclear engineers* to broadly refer to those who worked in the nuclear industry in Pittsburgh and subscribed to *Nuclear News*. The majority of subscribers had degrees in engineering, but many were also physicists, chemists, metallurgists, and other scientists. Nonetheless, they all worked alongside each other to develop nuclear technologies.

2. Minkler's first article in *Nuclear News* appeared in April 1966 and was not humorous. It reported on a panel of the Pittsburgh branch of the ANS that called for the "nuclear community" to work with the state of Pennsylvania to allow for further "nuclear growth." Bill Minkler, "Pennsylvania Panelists Ask: State Aid for Nuclear Growth?," *Nuclear News*, April 1966.

3. Bill Minkler, *The Best of Bill Minkler: Thirty-Five Years on the Back Page* (La Grange Park, Ill.: American Nuclear Society, 2002), xii.

4. Bill Minkler, interview by author, July 30, 2019.

5. Minkler, *The Best of Bill Minkler*, iii, iv.

6. Minkler interview.

7. Minkler, *The Best of Bill Minkler*, x.

8. Minkler interview.

9. Westinghouse Nuclear Energy Systems, "Man of Action," *ANS Annual Meeting Program*, June 1969, ellipses in original.

10. See, for example, Mariarosa Dalla Costa and Selma James, *The Power of Women and the Subversion of the Community* (Bristol, England: Falling Wall Press, 1973); Silvia Federici, *Revolution at Point Zero: Housework, Reproduction, and Feminist Struggle* (Oakland, Calif.: PM Press, 2012).

11. Nina E. Lerman, "Categories of Difference, Categories of Power," *Technology and Culture* 51, no. 4 (2010): 893–918; Erika Lorraine Milam and Robert A. Nye, "An Introduction to Scientific Masculinities," *Osiris* 30, no. 1 (2015): 1–14; Kara W. Swanson, "Rubbing Elbows and Blowing Smoke: Gender, Class, and Science in the Nineteenth-Century Patent Office," *Isis* 108, no. 1 (2017): 40–61.

12. Cindi Katz, "Vagabond Capitalism and the Necessity of Social Reproduction," *Antipode* 33, no. 4 (2001): 709–28; Katharyne Mitchell, Sallie Marston, and Cindi Katz, eds., *Life's Work: Geographies of Social Reproduction* (Malden, Mass.: Wiley-Blackwell, 2004); Katie Meehan and Kendra Strauss, eds., *Precarious Worlds: Contested Geographies of Social Reproduction* (Athens: University of Georgia Press, 2015); Jamie Winders and Barbara Ellen Smith, "Social Reproduction and Capitalist Production: A Genealogy of Dominant Imaginaries," *Progress in Human Geography*, 43, no. 5 (2019): 871–89.

13. Alison Blunt and Robyn Dowling, *Home* (Abingdon, UK: Routledge, 2006); Katherine Brickell, "'Mapping' and 'Doing' Critical Geographies of Home," *Progress in Human Geography* 36, no. 2 (2012): 225–44.

14. Minkler, *The Best of Bill Minkler*, 79.

15. Donald Kruger, interview by author, July 2, 2008.

16. Peter Copeland, interview by author, July 14, 2008.

17. Frank Sampson, interview by author, October 7, 2008.

18. Larry Johnson, interview by author, October 6, 2008.

19. Brian Hopkins, interview by author, February 12, 2009.

20. Martha and Otis Holland, interview by author, December 31, 2008.

21. Clarence Carter, interview by author, January 7, 2009.

22. Minkler, *The Best of Bill Minkler*, ix.

23. Bill Minkler, "Bill Minkler Reports on . . . Who Really Knows the Score in Big R&D," *Nuclear News*, October 1968.

24. Bill Minkler, "Bill Minkler Reports on . . . Why Our Computer, Here at the Research Foundation, Is the World's Fastest and Most Obedient," *Nuclear News*, May 1969.

25. Bill Minkler, "Bill Minkler Reports on . . . Typographical Terror," *Nuclear News*, June 1971.

26. Minkler, *The Best of Bill Minkler*, 86.

27. Doris MacArthur, interview by author, July 18, 2008.

28. *PoWeR Lines*, March 18, 1955, WECA, DL&A.

29. *PoWeR Lines*, May 13, 1955, WECA, DL&A; *PoWeR Lines*, May 27, 1955, WECA, DL&A.

30. *PoWeR Lines*, October 28, 1955, WECA, DL&A.

31. Kermit Garlid, "Analogies between a Neutron Population and a People Population," *Nuclear News*, August 1969.

32. Minkler, *The Best of Bill Minkler*, 49.

33. Bill Minkler, "Bill Minkler Reports on . . . the Impending Fall of the Hemline," *Nuclear News*, May 1970; Bill Minkler, "Bill Minkler Reports on . . . Our Fight to Save the Mini," *Nuclear News*, July 1970.

34. *PoWeR Lines*, May 13, 1955, WECA, DL&A.

35. *PoWeR Lines*, June 10, 1955, WECA, DL&A; *PoWeR Lines*, November 11, 1955, WECA, DL&A.

36. *PoWeR Lines*, June 10, 1955, WECA, DL&A.

37. *PoWeR Lines*, October 1, 1955, WECA, DL&A.

38. *PoWeR Lines*, June 24, 1955, WECA, DL&A.

39. Larry Goldblatt, interview by author, July 9, 2008.

40. Paul O'Connor, interview by author, July 1, 2008.

41. Alice Kessler-Harris, *Out to Work: A History of Wage-Earning Women in the United States* (New York: Oxford University Press, 1982).

42. "Ads Called 'Anti-feminist,'" *Nuclear News*, November 1972, 33–34.

43. "Discriminating Views," *Nuclear News*, December 1972, 25–26.

44. "Feminism, Fish, and Philosophy," *Nuclear News*, January 1973, 21.

45. When I interviewed Minkler, he could not recall this column and assured me LeLeur was not a real person.

46. Bill Minkler, "Women's Ad Lib," *Nuclear News*, January 1973, 86.

47. Carter interview.

48. See chapter 3 for S. M. Kinter's observations on the ideal research man.

49. Kruger interview.

50. Dr. Fred Forscher, interview by Anne Faigin and Harold Kimball, October 17, 1988, National Council of Jewish Women, Pittsburgh Section, Oral History Project #2, UPASC.

51. Dan Stein, interview by author, August 15, 2008.

52. David Lebowitz, interview by author, October 29, 2008.

53. Herman Schwartz, interview by author, August 15, 2008.

54. Schwartz interview.

55. Schwartz interview.

56. Schwartz estimated that there were one hundred Jewish families in Pleasant Hills at one time. He added that this community is aging and declining in size and that Jewish engineers are much less prevalent at Bettis than they once were. Schwartz interview.

57. Lebowitz interview.

58. Schwartz interview.

59. Hugh Gusterson, *Nuclear Rites: A Weapons Laboratory at the End of the Cold War* (Berkeley: University of California Press, 1998).

60. Stein interview.

61. One 1968 recruitment ad from United Nuclear Corporation even contrasted nuclear engineers with the 1960s counterculture, asking that before engineering students "try flower power, give a thought to nuclear power." If they did, they were certain to "find suburban Westchester more comfortable than Haight Ashbury." United Nuclear Corporation, "Don't Drop Out . . . Drop In!," *ANS Annual Meeting Program,* September 1968.

62. Johnson interview.

63. Stein interview; Tim Smith, interview by author, August 11, 2008.

64. Roger Johansson, interview by author, May 27, 2008.

65. See, for example, Elaine Tyler May, *Homeward Bound: American Families in the Cold War Era* (New York: Basic Books, 1988).

66. Lily Geismer, "Don't Blame Us: Grassroots Liberalism in Massachusetts, 1960–1990" (PhD diss., University of Michigan, 2010); Sylvie Murray, *The Progressive Housewife: Community Activism in Suburban Queens, 1945–1965* (Philadelphia: University of Pennsylvania Press, 2003); Joanne Meyerowitz, ed., *Not June Cleaver: Women and Gender in Postwar America, 1945–1960* (Philadelphia: Temple University Press, 1994); Paula Barker, "The Domestication of Politics: Women and American Political Society," *American Historical Review* 89, no. 3 (1984): 620–47.

67. David Freund, *Colored Property: State Policy and White Racial Politics in Suburban America* (Chicago: University of Chicago Press, 2007); Kevin Kruse, *White Flight: Atlanta and the Making of Modern Conservativism* (Princeton, N.J.: Princeton University Press, 2005); Lisa McGirr, *Suburban Warriors: The Origins of the American Right* (Princeton, N.J.: Princeton University Press, 2001).

68. On the Progressive Era politics of science and engineering, see David Noble, *America by Design: Science, Technology, and the Rise of Corporate Capitalism* (Oxford: Oxford University Press, 1977); and Robert H. Wiebe, *The Search for Order, 1877–1920* (New York: Hill and Wang, 1967). For a similar argument about the politics of scientists and engineers in the Cold War–era suburbs of Boston, see Geismer, "Don't Blame Us," 98–101.

69. For more on the technopolitics of nuclear engineering, see Gabrielle Hecht, *The Radiance of France: Nuclear Power and National Identity after World War II,* 2nd ed. (Cambridge, Mass.: MIT Press, 2009).

70. Lebowitz interview.

71. Minkler interview.

72. William H. Whyte, *The Organization Man* (New York: Simon & Schuster, 1956), 30.

73. Hopkins interview.

74. Roger Thompson, interview by author, August 20, 2008.

75. Thompson interview.

76. Robin D. G. Kelley, *Yo' Mama's Disfunktional! Fighting the Culture Wars in America* (Boston: Beacon, 1997).

77. McGirr argues that engineers in Orange County, California, had a similar affinity for bootstrap individualism and conservative politics. McGirr, *Suburban Warriors,* 88.

78. Ralph Murphy, interview by author, December, 10, 2008.

79. Herbert Marcuse, *One-Dimensional Man: Studies in the Ideologies of Advanced Industrial Societies* (Boston: Beacon, 1964), 32.

80. Smith interview; Sampson interview.

81. Sampson interview; Stein interview.

82. Johnson interview.

83. O'Connor interview.

84. Martin Robertson, interview by author, July 16, 2008.

85. Thompson interview.

86. Phil Thomas, interview by author, December 15, 2008.

87. Minkler, *The Best of Bill Minkler,* 82–85.

88. "Facing an Activist Training—Jack Hilton Associates," video, George Westinghouse Museum Collection, WECA, DL&A.

89. Pierre Bourdieu and Jean-Claude Passeron, *The Inheritors: French Students and Their Relation to Culture,* trans. Richard Nice (Chicago: University of Chicago Press, 1979); Pierre Bourdieu and Jean-Claude Passerson, *Reproduction in Education, Society, and Culture,* trans. Richard Nice (London: SAGE, 1990).

90. Bill Minkler, email correspondence with author, July 31, 2019.

91. Carl Poplowski, interview by author, January 21, 2009.

92. Thompson interview.

93. Thomas interview.

94. "1971 Bias Suit Start of Long Merger Fight," *Pittsburgh Press,* October 5, 1982.

95. Mary Stolberg, "Churchill, Edgewood Tax Rebates Stayed," *Pittsburgh Press,* July 6, 1981; Chet Wade, "East School Tax Refunds Unlikely," *Pittsburgh Post-Gazette,* July 15, 1981.

96. Vicki Jarmulowski, "Parents, Students Protest Merger," *Pittsburgh Post-Gazette,* August 1, 1981; Susan Mannella, "Merger Tour," *Pittsburgh Post-Gazette,* August 5, 1981.

97. Margi Stumpf, "Private Schools Resist 'Refugees,'" *Pittsburgh Press,* July 9, 1981.

98. Thomas interview.

99. Thompson interview.

100. Bill Jones, interview by author, July 7, 2008.

101. "Pittsburgh Education Panel," *Nuclear News* 8 (January 1965): 37. Of the 150 books ANS donated, 40 were given to Hillel Academy in Squirrel Hill. "Nuclear Society Donates 40 Books from A to Z to Hillel," *Jewish Chronicle of Pittsburgh,* February 5, 1965.

102. Jay W. Forrester, *Urban Dynamics* (Cambridge, Mass.: MIT Press, 1969), 1–11.

103. Johnson interview.

104. For other examples, see Jennifer S. Light, *From Warfare to Welfare: Defense Intellectuals and Urban Problems in Cold War America* (Baltimore: Johns Hopkins University Press, 2003).

105. Johnson interview.

7. Warplace/Workplace

1. "Science in World Is Forum Topic," *Milwaukee Journal,* April 18, 1946; Edward H. Martin, "Westinghouse Forum Is Given Warning by Research Scientists," *Pittsburgh Post-Gazette,* May 17, 1946; "U.S. Was Ready to Wage War with Deadly Germs," *Pittsburgh Post-Gazette,* May 17, 1946.

2. "World Power Too Restricted, Forum Is Told," *Pittsburgh Post-Gazette,* May 17, 1946.

3. "Westinghouse Fete Closed by Art Tour," *Pittsburgh Post-Gazette,* May 16, 1946, 29.

4. Jessica Wang, *American Science in an Age of Anxiety: Scientists, Anticommunism, and the Cold War* (Chapel Hill: University of North Carolina Press, 1999), 5. See also Sarah Bridger, *Scientists at War: The Ethics of Cold War Weapons Research* (Cambridge, Mass.: Harvard University Press, 2015).

5. Internationalism and a left politics of science were on clear display at a meeting sponsored by the Association of Pittsburgh Scientists in December 1946; a University of Pittsburgh psychologist told attendees that as a result of "scientific and technological progress," people had become so interdependent that they "must learn to live in one world." "To survive," he called for Americans to "transform our nationalistic sovereignties to a one-world sovereignty" and "eradicate from our minds those ideas which have produced cultural barbarism and national stubbornness." "Council of Federation of American Scientists Meet," *Bulletin of Atomic Scientists* 1 (May 1, 1946): 14; "Atom Control Discussed at Women's Conference," *Pittsburgh Post-Gazette,* July 19, 1946; "Scientists Show Atom Age of Perils," *Pittsburgh Post-Gazette,* December 13, 1946.

6. See John W. Simpson, *Nuclear Power from Underseas to Outer Space* (LaGrange Park, Ill.: American Nuclear Society, 1995), 8; Richard G. Hewlett and Francis Duncan, *Nuclear Navy: 1946–1962* (Chicago: University of Chicago Press, 1974), 97.

7. Paul Forman, "Behind Quantum Electronics: National Security as a Basis for Physical Research in the United States," *Historical Studies in the Physical Sciences* 18, no. 1 (1989): 150.

8. Matthew Farish, *The Contours of America's Cold War* (Minneapolis: University of Minnesota Press, 2010), xxxiii.

9. As Scott Kirsch, Colin Flint, and others note, there is a need to "challenge the false dichotomy between war and peace" and to consider war "a more or less permanent process . . . premised ideologically on a distinct horizon of peace, and the closure of war as a discrete event." The notion that war and peace are geographically and historically discrete legitimates the omnipresence of violence in times and places of "war" and "peace." Scott Kirsch and Colin Flint, "Introduction: Reconstruction and the Worlds That War Makes," in *Reconstructing Conflict: Integrating War and Postwar Geographies,* ed. Scott Kirsch and Colin Flint (Surrey, England: Ashgate, 2011), 3–28; Jenna M. Loyd, "'Peace Is Our Only Shelter': Questioning Domesticities of Militarism and White Privilege," *Antipode* 43, no. 3 (2011): 845–73; Mark Neocleous, "War as Peace, Peace as Pacification," *Radical Philosophy* 159 (January/February 2010): 8–17.

10. Steven Shapin, "Following Scientists Around," *Social Studies of Science* 18, no. 3 (1988): 546. On the absence of work and labor from STS, see also Steven Shapin, "The Invisible Technician," *American Scientist* 77, no. 6 (1989): 554–63; and Stephen R. Barley and Beth A. Bechky, "In the Backrooms of Science: The Work of Technicians in Science Labs," *Work and Occupations* 21, no. 1 (1994): 85–126.

11. Michael Mann, "The Roots and Contradictions of Modern Militarism," *New Left Review* 162, no. 1 (March–April 1987): 35–50; Patrick Vitale, "Wages of War: Manufacturing Nationalism during World War II," *Antipode* 43, no. 3 (2011): 783–819.

12. Forman, "Behind Quantum Electronics," 178; Peter Galison and Bruce Hevly, eds., *Big Science: The Growth of Large-Scale Research* (Stanford: Stanford University Press, 1992); Stuart W. Leslie, *The Cold War and American Science: The Military-Industrial-Academic Complex at MIT and Stanford* (New York: Columbia University Press, 1993).

13. Mark Neocleous, "'What Do You Think of Female Chastity?' Identity and Loyalty in the National Security State," *Journal of Historical Sociology* 19, no. 4 (2006): 374–96.

14. "Atomic Power, Conversion of Matter to Energy," *Westinghouse Engineer,* February 1943, 7; E. U. Condon, "Physics Gives Us—*Nuclear Engineering,*" *Westinghouse Engineer,* November 1945, 167–73; C. F. Wagner and J. A. Hutcheson, "Nuclear-Energy Potentialities," *Westinghouse Engineer,* July 1946, 125–27.

15. Simpson, *Nuclear Power from Underseas to Outer Space.*

16. Richard G. Hewlett and Francis Duncan, *Nuclear Navy: 1946–1962* (Chicago: University of Chicago Press, 1974), 35–36.

17. Quoted in Scott Frickel, "Engineering Heterogeneous Accounts: The Case of Submarine Thermal Reactor Mark-I," *Science, Technology, and Human Values* 21, no. 1 (1996): 45.

18. Frickel, 45.

19. U.S. Navy Bureau of Ships, "Steam Products," Order #61440-T, June 2, 1948, WECA, DL&A.

20. Hewlett and Duncan, *Nuclear Navy,* 92.

21. Simpson, *Nuclear Power from Underseas to Outer Space,* 21.

22. E. L. Harder, "Nuclear Power: Events Leading Up to the Nautilus and Shippingport, a Pittsburgh Heritage," adult class at Calvary Lutheran Church, April 10 and 24, 1983, WECA, DL&A.

23. Hewlett and Duncan, *Nuclear Navy*, 99–100.

24. Tim Smith, interview by author, August 11, 2008. Hewlett and Duncan also note that Bettis's "ties to the naval reactors branch in Washington were much closer than to the company headquarters in Pittsburgh." Hewlett and Duncan, *Nuclear Navy*, 120.

25. In January 1949, Bettis had 30 employees; in 1951 it had around 2,000; in 1955 it had 2,100; in 1956 it had 2,800 and an additional 1,500 at Large, Pennsylvania; in 1958 it had 4,000; and in 1964 it had 2,905 employees. Employment peaked during the late 1950s, when twenty reactors were under development at the lab. The development of Westinghouse's Plant Apparatus Division (PAD) and the movement of most manufacturing outside Bettis decreased employment during the 1960s, and it decreased further in the 1970s as it became more of a "caretaker" of the nuclear fleet. Hewlett and Duncan, *Nuclear Navy*, 283; Harold Orlans, *Contracting for Atoms* (Washington, D.C.: Brookings Institution, 1967), 74.

26. While this project seemed "disarmingly simple," "the trouble was, none of this theory was well enough advanced to know how much or how many, or how big or how small, or how hard or corrosion resistant everything had to be." Building a nuclear reactor reliable enough to go to sea and operate in the confined space of a submarine, while theoretically possible, was an immense engineering challenge. Simpson, *Nuclear Power from Underseas to Outer Space*, 31.

27. WEC, "They Harnessed the Atom," September 1954, 2, WECA, DL&A. Simpson also likens the development of the U.S.S. *Nautilus* to Kitty Hawk, where the Wright brothers first flew. Simpson, *Nuclear Power from Underseas to Outer Space*, 53. For a full account of the Mark I, see Martin Mann, "Feature of True Science Adventure: The Daring Voyage of a Secret Submarine," *Popular Science* 178, no. 5 (June 1961): 108–16.

28. Simpson, *Nuclear Power from Underseas to Outer Space*, 68.

29. "Highlights of the 1965 AEC Annual Report," *Nuclear News* 9 (March 1966): 16.

30. Frank Sampson, interview by author, October 7, 2008.

31. Hewlett and Duncan, *Nuclear Navy*, 100.

32. See, for example, Captain John W. Crawford and Steven L. Krahn, "The Naval Nuclear Propulsion Program: A Brief Case Study in Institutional Constancy," *Public Administration Review* 58, no. 2 (1998): 159–66.

33. David Lebowitz, interview by author, October 29, 2008.

34. Simpson, *Nuclear Power from Underseas to Outer Space*, 90; Hewlett and Duncan, *Nuclear Navy*, 120.

35. Hewlett and Duncan, *Nuclear Navy*, 163; Dan Stein, interview by author, August 15, 2008.

36. Bill Jones remembered visiting Rickover's office in a crumbling World War I–era building: "They had light bulbs hanging down with the old Mazda lamps. You went in his offices and there wasn't a single bit of furniture that matched. Everything was a cast off, worn off here or there, arm things duct-taped in place, or a book under

the corner of a chair. He made . . . a display of being extraordinarily frugal. And he loved to have Congressional people come into his office to see how he was not wasting federal money. And . . . he didn't waste any federal money, but in one sense he carried it a little bit to the extreme." When Rickover's office moved to a new "beautiful set of buildings" in Crystal City, he furnished it with the same "old mismatched furniture." Another popular Rickover story were accounts of his interviews of potential submarine captains. He kept a special chair for these interviews "with the front legs too short so you would be uncomfortable" during the grilling that he inevitably meted out. Bill Jones, interview by author, July 7, 2008; Larry Johnson, interview by author, October 6, 2008.

37. Hewlett and Duncan, *Nuclear Navy,* 33; Orlans, *Contracting for Atoms,* 123.

38. Rickover first pursued establishing the Naval Reactor Engineering School at North Carolina State University, where one of the country's first nuclear engineering programs and testing reactors was established, but, according to Bettis lore, he was unimpressed and informed the university's president that he would not send his dog there. By 1973 forty thousand naval personnel had passed through the Reactor School at Bettis. Stein interview; Simpson, *Nuclear Power from Underseas to Outer Space,* 51–52.

39. Stein interview.

40. Simpson, *Nuclear Power from Underseas to Outer Space,* 35.

41. Zalman Shapiro, interview by Harold Kimball and Jean Meth, June 21, 1984, National Council of Jewish Women Oral History Project, UPASC. Bettis developed techniques to manufacture zirconium alloys in large quantities during the early 1950s. Because zirconium was transparent to neutrons, it was a perfect material to clad fuel rods within reactors.

42. Hewlett and Duncan, *Nuclear Navy;* Thomas B. Allen and Norman Polmar, *Rickover: Father of the Nuclear Navy* (Washington, D.C.: Potomac Books., 2007).

43. Jones interview.

44. Stein interview.

45. Johnson interview.

46. Simpson, *Nuclear Power from Underseas to Outer Space,* viii, 37.

47. Jake Hubert, interview by author, November 11, 2008.

48. Lebowitz interview.

49. Peter Copeland, interview by author, July 14, 2008.

50. Jones interview.

51. Like many employees, Thomas escaped Bettis by leaving the lab to work for an outside company and then later being rehired by Westinghouse, in his case after a very short period. Phil Thomas, interview by author, December 15, 2008.

52. Simpson, *Nuclear Power from Underseas to Outer Space,* 22; Hewlett and Duncan, *Nuclear Navy,* 97–98.

53. Smith interview.

54. Smith interview.

55. Ralph Murphy, interview by author, December 10, 2008.

56. While Rickover's draconian influence was a key drawback of work at Bettis, a key benefit was the resources he provided. In its early years, one of Bettis's "biggest advantage was we had dollars available to us that universities didn't." This advantage included funding and access to materials, such as zirconium, that the state prioritized for military use. Herman Schwartz, interview by author, August 15, 2008.

57. Hubert interview.

58. Stein interview.

59. Copeland interview.

60. Gusterson had similar reflections when he began his research at Lawrence-Livermore. He assumed that most scientists were conservative, only to discover that "the laboratory is a place where Reagan-Bush supporters, those with no great interest in politics at all, and liberals who had struggled for Civil Rights and against the Vietnam War all worked together in the development of nuclear weapons." Hugh Gusterson, *Nuclear Rites: A Weapons Laboratory at the End of the Cold War* (Berkeley: University of California Press, 1998), 40.

61. Smith interview.

62. Gusterson, *Nuclear Rites,* 41, 43, 67.

63. Tom Boreland, interview by author, July 2, 2008.

64. John Peters, interview by author, November 5, 2008.

65. John W. Dower, *War without Mercy: Race and Power in the Pacific War* (New York: Pantheon Books, 1986).

66. Peters interview.

67. Peters interview.

68. Herbert Marcuse, *One-Dimensional Man: Studies in the Ideologies of Advanced Industrial Societies* (Boston: Beacon, 1964), 32.

69. Schwartz interview.

70. Johnson interview.

71. Stein interview.

72. Stein interview.

73. Hubert interview.

74. Sampson interview.

75. Copeland interview.

76. Johnson interview.

77. Copeland interview.

78. Johnson interview.

79. Ann R. Markusen et al., *The Rise of the Gunbelt: The Military Remapping of Industrial America* (Oxford: Oxford University Press, 1991).

Epilogue

1. "Extreme Metropolitan Makeover," *National Geographic Traveler,* October 2011.

2. See, for example, Glenn Thrush, "The Robots That Saved Pittsburgh," *Politico Magazine,* February 4, 2014, http://www.politico.com.

3. Key examples include Donna Haraway, *Modest_Witness@Second_Millenium. Femaleman_Meets_OncoMouse: Feminism and Technoscience* (London: Routledge, 1997); David Livingstone, *Putting Science in Its Place: Geographies of Scientific Knowledge* (Chicago: University of Chicago Press, 2003); and Steven Shapin, "The House of Experiment in Seventeenth-Century England," *Isis* 79, no. 3 (1988): 373–404.

4. Slava Gerovitch, "Parallel Worlds: Formal Structures and Informal Mechanisms of Postwar Soviet Mathematics," *Historia Scientiarum* 22, no. 3 (2013): 181–200; Shapin, "The House of Experiment in Seventeenth-Century England."

5. Kate Brown, *Plutopia: Nuclear Families, Atomic Cities, and the Great Soviet and American Plutonium Disasters* (Oxford: Oxford University Press, 2013); Lindsey A. Freeman, *Longing for the Bomb: Oak Ridge and Atomic Nostalgia* (Chapel Hill: University of North Carolina Press, 2015).

6. "Briefing by White House Press Secretary Robert Gibbs," May 28, 2009, https://obamawhitehouse.archives.gov.

7. Barack Obama, "Statement by the President on G-20 Summit in Pittsburgh," September 8, 2009, https://obamawhitehouse.archives.gov.

8. Barack Obama, "Remarks by the President at G20 Closing Press Conference," September 26, 2009, https://obamawhitehouse.archives.gov.

9. Bill Flanagan, "Transformational Visuals," Pittsburgh G20 Partnership press release, September 20, 2009, copy in possession of author.

10. Many of them drew very closely from the partnership's press release. Pittsburgh G20 Partnership, "Transformed Pittsburgh: The Perfect Host for World Economic Summit," September 24, 2009.

11. Mitch Potter, "How Pittsburgh Got Its Green Back," *Toronto Star,* September 21, 2009; Howard Fineman, "Pittsburgh Stars at the G20," *Newsweek,* September 21, 2009; Kevin Connolly, "Pittsburgh Steeled to Be Host City," *BBC News,* September 23, 2009; Caitlan Smith, "Pittsburgh, City of Renewal," *The Atlantic,* September 24, 2009. See also Michael McKee, "Pittsburgh's Economic Revival, Bond Debt Offer Lessons to G-20," *Bloomberg News,* September 22, 2009, http://www.bloomberg.com; Ian Urbina, "For Pittsburgh, G-20 Meeting Is a Mixed Blessing," *New York Times,* September 24, 2009; "Pittsburgh, Città Del Futuro," *Corriere Della Sera,* September 10, 2009, http://www.corriere.it.

12. Connolly, "Pittsburgh Steeled to Be Host City."

13. Obama, "Remarks by the President at G20 Closing Press Conference."

Index

Page references in italics refer to illustrations

PATRICK VITALE is assistant professor of geography at Eastern Connecticut State University.